Vice, Crime, and Poverty

European Perspectives

European Perspectives
A Series in Social Thought and Cultural Criticism
Lawrence D. Kritzman, Editor

European Perspectives presents outstanding books by leading European thinkers. With both classic and contemporary works, the series aims to shape the major intellectual controversies of our day and to facilitate the tasks of historical understanding.

For a complete list of books in the series, see pages 279–280.

Vice, Crime, and Poverty

How the Western Imagination
Invented the Underworld

Dominique Kalifa

Translated by
Susan Emanuel

Foreword by
Sarah Maza

Columbia University Press   New York

COLUMBIA
UNIVERSITY
PRESS

Columbia University Press gratefully acknowledges the generous contribution for this book provided by Publisher's Circle member Jeanine Plottel.

This work received the French Voices Award for excellence in publication and translation. French Voices is a program created and funded by the French Embassy in the United States and FACE Foundation (French American Cultural Exchange).

Columbia University Press
Publishers Since 1893
New York   Chichester, West Sussex
cup.columbia.edu
First published in French as Les Bas-fonds: Histoire d'un imaginaire
© 2013 Editions du Seuil
English translation copyright © 2019 Columbia University Press
All rights reserved

Library of Congress Cataloging-in-Publication Data

Names: Kalifa, Dominique, author. | Emanuel, Susan, translator.
Title: Vice, crime and poverty : how the Western imagination invented the underworld / Dominique Kalifa ; translated by Susan Emanuel.
Other titles: Bas-fonds. English
Description: New York : Columbia University Press, [2019] | Series: European perspectives | Translation of: Bas-fonds. | Includes bibliographical references and index.
Identifiers: LCCN 2018042782 (print) | LCCN 2018051325 (e-book) | ISBN 9780231547260 (e-book) | ISBN 9780231187428 (cloth : alk. paper)
Subjects: LCSH: Urban poor—History. | Marginality, Social. | Marginality, Social, in literature. | Criminals–History. | Criminals in literature. | Inner cities–History. | Crime–History. | Inner cities in literature. | Social representations. | Deviant behavior in literature.
Classification: LCC HV6963 (e-book) | LCC HV6963 .K347 2019 (print) | DDC 305.5/69091732—dc23
LC record available at https://lccn.loc.gov/2018042782

Columbia University Press books are printed on permanent and durable acid-free paper.
Printed in the United States of America

Cover design: Julia Kushnirsky
Cover image: originally appeared on the cover of *Les Bas-fonds du crime et de la prostitution* by Mr. Jean (Paris: P. Fort, 1901). Collection Kharbine-Tapabor.

For Alain Corbin

Contents

Acknowledgments

Several chapters in this book, in earlier versions, were given as papers and lectures. My thanks go to many colleagues who gave me the opportunity to discuss some aspects of this work: Lise Andriès at the Université Paris-Sorbonne; Lucia Granja at the University of Sao Paulo in Rio Preto; J.-P. Daughton at Stanford University; Cathy Nesci and Dominique Julien at the University of California at Santa Barbara; Daryl Lee, Corry Cropper, and students at Brigham Young University, who participated in a seminar on this subject; Michel Porret at Geneva University; Corinne Legoy at the University of Orléans; Walburga Hülk-Althoff at the University of Essen; Robin Walz, Sarah Maza, and Miranda Spieler, who organized a session at the Western Society for French History at the University of Louisiana at Lafayette; Andrea Goulet and the Nineteenth-Century Society for French Studies; Jann Matlock at University College London; Laure Murat at the University of California at Los Angeles; Andrew Pepper and Dominique Jeannerod at Queen's University, Belfast; Alex Gagnon and Pierre Hébert at Sherbrooke University; Vanessa Schwartz at the University of Southern California; Laura Suarez de la Torre at the Instituto Mora, Mexico; Guillaume Pinson at Laval University, Québec; Maire Cross and Steve Wharton at

Bath University; Marta Caraion at Lausanne University; Deivy Carneiro Ferreira at the Uberlandia University, Brazil.

Other aspects of this book have been subjects I have taught in courses and a cycle of seminars at the Université Panthéon–Sorbonne. My thanks also go to the students who attended them, and whose suggestions and research papers enabled me to deepen several points. A special mention goes to Louise Auvitu, Camille Boucher, Emilie Braga, Damien Cailloux, Corinne Doria, Laure Dubesset, Fabienne Giuliani, Lucia Katz, Agathe Lecoeur, Mathilde Meheust, Hadrien Nouvelot, Marie-Charlotte Parpaite, Nicolas Picard, Alicia Potin, and Jérôme Triebel.

Many colleagues and students gave me the benefit of their erudition or have transmitted documents to me. So thanks to Marcos Bretas, Lila Caimari, Leonardo Carvalho-Goncalves, Jean-Claude Caron, Jacques Carré, Glenn Close, Stéphanie Demange, Mélodie Simard-Houde, Laura O'Brien, Michel Porret, Jean-Noël Tardy, and Jean-Claude Vimont.

I also wish to thank Alberto Gabriele for introducing me to Gladstone Library, and my editors at Le Seuil, Hughes Jallon and Severine Nikel, who had trust in this project.

Obtaining the "French Voices Award" in 2016 greatly facilitated the translation of this book into English. Therefore, my thanks go to the Cultural Services of the French Embassy, as well as to American colleagues and friends who helped me in this enterprise: Venitta Data Stephane Gerson, Robin Holding, Philip Nord, and John Merriman. Larry Kritzman and Jennifer Crewe agreed with enthusiasm to publish this book in this collection, and Susan Emanuel devoted her knowledge—and her patience—in offering a magnificent translation.

Foreword

In 1958, Louis Chevalier published his *Laboring Classes and Dangerous Classes*, a book that instantly became a classic whose influence has endured to this day. A study of urban change and poverty in Paris in the first half of the nineteenth century, its lasting impact came from Chevalier's unprecedented and unorthodox mixing of sources. Alongside the classic materials of urban history such as administrative and demographic sources, Chevalier also drew upon a range of literary texts, from the canonical such as novels by Balzac and Hugo to serials and other pulp fictions. These works were not to be used as documentary evidence, he argued; rather, they provided a way of understanding the terrors the Parisian middle classes experienced in response to the dramatic post-revolutionary swelling of the capital's poorer population. Victor Hugo's hallucinatory depiction of the city's sewers in *Les Misérables*, for instance, tells us less about urban sanitation than about fears of a dark and dangerous world below the streets, a metaphor for the unknown hordes of the angry poor. Inserting fiction *as* fiction into his analysis, Chevalier pioneered for historians what has since become known as the study of the "social imaginary."

Dominique Kalifa, whose work, especially in the present volume, has addressed some of the same themes as Chevalier's, is today's leading historian in France of the "social imaginary." If Chevalier's legacy haunts *Vice, Crime, and Poverty*, Kalifa's study is also a much broader-gauged work, with a geographic purview anchored in Paris but ranging to London, New York, Buenos Aires, and Algiers, and a time-span that extends from the 1830s into the early decades of the twentieth century. This magisterial survey and analysis of the Western literature of the "lower depths" in the century of its most ubiquitous presence is also the work in which Kalifa most specifically deploys the concept of "the social imaginary" both in theory and in practice. Among his previous works, his first book, *L'Encre et le sang*, explores the culture and themes of crime journalism in the Belle Époque seeking to pin down exactly why a repertoire of stories told in certain ways grabbed the attention of the fin-de-siècle reading public; his 2009 *Biribi* offers an engrossing social history of the notoriously brutal military prisons in French North Africa but is equally concerned with decrypting the meaning of the pulp novels and sensational journalism that made these institutions an object of horrified fascination for French readers from the Belle Époque to the interwar years.

Of Dominique Kalifa's many books, *Vice, Crime and Poverty* most explicitly seeks to delineate "the social imaginary" as an object of historical investigation. In his opening pages, he defines the concept as "a coherent and dynamic system of representations of the social world, a sort of repertoire of collective figures and identities that every society assembles at given moments in its history." Kalifa insists that such representational clusters must always be carefully historicized: what matters is not only which "collective figures and identities" recur insistently but exactly why they appear and cluster at a certain point, and when and why they wane and disappear. This study accordingly asks why the period between 1830 and 1930 in the Western world produced so many descriptions and stories of the miserable, corrupt and dangerous para-societies said to exist beside or below the normative urban world of safe and respectable folk. Obviously, any such long-lived fictions have deep roots and tenacious afterlives, which Kalifa also evokes. He traces fears of urban vice back to the Biblical contrast between the heavenly city of Jerusalem and the degeneracy of Sodom and Babylon, taking us on a tour of portrayals of medieval and early modern *gueux*, *picaros*, and other menacing paupers and of the Courts of Miracles they were said to form; at the other end of the story, he show the *bas-fonds* motif surviving in the fear of cartels and other crime syndicates, the construction of a late twentieth-century American "underclass," and the contemporary fascination with gangs and prisons.

Kalifa posits that images of criminal underworlds always mirror the salient power structures of their time: early modern "courts of miracles" and their rulers mimicked actual royal courts, the early nineteenth-century idea of "dangerous classes" spoke to new understandings of bourgeois social dominance, while later obsessions with "armies of crime" reflected burgeoning nationalist militarism, and "crime syndicates" got their moniker from labor unions and industrial cartels. In a sharp insight toward the end of the book, Kalifa proposes that "these representations are particularly propagated in periods of social opacity and confusion, such as the first third of the nineteenth century." Myths of the underclass perform a "normalizing role," helping to define the normative core of society in periods of deep social change. The age of political and industrial revolutions with its massive patterns of urban growth upset longstanding social landscapes; the mythology of the lower depths both expressed and helped manage the resulting fears among the well-to-do.

Navigating through the often lurid nineteenth-century literatures of the "lower depths," Kalifa never loses sight of their connections to the social realities that gave birth to them. He notes how often the metaphor for a dangerous underclass is that of stagnant, putrid water—swamps, sewers, all of the stinking overflow of civilization—while noting that the poorer sections of cities were indeed often located "lower," near rivers and ports. He traces the links between imperialism and the mythology of the underclass, starting with the initial French conquest of Algeria in 1830, proceeding to countless analogies between the "dangerous classes" and native Americans, then shifting to metaphors of Africa ("darkest London") starting in the 1880s. He details the ways in which waves of eager professionals—policemen, philanthropists, reformers, journalists—all contributed to describing and sensationalizing the lives of the poorest citizens of the West's major cities. Most importantly, he notes that the flowering of this "underclass" mythology has everything to do with the birth of certain forms of mass culture—newspapers and popular fiction—produced for the benefit of emerging groups of middling readers both fascinated and repulsed by the culture of poverty they themselves had escaped.

While the "lower depths" certainly existed, Kalifa shows us, they were often pressed into the mold of upper-class fantasies. Central sections of the book detail the elite practices that gave birth to recurrent images of misery. Upper-class men and women "produced" the poor by trapping them within taxonomies, elaborate classifications of denizens of the underworld that the celebrated criminologist Eugène-François Vidocq likened to "the Linnaen method." Aristocrats, journalists, and philanthropists acted out the fantasy of the "prince in disguise," going undercover ostensibly as agents of justice and reform but often mostly to indulge their voyeurism. Other members of the elites openly fed their prurient interests by engaging in the earliest forms of slum tourism, known at the time as the "Grand Dukes' Tour"; clever entrepreneurs gave them what they wanted by staging barroom brawls and erotically charged nightclub scenes.

Paying careful attention to all their regional variations, from London's Whitechapel to New York's Five Points to the notorious "Zone" around the edges of Paris, Kalifa shows us how and why dark fantasies of the underside of urban life came to haunt Western culture in the age of revolution and industrialization and how and why they receded in the age of mass warfare. His is an exemplary study of the process whereby anxieties bred of changes in class relations are managed through the production of characters and stories that make the social world manageable, intelligible, and yes, entertaining. In *Vice, Crime, and Poverty*, Kalifa brings together all the myths, from Jack the Ripper to London's urchins, from *The Mysteries of Paris* to *The Gangs of New York*, that made up so much of nineteenth-century culture in the West. Along the way, he gives us a master class in how to track the "social imaginary."

Ladies and gentlemen, welcome to the Lower Depths. You could have no better guide than Dominique Kalifa.

Sarah Maza
Northwestern University

Vice, Crime, and Poverty

I

Introduction

The "lower depths" . . . we instantly understand this expression. Unfortunately, we can easily imagine the reference to hovels and slums: limp bodies living in dives that smell of dirt and urine, existences degraded by poverty and alcohol, poorhouses and prisons, the morbid flesh of prostitutes—intolerable situations in which deprivation mingles with immorality, desperation, crime, and incest. The lower depths connotes the hell down into which hordes of vagabonds, wretches, mendicants, "lost" girls, criminals, and convicts seem to be constantly dragged—all of them hideous figures in a hellish landscape that is partly real and partly fantasized.

The French expression *bas-fonds* (meaning "lower depths" and later "underworld") is immediately comprehensible, but it is also diffuse and uncertain. There has never been an objective definition of *bas-fonds*, and no official boundary has ever circumscribed it. No map or census of this frightful world exists. The lower depths stretch across a fluctuating wasteland, and the underworld contains the worst of realities because it is partially linked to the imaginary—a terrain in which the "social" is constantly redefined by the "moral" and in which flesh-and-blood beings merge with fictional characters.

This territory, which I have been exploring for more than twenty years, was long merely a backdrop for my work as a historian of crime and of the social margins. But one day the setting itself became the object of my research. What exactly were these "lower depths" that seemed self-evident, complacently described by so many novelists, journalists, and social observers? To what social realities, to what moral imperatives, did they correspond? This book arose from these questions.

I take the grim setting seriously and try to understand its construction, to grasp its meanings, and to illuminate the long-standing fascination it has held in our imaginations. The "lower depths" expression itself will necessarily be our point of departure. What do dictionaries (an always precious source) tell us? The French term *bas-fonds* at first belonged to the register of topography and landscape, and so the bas-fonds (in English, lower depths) were "places." The first meaning arose in a maritime context: it meant a shallow depth of water, "which is dangerous, where it is easy to run aground," explained Furetière in his 1690 *Dictionnaire*, a meaning soon adopted by subsequent lexicographers. Gradually a shift was made from the waves to terra firma. The term refers to "low and sunken terrains," noted the dictionary of the Académie française in 1798, meaning depressed and less-elevated zones that were often flooded by water, therefore swampy and unhealthy. The *social* meaning—the modern lower depths that interest us here—did not emerge until the nineteenth century. It refers to a "class of vile and contemptible men," writes Émile Littré in 1863; a "class of men degraded by vice and poverty" is a more specific gloss made three years later by Republican encyclopedist Pierre Larousse, who was more sensitive than Littré to the social and moral mechanisms that engendered baseness. Although the term slipped from topographic to social meanings, the spatial dimension was never lost. The lower depths always correspond to places—hovels, underground Courts of Miracles where outcasts thrive, nighttime refuges, basement sweatshops—marked by a natural propensity to sink even lower.

What is "beneath" (i.e., the underworld or the lower quarters) is sunk in the depths of what Balzac called the "social cavern." But corresponding to the environmental conception that has long dominated medical thinking, places also correspond to characters, and physical topographies are also moral views. Three closely interlaced traits seem to define this fallen state: poverty, vice, and crime. These three terms recur almost obsessively in authors' writings: *An Inquiry Into Destitution, Prostitution, and Crime* was written by a Scottish doctor who explored the sordid places of Edinburgh in 1851;[1] "Vice, Crime and Poverty" were the terms American journalist Edward Crapsey used in the title of his book to define the New York lower depths into which he delved in 1868.[2] Finally, in 1896 an editor of a serious French penitentiary journal described the police prefecture's storage basement as the "great receptacle of vice, poverty, and crime in the capital,"[3] which was restated by the novelist Pierre Zaccone as a place "of theft, debauchery, and crime."[4] It is "the pit down into which Paris shakes its vices, its crimes, and its poverty," stated the journalist Maurice Aubenas in 1934.[5] The conceptual dose of each of these three elements may vary, as does the writer's focus, but their intersecting presence is an indispensable constant. Moreover, their interrelations sketch the dynamic of how the bas-fonds occur: "So poverty initiates the misery of everybody. Then vice arrives, and crime is not far behind," explains the novelist Octave Féré.[6] But others obviously supported the reverse order: first vice, then crime, and finally poverty. All combinations are possible, which the invention of "degeneration" came to legitimate in the middle of the nineteenth century. So now we have a triad: places, states of existence, and (finally) individuals. The people of the bas-fonds are classified in an interminable list; the legion of miscreants includes all those prostitutes, beggars, thieves, assassins, prowlers, rag-and-bone men, convicts, and so on who are all born from the unclean cross-fertilization of vice, crime, and poverty.

This meaning of bas-fonds is intimately linked to the nineteenth century. Most of the puzzle pieces existed previously, but something happened during this century that assembled them in a coherent fashion, gave them a name, and hence an identity and a visibility. The expression *bas-fonds*, in its social sense, emerged in the course of a single year (1840) in the writings of three authors, a sign that it was reaching maturity within the Zeitgeist. Balzac used the expression in 1840 in his novelette *Z Marcas*;[7] Constantin Pecqueur, one of the "utopian" socialists of the day, used it in an essay on political economy;[8] and Honoré Frégier used it in his famous book on *Des classes dangereuses de la population dans les grandes villes*.[9] Thus, in the year 1840, a novelist, a theoretician of social reform, and a policeman all use the term *bas-fonds*, and it is worth noting that the expression appears simultaneously in the three registers (fiction, social theory, and policing) that become responsible for its rapid spread. In fact, the expression is quickly taken up by writers such as Proudhon, Eugène Sue, and Constant Guéroult. By 1862 it had become of sufficiently common usage for Henry Monnier, the inventor of M. Prudhomme, to make it the title of a series of stories evoking diverse moral and social sores—*Les Bas-Fonds de la Société: Scènes populaires*[10]—and for Victor Hugo to use it as a title for one part of *Les Misérables* (1862): *Le bas-fond*. This surge in the middle of the nineteenth century was not limited to France. Most of the Romance languages adopted it with similar meanings—*bajos fondos* in Spanish, *bassi fondi* in Italian—and with explicit references to its French origin.[11]

The situation is more complex in England, which already possessed a whole lexical battery to refer to slums and hovels: rookeries, dens, dives, and low life. But England in the nineteenth century proved just as inventive as France; it forged two new terms that would come to supplant all the others. The word *slum*, attested in 1812 with an imprecise meaning ("a room where low goings-on occur"), quickly spread in the 1830s and 1840s to designate "low neighborhoods" and then the "slums" of the city.[12] The term *underworld*, still closer to the French bas-fonds, had been in use since the seventeenth century, notably by playwright Ben Jonson, to refer to pagan hells.[13] But its social meaning did not appear until 1869, from the pen of American novelist George Ellington in *The Women of New York*,[14] then it appeared again twenty-some years later in a work by philanthropist Helen Campbell, which was subtitled *Lights and Shadows of New York Life*.[15] *Underworld* had come into current usage by the end of the century, which saw a multitude of "true stories of the underworld."[16] The term also spread throughout England, especially during the Jack the Ripper affair in 1888. It designated a clandestine place "devoted to crime, to debauchery, or to conspiracy," as *Chambers' Dictionary* signaled at the beginning of the twentieth century.[17] Like its German equivalent *Unterwelt*, "underworld" gradually acquired a different meaning, which was synonymous with "organized crime," but this was not so when it first appeared in the last third of the nineteenth century. At that time, the association of poverty and crime nourished many representations of the underworld, and most accounts (for example, Thomas Archer's in 1865) mingled descriptions of the poor, the imprisoned, and criminals.[18] When journalist Thomas Holmes published his celebrated *London's Underworld* in 1912, he evoked almost exclusively the fate of the poor and indigent.[19] Dictionaries of slang, which were numerous between the two world wars, were not mistaken about the link: the term *underworld* also served to designate the *argot* (slang) of vagabonds, beggars, and marginal people.[20] Thus it is as a quasi-synonym of bas-fonds that I will use "lower depths" and then "underworld" in this book.

In the nineteenth century, Western societies everywhere felt the need to forge new terms to rename real situations linked to poverty and transgression. This lexical exigency, arising within a very dense system of representation, is one of the principal historical issues at the heart of this book. How and why did the century of positivism, industry, democratization, and mass culture reorganize the ways it thought about its margins? It is important to understand why at a given moment descriptions of social realities were reconfigured, but it is just as essential to identify the recurrent motifs that characterized their long-term history. Obviously, the realities in question— indigence, delinquency, debauchery—existed well before the term *bas-fonds* came along to refer to them. In this respect, two historical stages appear decisive: the invention of the concept of the "bad poor" at the beginning of the thirteenth century to designate the ever-growing troupe of beggars and vagabonds, and then the concept of "beggary" at the turn of the fifteenth and sixteenth centuries. The end of the Middle Ages and the start of the modern period are in effect marked by the intensification of social fears and the multiplication of images of marginal people. As the term *gueux* (beggar) came to predominate, it was invested with a strong connotation of duplicity: these people were indigent but also rascals, contemptible individuals, *misérables*. Pierre Larousse explained that "the word *gueux* (beggar) presents poverty as something dirty and vile; often compounded by the idea of begging." *Beggary* covers the same semantic register as bas-fonds, connoting misery and poverty, but it also connotes vice, trickery, and delinquency. On top of this comes the idea of a hierarchical countersociety, a "world turned upside down," and a language—slang—that was thought to dissimulate guilty actions. When projected at the core of a swelling print production that quickly spread throughout modern Europe, the world of the wretched heralded that of the bas-fonds.

One difficulty starts to loom. Did these bas-fonds and these wretches actually exist? That there were indeed poor people, thieves, prostitutes, and organized bands is unfortunately not in doubt, but whether they actually resembled the picturesque and horrified descriptions offered in the principal accounts is less certain. Essentially, the underworld arose from a *representation*, a cultural construction that was born at the intersection of literature, philanthropy, the desire for reform, and the moralizing of elites, but it also arose from a thirst for escape and for social exoticism, an avidity to exploit the potential of the "sensational" emotions that these milieux have always carried, both then and now. This is the reason the social sciences have never taken this expression seriously. A few historians of crime or poverty (such as Louis Chevalier or John Tobias) used "underworld" in the 1940s and 1960s, but without truly questioning its nature or meaning.[21] This is also the case with studies devoted to the marginal milieux of large cities such as London, New York, or Berlin.[22] When these expressions are explicitly considered (especially "underworld"), historians tend to reject them as vague, ambiguous, and nebulous; they are correctly seen as a "literary" creation, a sort of formidable figure invented by the elites to depict a working-class world that is brutal, menacing, and artificially isolated from the rest of society. As such, the underworld teaches us nothing about the life or experiences of the real world. This rejection has been accentuated by the public fascination with stories of the underworld and the multiplication of graphic tales and true crime stories that flourish in the English-speaking world. "Underworld, as a term, has fallen out of favor among scholars who associate it with 19th century writing about the criminal classes, and especially unscholarly writing about denizens of the underworld, as if they lived in a geographically separate area," writes a British historian.[23] The rejection is even stronger on the part of sociologists, especially due to the emergence at the end of the 1970s of the related expression "underclass," which was accused of being key to a neoliberal reading that masked the social workings of the new poverty.[24]

Therefore, we will not seek the traces of tangible experiences of poverty or crime in these tales of the underworld. Of course these realities arise incidentally because places and human stories may allow glimpses of the realities; some historians have endeavored to gather data from them, notably with respect to organized criminality.[25] But the lower depths are essentially a representation in which are intermingled the fears, desires, and phantasms of all those who are interested in these places. It is a "confused heap of residual elements of all kinds and of all origins," wrote the Argentinian psychologist and criminologist Francisco de Veyga in 1903.[26] It is an "imposture," added Henry James in *The American Scene* in 1907; in his account of a trip along the Atlantic coast of the United States, James lingers in New York City's Lower East Side and criticizes stories that invent an artificial and sinister world.[27] And that is how the underworld has to be taken, as "an aggregate of figures and scenes issuing from the urban imagination,"[28] a place where a thousand images are entangled: a thousand literary references, social inquiries, studies of public hygiene, news snippets, the moral and political sciences, songs, and films. Historians of culture have proved to be more interested in representations that express disquiet and anxieties among the elites, and substantial studies have been devoted to the consequent figures of repulsion, of crime, of danger, and to the practice of "slumming."[29] However, no one has considered the lower depths as a whole to be a *social imaginary* that is subject to an overall reading, and this is what I intend to provide.

The notion of a social imaginary merits more precision at this stage, particularly because it has scarcely been a subject examined in detail, and it also suffers from the strongly ahistoric dimension that philosophers and anthropologists have given to the imaginary.[30] Here I define it, in accordance with work in historical anthropology, as a "coherent and dynamic system of representations of the social world," a sort of repertoire of collective figures and identities that every society assembles at given moments in its history.[31] Social imaginaries describe the way in which societies perceive their components—groups, classes, and categories— and hierarchize their divisions and elaborate their evolutions. Thus they *produce and institute* the social more than they *reflect* it.[32] To do this, social imaginaries need to be incarnated in plots and recounted in stories so that they are heard, read, and seen. The social imaginary is above all (as Pierre Popovic suggests) an "interactive ensemble of correlated representations, organized into latent fictions."[33]

Here, the lower depths and underworld offered for exploration arise from such a conception of the imaginary. Produced by troubled societies at times of crisis or turbulence, they offer at their margins a series of tales that aim to either qualify or disqualify, so they speak of the intolerable as well as the tolerable in order to conceive and formulate possible lines of escape from the abyss. But no overseer has the upper hand in the elaboration of these tales; they are collective only by default and sometimes such tales take back roads. The plurality of their inspiration and especially of their uses accounts for their complexity as well as for their richness.

The three eras covered in this book invite us to understand how Western societies have thought about their underbellies at tipping points in the industrial order. Centered on the advent of the lower depths, the first part plunges as deeply as possible into this imaginary—places, décors, actors, motifs—and probes the contexts that explain its emergence in the mid-nineteenth century. It also shows the recurrence of certain representations, some of which are anchored in an immemorial past. But here, the lower depths surge up in their insidious mid-nineteenth century present. Then, exploring the idea that a social imaginary functions through the plots that endow it with form and meaning, the second part of the book identifies four scenarios, four remarkable scripts that organize the stories of the lower depths. I am not implying that these four exhaust the terrain, other choices and other basic outlines were no doubt possible, but the four sequences I have chosen illuminate the broader scenography of these social undersides. If it has a beginning, a social imaginary must also have an ending so that its historical evidence can be perceived with the same acuity. Although most of its motifs and components persist or are reconfigured or adapted to new contexts, the specific combination born around the lower depths at the beginning of the nineteenth century gradually exhausts itself around the middle of the following century. The welfare state instituted after World War II left almost no place for it. The final part of the book is devoted to the history of this gradual effacement and its remnants. Along the way, I also speculate about the uses of such a social imaginary, the often very different ways of investing meaning in it—that is, its "practical sense."

PART I

The Advent of the
Lower Depths

In the Den of Horror

The history of the lower depths is complex. It interweaves a thousand motifs, a thousand references—some are lost in the darkness of time, but others continue to envelop us. My ambition is precisely to unpick the subtle weave of their interlacing. First we have to enter into the heart of this sordid universe to describe more closely the horrid images that were forged by contemporaries. In this chapter I invite you to explore the underworld in all its forms in the era of its heyday—between the 1830s and the Second World War. This voyage is sometimes difficult, but I will try to be neither complacent nor sensational. First I describe, expose, and unflinchingly paint the content of the lower depths. We must enter (without shuddering or flinching) the "world underneath the world" evoked by the Goncourt brothers in 1864[1] and discover the main characters who dwelt there. The description provided here is a place that does not actually exist anywhere; rather, it emerges from a multitude of inquiries, accounts, reporting, and also from myriad fictions that endeavored for more than a century to depict the places of poverty and perdition. This is what I call the *social imaginary*, which I am trying to restore in letter and spirit, just as Eugène Sue announced on the threshold of writing his *Mystères de Paris*: "Readers [are] forewarned about the excursion that I am offering among the [inhabitants] of this infernal race that peoples the prisons and penal colonies, and whose blood reddens the scaffolds."[2]

CITIES IN CRISIS

The underworld, as stated in the introduction, refers simultaneously to places, individuals, and behaviors. But *places* come first: they constitute the décor in which the whole history is rooted. The expression first appeared at the beginning of the nineteenth century, the heyday of neo-Hippocratism, a medical theory that closely linked topographies and moral characteristics. Therefore, the *bas-fonds* were embodied in precise spaces that were intrinsically linked to the experience of the city. This point is crucial. In the peasant and rural societies of France and modern Europe at that time, there was no underworld. Poverty, crime, rape, and incest did indeed dwell in the depths of the rural world—and perhaps especially there—but the lower depths and underworld existed only in large cities. The children of Sodom and Babylon bear the mark of an "urbanophobia" that was exacerbated in the nineteenth century.

The corrupting influence of the city had been long decried, but the threat was most markedly perceived at the heart of the "urban crises" in the first half of the nineteenth century. The city that engendered the *bas-fonds* is always the "old city": aging, congested, saturated, agitated by social tensions, and enflamed by the impulses of its imagination. Before Baron Haussmann redesigned Paris in the 1870s, it was overpopulated and overheated, dirty, oozing, and labyrinthine—and no doubt constituted the archetype of this city "in crisis." It was "Gothic, black, dark, obscure, muddy and feverish, the city of shadows, disorder, violence, poverty, and blood!" wrote Jules Janin in 1843, who, like so many others, depicted the "intersections of houses, dead-end and forked streets, mazes, crossroads [as] . . . great muddy and bloody spaces in which various tricksters of both sexes were stewing."[3] Thus the standard scene became implanted. This is the Paris of police inspector Vidocq and novelist Balzac, the heart of a *cité* that was described by a chief of police as a maze of "murderous streets," stinking alleys, dark staircases, "humid and infected backstreets, with houses the color of mud," and peopled with indigents, brigands—in short "human vermin among whom the most monstrous crimes were engendered."[4]

So it was not by chance that Paris in 1840 spawned the "bas-fonds" expression. In the following year, in the first police story in Western literature, Edgar Allan Poe situated the action of "Murders at the Rue Morgue" in Paris (although he never went there). And one year later, in 1842, Eugène Sue inaugurated the genre of "urban mysteries" that in less than two decades came to cover all the cities of the world. It was in this Parisian "labyrinth of obscure, narrow, and winding streets which extends from the Palais de Justice to Notre-Dame"[5] that the bas-fonds befell modernity.

But Paris's preeminence lasted for only a short time. Although Walter Benjamin would later promote Paris as the "capital of the nineteenth century," at the time it had to share the title of "capital of the lower depths" with many other cities. All the old Gothic cities in France demonstrated their claim to the title: Rouen's Martinville and Saint-Hilaire neighborhoods assembled "what the city has that is most shameful and saddest: vice and crime."[6] Ports and manufacturing cities quickly entered the contest. Social inquiries at the beginning of the century showed how Lille, Nantes, Amiens, Saint-Étienne, Lyon, Mulhouse, and so many others had crammed into their peripheral areas or into their cellars the new "barbarians" begotten by industrialization. Southern France was not spared; into the "labyrinth of thousands of dirty, dark streets that comprised primitive Marseille" pressed a population of drunkards, beggars, sailors, thugs, and prostitutes. "It seemed as if Eugène Sue had passed this way to glean some sensational scenes."[7]

And then there was London, which in this respect had no reason to envy Paris. Although the bas-fonds were unknown there, the city did have its slums, dens, rookeries—and soon its underworld—to make it a hive of vice. London was the great dark Babylon, "the Great Wen" as the radical William Cobbett called it in 1820. Rarely had the city been invested with such a corrupting influence: citizens denounced its denizens' criminality, laziness, immorality, debauchery, drunkenness, and irreligion. Later on, in the 1880s, it would be the universal whore-shop, the world's bordello, notable for perversion and prostitution. It was a hideous city, ragged, corrupt, perverted, "a gigantic laboratory of corruption of all kinds of crime [. . .] which pulls the rest of England to the bottom with it," as Charles Trevelyan wrote in the *Times*.[8] Throughout the century, London was subject to almost obsessional mapping to describe in menu fashion the convolution of beggary, workhouses, backstreet slums, and infamous pubs where gin flowed freely. Around 1840, the St. Giles and Covent Garden areas in the heart of the old city constituted an immense slum of more than 4 hectares, nicknamed the Holy Land: "A very dense mass of shacks so decrepit that they had to avoid collapsing, narrow and sinuous alleys, rivulets of stagnant water, trash, discolored walls."[9] The city entered by the youth at the beginning of the *Mysteries of London* is a "labyrinth of dirty and narrow streets which lies in the immediate vicinity of the northwestern angle of Smithfield-Market." Further on someone recalls "revolting streets which branch off from that Smithfield. It seemed to me that I was wandering amongst all the haunts of crimes and appalling penury of which I had read in romances, but which I never could have believed to exist in the very heart of the metropolis of the world."[10] When part of the neighborhood was torn down in 1847, the center of gravity shifted to the east, toward the East End, a mixture of quays, docks, shacks, abattoirs, and tanneries. "A vast continent of vice, crime, and poverty,"[11] which at the end of the century incarnated the whole horror of London and which the crimes of Jack the Ripper in 1888 would make known to the entire world.

What London did on a grand stage, other British cities realized on a more modest scale—Liverpool with its Waterloo Road area, Birmingham with St. Mary and St. Lawrence—and Edinburgh resonated with the terrible murders of the "resurrectionists" Burke and Hare, who, in 1827, assassinated their tenants and sold their bodies for dissection. Manchester was no better, with its low quarters "with repugnant visions/sights and intolerable stench, where all the garbage, filthy water and muck of houses and basements were putrefying in the streets," as Geraldine Jewsbury described in *Marian Withers* in 1851.[12] Nineteenth-century cities everywhere, which had become gangrenous due to an expansion that piled up migrants in unfit living conditions, were exhibiting their lower depths.

The Old World soon had rivals. The resumption of colonial expansion quickly accentuated the ports and major colonial cities, such as Bombay, Algiers, Tangier, and Manila, where indigence and prostitution were tinged with racist overtones. Shanghai became the "brothel of Asia" and had both sumptuous mansions and sailors' hovels, nailed-together huts, and whorehouses "made of woven bamboo and daub."[13] Leopoldville in the Belgian Congo was a lair of thieves, pimps, and a "rabble of downgraded and lazy blacks who have taken from civilization what is least good."[14] International migrations generated the exceptional growth in the lower depths of the New World. New York, the bridgehead of immigration to the United States, was the first affected. By 1830, Five Points, a muddy intersection in the south of Manhattan, concentrated all the evils that assailed the young nation: poverty, violence, prostitution, and crime. It was the "cesspool of all the depravity of human nature" declared Thomas Jefferson.[15] Henceforth (and for a long time) New York was *the* wicked city. But soon all U.S. cities were affected to the extent that by 1850 almost every one already had a "mysteries" publication: Boston, Philadelphia, St. Louis, New Orleans, Rochester, Charleston, Lowell, and so on.[16] In South America in the 1880s, Buenos Aires was counted as the epicenter of new underworlds, as an immense bordello fallen into the hands of procurers and ruffians, but also containing a population of professional thieves, children of the streets, scrawny migrants, and fanatical anarchists.[17] Elsewhere in the Americas, Rio, Montevideo, Caracas, and Panama each possessed its neighborhood known for poverty and debauchery.

"A WORLD UNDERNEATH A WORLD"

As an urban reality, the lower depths did not occupy the entire city. Two types of spaces were reserved for it: on one hand, downtrodden zones that were depressed, dirty, poor, and forsaken, the sordid margins with their muddy alleys, dives, and wastelands, and "mucky holes with unfinished constructions";[18] and on the other hand, places of authority, veritable legal underworlds that unwillingly concentrated all sorts of marginal types: prisons, penitentiaries, hospices, asylums, and workhouses.

A common trait, inscribed in the same "lower" term that designated them, located these repugnant places as essentially "down below": caves, cellars, underground passages, pits, chasms, catacombs, sewers, and "mines." Hundreds of examples could be taken from all kinds of sources. In Nantes, all the vices, urban infamy, and immorality seemed to be concentrated around the "quay of the Pit"—whose name says it all. It was the lowest part of the city that bordered the port, and it contained the hovels, shacks, whorehouses, dives, greasy streets, and garbage.[19] "We are leaving out the black walls that retain the viscous air, the basest human odors, the mildew exhaled by superimposed cellars [. . .]. In the evening, the knives are out somewhere or other."[20] In Lille, it was the cellars—"this bleak hell" so disgraceful to Victor Hugo in the *Châtiments* (*Punishments*, 1853)—where the poor were described as "phantoms who are there in underground rooms." In Paris, the worst places are those into which one can sink. The *tapis-francs* (grog shops) are "cabarets on the lowest floor," dens such as the Bras-Rouge, the "Bloody Heart" (the subterranean cabaret of *Mystères de Paris*), or the Trou-à-vin (Wine Hole) in *Mendiants de Paris* (Beggars of Paris), a "cavern," a "low room." Everywhere in the city were "foul cellars, lit by basement windows reaching the daylight only at the level of gutters," and, of course, the catacombs celebrated in the stories of Elie Berthet and Pierre Zaccone.[21] Even in 1929 Henri Danjou still took pleasure in leading the reader into this "city of the dead, [. . .] a city of labyrinths," with its cadavers and its mysteries.[22] In Buenos Aires, the most sordid quarter was La Boca, which Albert Londres described as the "bottom of the bottom," where one could not "reasonably descend lower."[23] And yet a few years earlier there had been worse. Jules Huret remembers El Bajo, "a working-class quarter, partly taken back from the waters of the Rio [. . .] It was the dumping ground for dead animals, garbage, and rotten fish. Disreputable people gathered there in the lowest sort of dives."[24] The Berlin *Unterwelt* was "truly a subterranean world which from cellar to cellar, from dive to dive, from one cut-throat area to another, extended its ramifications under the surface of Berlin."[25] Of course, a few places could prove the exception. Squalid and repulsive in Western eyes, the Kasbah of Algiers was in fact on a promontory with an interminable stairway that rose toward increasingly sordid heights. The worst one was the highest, the street of the Zouaves where "a tribe of gypsies camped on the summit."[26] In effect, the Kasbah was an inverted lower depths that resulted from its colonial nature.

Of course, the concentration of marginal people in depressed places was due to social constraints: these were often the only places left to them. Some places might serve as refuge, such as the Parisian perimeter's "American quarries" and their plaster ovens, which were occupied in the nineteenth century by Parisian vagabonds, or the dens used for fomenting crimes. In London, the Adelphi arches played the same role. The Orgères Band— a "horde"—lived underground.[27] In Paris, a criminal gang known as the "Grouilleurs" arranged its den in a disaffected sewer along the banks of the Seine.[28] The international brotherhood of thieves described by Darien in *Le Voleur* favored "houses where the light of day never penetrated, with triple doors and windows boarded up with planks nailed from the inside; mysterious shops that were perpetually for rent, with shutters always closed, into which one slipped by giving a password; cellars with smoky vaults."[29] The gang in *The Silver Wedding*, a U.S. film of 1906, chose to operate from the sewers of New York because there one could move undetected and slip away easily.[30]

Places of incarceration also tended to be tucked under cliffs. Prisons "often occupy the borders of humid ditches," noted Villermé;[31] many jails are underground, as are all the dungeons and *oubliettes*. In Paris, the cells of the police prefecture occupied a vast "low, dark room, long and narrow and gloomy,"[32] whose "ceiling formed a vault, rather like the lid on a coffin," according to Gustave Macé.[33] "The depot is indeed in the pit, as they say in the theater, since it has been judged appropriate to locate it in the substructure of the Palais de Justice," noted the Vicomte d'Haussonville,[34] and others described it as a "bottomless pit."[35] Farther away, at La Force, the most dangerous prisoners were shut up in the "lion's den."[36] At Montfaucon, the horror was less to do with the sinister forks of the gibbets than with its cellar, into which "were thrown not only the human remains which came off the chains at Montfaucon, but the bodies of all the wretches executed at the other permanent gibbets of Paris."[37] But there is always something worse. In Rouen, the hospice of Saint-Yon that imprisoned mad people was a "tomb into which the living descended, whose cellar doors fell on their heads like a casket lid on a cadaver."[38] In Peru, the penal colony of Casas-Matas was a network of narrow subterranean galleries of daub and sand that received light only through the trapdoor and two apertures at the entry.[39]

As topographical realities, these locales derive from symbolism relating to Hell, to that *katabasis* (underworld) into which every hero since Greek Antiquity had to descend,[40] but they also derive from the terrible places— tombs, subterranean vaults, oubliettes—that the Gothic novel popularized at the end of the eighteenth century. Many of the lower depths and their mysteries were inspired by *The Mysteries of Udolpho* by Ann Radcliffe, published in 1794. The underworld meant darkness, night, blackness. The interminable undergrounds that comprised the lower depths were thus simultaneously moral, religious, sociological, and topographical. We are in an inverted world, an antiworld, the locus of impurity.

Moreover, this world is not just down below but is being pulled toward the bottom in an ever-descending movement. People's future is degradation, alcoholism, sickness, madness, and death itself, which often occurs down there, in the "common pit into which the bodies of men, women and children, in frightful promiscuity, mingle in the fermentation of death."[41] It is a world entrained in the Fall, in the Christian sense, which is plunged in darkness and evermore perverted in this downward slide until it is concentrated in a foul residue. The term *residuum* was used by the Liberal member of Parliament John Bright in the debates on the Reform Bill of 1867, and the Victorians used it to categorize the worst criminals and indigents. But the French did not lag behind, and the debates about penitentiaries in the 1840s compared the prison to a "drain."[42] Here is how Prison Inspector Moreau-Christophe expressed himself in 1839:

> Below all social classes, there exists a tiny and abnormal class, outside any regular action of the social apparatus. [It] is composed of sediment, of residue, of the dregs of all the classes placed above it and into which is poured the overflow of their immoralities. Down there is the receptacle of all the vices that flow from above, which are distilled or infused there.[43]

At the very bottom, water is found, but it is stagnant, stinking and putrid, a "cesspool" that reaches back to the initial and maritime meaning of "lower depths" but also to the classic representations of Hell, reached by the Styx, the river of the dead. The whole lexicon here is liquid: pits, sewers, chasms, abysses. It is an ocean that engulfs the weakest and the most vicious, as in the famous frontispiece of *In Darkest England* (1890) by William Booth, the founder of the Salvation Army. Here the poor are described as shipwrecked, derelicts, "the submerged tenth." Poverty is a stagnant pool, a sea of human misery; the poor are swathed in mud, a "heap of muddy matter and depraved bodies."[44] Those who escape the abyss remain "float-ing" populations. Everywhere the most sinister sites are oozing, gorged with humidity, overrun by waste and dirty water. In London, the most mis-erable part of Bethnal Green formed a "rotting lake, an enormous pit, a pool of stagnant water thickened with putrefying matter [that] is dented by the bodies of dogs and cats in all stages of decomposition."[45] In New York, the Five Points neighborhood where shacks started sprouting in 1820 was built on swampy ground.[46] In Madrid, the sinister alleys of the south-ern areas are a "fetid marsh, inhabited solely by reptiles and by savage and ragged Moors."[47] In Buenos Aires, the lower depths of La Boca was an area "surrounded by marshy land on which [structures] have been built, against all the most elementary rules; it is also home to fevers and other maladies."[48] A multitude of examples could be added to this list. The interiors are no better. "The whole topography of mysterious Paris is composed of descend-ing levels, steps that can only go down."[49] The cellars of the Lapin Blanc cabaret, explains M. Claude, lead to the sewers. And when Rodolphe, the hero of the *Mystères de Paris*, is to be gotten rid of, he is dumped in the cel-lar of the Bras-Rouge, which the waters of the Seine periodically inundate.

This water symbolism is omnipresent for three interrelated reasons. The first is historical; we should not forget that the lower depths draw a portion of their imaginary from the galleys that from Antiquity to the eighteenth century banished to the ocean a substantial number of their undesirables: slaves, vagabonds, criminals, deserters. The universe of the galleys extended to the port penal colonies of Brest, Rochefort, and Toulon, located on pon-toons or on mothballed British ships. The "hulks"—those frightful prison ships anchored on the coasts or along the banks of the Thames River (more than forty of them existed around 1800, and the number of prisoners was estimated at around 4,500 in 1828)[50]—dismayed the British public. In Aus-tralia, New Caledonia, and Guyana, the colonial penal system prolonged this tradition, stockpiling convicts during the crossing (and often upon arrival) in floating penitentiaries.

Second is the infernal dimension of water, long attested to in Western culture and nourished by images of the Flood and the River Styx and by tales of barbarian coasts. The *Nef des fous* composed by Sébastien Brant in 1492, when the social imaginary about paupers was being constructed, associated madness and banishment with unhealthy and demoniac waters. Western cultures have long distrusted the ocean.[51] From Ulysses and Orpheus to Dante, the descent to the Underworld was a major metaphor of Western culture, partly governed by a katabastic imagination.[52] "Images of water, and a heavy and maleficent water, usually accompany this trajectory of fatal descent," writes Alain Pessin.[53] Certain sinister events occur periodically to give body to these ideas. In September 1878, the *Princess Alice*, a ferry that linked Gravesend to London, sank in the Thames with more than seven hundred passengers on board. The sinking took place in a stretch of the river very polluted by industries and sewer outflow, and more than five hundred passengers perished from the infected waters.[54]

Finally, somber poetry often evokes the verges of bad waters and confers on them a sad and sinister aspect. Rivers such as the Seine and the Thames, with their docks and canals, arouse despair.

> In the outlying areas of the great agglomerations, the canal magnetizes the fog, the dust, the rain, the wind, the grubby air, the odors of charcoal, dust, gasoline, diesel, and in it float dead animals, garbage, old carcasses, and dead wood; it deposits on its banks scree, coal, bricks, rubble, sacks of plaster, girders—the canal is enveloped in a cage of metal, of workshop and shack rubbish, old trolley tracks, wrecked wagons and fencing; it has worksites forbidden to the public, seedy hotels, buildings blackened with smoke. . . . The great garbage dump.[55]

THE GREASY, THE FILTHY, AND THE PERVERSE

These sinister places breed poverty, vice, and crime, although the dose of each of the three components may vary. Everyone, according to political or religious culture (and also to social context), would stress one or another of these components. For philanthropists, poverty was most important, whether they were romantics or socialists, but for other groups, vice and debauchery were prime, and they were equally prolix about them. Vice, explained Honoré Frégier in his famous treatise on the *Classes dangereuses*, was the state of someone no longer guided by conscience or religion, one who lived only for pleasures and the senses,[56] and in 1840 he estimated the "vicious class" of Paris at sixty thousand persons (men and women combined). In his *Monde des coquins*, published in 1862, Moreau-Christophe also denied any link between poverty and crime: the sole cause resided in vice and immorality.[57] However, it was always by filth, stench, and perversity that the lower depths were manifested. Pulled downward, this was also a world of the "bodily lower stratum," in the sense Mikhail Bakhtin gave to this term.[58] It was the universe of grease, dirt, excrement, the scatological. Hence the grotesque dimension of the lower depths was very present under the *ancien régime*, with the stress on orgy, prostitution, sexual perversion, and bestiality. What remains is a sense of the "residue" of everything that is expelled from the body, including blood, sperm, and excrement.

Dirt is the omnipresent motif, as much on the social level as on the psychological or moral level. It bespeaks savagery, a depravity of places, people, and activities. Mud, muck, and garbage are everywhere. Reinventing the Cour des Miracles (the place in the medieval city where all the beggars, vagrants, criminals, and prostitutes gathered at night) in 1826, G. de la Baume insists in his novel *Raoul* on the smelly and unhealthy dimension of the place: "a contaminated sewer that drained all the vermin, all the disgusting garbage generated by a huge city, and which experience has proven that it is hard to be rid of."[59] Descriptions of real places match each other. In Rouen, the low quarters are cesspools, "receptacles of garbage and manure; the foot seeks in vain for solid stone; trash invades everything."[60] One of the worst places in Paris, Montfaucon, the old site of the gallows, had become a dump, a latrine, and a slaughterhouse. The whole city was contaminated by its nauseous vapors. In London, one saw nothing but rotting shacks, "courtyards reeking with poisonous and malodorous gases arising from accumulation of sewage and refuse scattered in all directions and often flowing beneath your feet"; you have to ascend "rotten staircases, which threaten to give way beneath your every step," to grope your way along "dark and filthy passages swarming with vermin."[61] Moreover, the people who live there are given to all sorts of activities that relate to waste or garbage. Henry Mayhew, when he described the small trades of Whitechapel in the 1860s, identified them as the collectors of dog turds, the rag-and-bone men, the rat killers, the slaughterers, those who hunt for worms and eels in the Thames. Filth carries vermin, infection, scabies and other skin maladies. This is the reason any new arrival in an asylum or workhouse is first stripped of his rags and then led into disinfecting steam. "One has to see them to understand to what point certain individuals can be ignorant of the use of water, and see their fearful air, their anguished fear, their terrorized expectations. [...] There are some who scream as if they were being flayed."[62]

Dirt also relates to the mingling of races, to ethnic impurity. Immigrant neighborhoods such as Five Points in New York, to which new arrivals streamed (first the Irish, then Italians, Chinese, Jews, and so on), and, even worse, the indigenous quarters of colonial towns, are made into veritable hells. There exists in Algiers a zone of lugubrious shacks "with muddy or dusty paths, depending on the season, but continually infected with excrement."[63] Everywhere in the city the ground is "slippery, mucky, piled with garbage," covered with "sticky things," "organic detritus overheated by the sun."[64]

This omnipresent dirtiness feeds the unhealthiness and corruption of places. It hurts all the senses, saturates the space of vision, of sounds, of intolerable odors. The stench is the most shocking thing, and the smell of poverty sticks to individuals: "something of the faded and cadaverous impregnates your clothes, your hair, your beard, and which all the strongest fragrances can hardly dissipate."[65] Fradin's place, a dive on the Rue Saint-Denis where the destitute may knock themselves unconscious with wine all night long, "exhaled an odor of the hospital and of wild animals, flesh never washed, sordid and damp clothing, old wounds, wine-soaked breathing, sick organs."[66]

The most tenacious odors are those that emanate from sex or from excrement. Most hovels exude the "odors of vice that grab you by the throat"[67]— the smells of vice and death. In Algiers, the Marine quarter smells of the "transpiration from the most secret feminine folds."[68] In old and insalubrious quarters such as the center of Paris, the smell of excrement dominates all the others. In the houses described by Frégier in 1840, "the broken latrines on the fifth floor let fecal matter fall on the stairs, which is swamped all the way down to the ground floor."[69] In *Les bas-fonds de Paris*, a novel that does not fear to play on exaggeration, Bruant has a toilet collapse on a group of revelers who had feasted in the catacombs.[70] But the reality is sometimes worse: in 1866 in the Lambeth workhouse, the whole lower floor was inundated with excrement due to the chronic diarrhea provoked by the residents' poor water and food.[71] Everywhere the atmosphere is full of putrid miasmas. "It is an infernal stench that nothing can chase away; it is inherent in these quarters, everything from there exudes it, and this compresses your chest and strangles you."[72] The worst is in the colonies, where the stench of the lower depths is compounded by the smell of indigenous "races" who are conceived as dirty, impure, sick. In the Kasbah of Algiers, the stench is "killing."[73] The air is tainted, full of nauseous emanations from excrement, decomposing animals, and the lingering smell of bad meat relents. The Kasbah remained this most repugnant place until late in the twentieth century: "In this house that stank of warmed muck, rotten food, cockroaches, and urine, each wall seemed filled with stinking matter, for the smell comes from the walls and windows as well as from mouths; there is not a molecule of this house that does not stink, and no inhabitant who is not approaching a permanent state of asphyxia."[74]

Certain specific places are recognizable by their odor, for example, the British workhouses where the "concentrated and almost fecal stench of the asylum" reigns.[75] Prison is also an olfactory world where one breathes air "infected and saturated with the mortal miasmas exuded from rotted earth, from humid high walls, and from their own filth," explained the inspector from the Committee of Public Assistance in 1791.[76] It seemed nothing could be done. Despite the progressive "improvement" of prisons, the space of incarceration was, above all, foul smelling. "No sooner had the door been opened than it exuded a fetid odor that almost extinguished the light the jailer held up," wrote Louis-François Raban in 1826. The principal cause was what in prison argot was called *griarches*, the pails and buckets that served for detainees' waste, which very often were uncovered and were rarely emptied. "Consequently, the matter they contained is almost continually slopping about and thus they are transformed into contaminated latrines,"[77] explained Villermé in 1820. Even a century later, hygiene, black soap, and creosol disinfectant had not taken care of the problem,[78] a sign that time has little control over that smell. Genet still noted this in 1948: "The odor of prison is the odor of urine, formalin, and paint. I recognized it in all the jails of Europe." And it still remains so: "Prison is first of all an odor; it stank more and more and I had a strong desire to puke."[79]

Filth, both physical and moral, bleeds into the bodies—shapeless, deformed, monstrous—and into characters. The horror of the soul relates to that of bodies and was linked to physiognomic theories that constructed a hideous anthropology of the lower depths. But the horror was indeed there. Jack London, a scrupulous observer, described the emergence in the East End of "a new and different race of people, short of stature and of wretched or beer-sodden appearance.... Here and there lurched a drunken man or woman."[80] A little later, the French journalist Elie Richard mentions "sub-men."[81] Is this world even human? Animalism is general. "Vermin at its most hideous flounders in this muck:"[82] fleas, worms, stinkbugs, often in competition with rats, all bearing germs and sickness. Dogs and cats also wander about in quantity. In the Kasbah of Algiers lived donkeys, dogs, cats, and sheep. In a cellar of London, Reverend Andrew Mearns reported, a sanitary inspector found a father, a mother, three children, and four pigs.[83] Even Friedrich Engels explained that the Irish have not only imported into England alcoholism and dirtiness, they also share their habitats with pigs. "The Irishman loves his pig [...] he eats and sleeps with it, his children play with it, ride upon it, roll in the dirt with it, as any one may see a thousand times repeated in all the great towns of England."[84] Animalism proliferates in the state of carrion. In Paris, noted Honoré Frégier, all one saw "in one house's courtyard was debris from animals, intestines, and the residue of slop, all in full putrefaction."[85]

Animality infects the inhabitants of the lower quarters, as witnessed by the rhetoric of swarming and proliferating that saturates most descriptions. In the "rotten and stinking tenements" of London's East End, "every room houses a family, often two. In another room, a missionary found a man ill with smallpox, his wife just recovering from her eighth confinement, and the children running about half-naked and covered with dirt. Here are seven people living in one underground kitchen, and a little dead child lying in the same room."[86] In Naples, the dangerous classes are compared to maggots.[87] Criminals are described as hyenas, wild animals, vipers, ferocious beasts. Prostitutes are confined like bitches in the pens of brothels, "sorts of economical kennels."[88] "Any human form is erased in a flesh without individuality. It is the jumble of a herd."[89]

In these conditions, how can we imagine that this world is not governed by the bestial and transgressive sexuality of "spoiled flesh"?[90] In the hovels as in the penal colonies, people live "in a world where vice reigns like a destructive miasma."[91] The promiscuity, the piling up of bodies, is the main cause of animal behavior and instincts. In the lower depths of Madrid, the inhabitants "sleep in the same bed just as they eat at the same table—until one night, a man awakens in a state of excitement, and in a semi-conscious state he throws himself into the arms of his daughter or sister or the nearest woman, without the shadow of a marriage, or mingles this with homosexual love."[92] Everywhere vice takes the upper hand, arousing "guilty acts, obscene touching, grave disorders" that the world of the prisons and penal colonies carry to their paroxysm. On top of incest, which people do not dare to mention, comes prostitution, which is overrepresented. As for homosexuality, it too remains barely visible. Only the penal colonies, the prisons, and later the houses of correction permit long reports on the corruption aroused by the "shameful vice." As an example, in the Saint Denis depot in 1834 "the hideous mélange of childhood, decrepitude, and virility" forms there "a monstrous assemblage, swarming with vice and infamy."[93] Yet there existed in London, as in the other capitals of Europe, many homosexual bordellos, modeled on the White Swan in Oxford Street or the Rose Tavern, the "black hole of Sodom" described by the writer Thomas Brown,[94] and police officers like Canler in their memoirs evoke the milieu of "queer" activity. But it was not until the beginning of the twentieth century that the homosexuality of the lower depths was more freely expressed. *Jésus-la-Caille* (1914) by Francis Carco inaugurated tales dramatizing the young ambiguous louts of Montmartre. Twenty years later, the American novelist Djuna Barnes, who had given to the *New York Sun Magazine* many tales of the homosexuals of Greenwich Village, offered a brutal and cruel representation of Parisian lesbians in *Nightwood*.[95] This was a dirty, marginal, and *queer* (in all senses of the word) world at the heart of the lower depths that Haussmann's urban renewal had not reached, a "veritable monstrous parade" of transvestites, lesbians, beggars, and moronic or degenerate children.

THE PEOPLE OF THE LOWER DEPTHS

At the bottom of these unnamable places flourished a frightful "human vegetation."[96] The inhabitants of the lower depths were categorized in interminable lists that I cannot hope to exhaust here. Let me merely mention various "species" to be encountered later on in this book. Five principal families can be distinguished.

The most numerous is incontestably that of the poor, under their multiple identities as indigents, vagabonds, destitute persons, paupers, beggars, the homeless, "the 'empty-stomachs,' . . . the worn out, the incomplete, the 'scum of the bidet.' "[97] The society they composed is as complex and hierarchical as that above, and I cannot cover all its aspects. Most of the tales agree on setting aside those who work, whatever the nature of the job, who manage to escape the world of idleness and indignity. Thus the ragpickers sometimes attract sympathy, as do all those with small jobs, however meager, because regular activity saves them from the abyss. An immense structural fracture separates all the others: on one side the truly poor, victims of life; and on the other, the false ones, all those whom idleness and vice have led into poverty. The former are social wrecks, broken by life, alcohol, or hard luck. "Women with a blank gaze, ageless under their rags, men broken by endless labor, without hope, poor martyred kids with faces of terrible gravity."[98] In Buenos Aires, they call them *atorrantes* because they sleep at night in water supply pipes manufactured by the firm A. Torrent.[99] All of them—or almost all—are condemned to very short lives. Gaunt, in tatters, excluded from the social pact, they play the role of pitiful and pitiable figures: "alone, resigned or timid, inoffensive due to frailty, they wait for nothing more than their turn to die."[100] All the others are the "false poor," children of the Court of Miracles, exploiters of public charity, those who make begging an industry, "those who have managed to falsify poverty itself."[101] These latter constitute the bulk of the herd, even its breeding ground, from which comes the whole society of the lower depths. In their dens "are constantly trained, exercised, and recruited the army of vice, of debauchery, crime, and no doubt also the army of revolt, insurrection, and anarchy."[102] They beg in the street in their rags starting in infancy, they invent all the con tricks to fool public credulity, becoming "falsely legless, falsely armless, falsely maimed."[103] The girls prostitute themselves, the boys will be thieves; all of them will end up in the asylum, the penal colony, or on the scaffold.

The thieves form the second and most powerful nation, which reigns over the people of the lower depths. They are the incarnation par excellence of the crime "professions" of which they bear all the stigmata and vices. Subtle hierarchies pervade them, running from the street urchins who are vicious by nature and by essence, who are said to be irredeemable by the age of fourteen, up to the adventurers and "high-flying" swindlers, whose poise and audacity are fascinating. But all of them "have only their perverse instincts for rules, [...] and tend always to the same goal: theft."[104] The detective Vidocq in *Les voleurs* divides them into three main categories: the weak, who steal under the influence of some passion, principally gambling; the necessitous, whom poverty alone has made guilty of robbery; the professional thieves, who are "from ten to twelve quite distinct species, without counting the sub-varieties, and then come the nuances." It is the latter, incorrigible due to their frequent presence in prison, who dominate the lower depths. The most violent live in bands and fight each other for control of territories: Parisian thugs and then *apaches*, Marseilles' *nervis*, New York's Dead Rabbits and Bowery Boys, British Scuttlers, Ikers, Peaky Blinders, and Hooligans. The most intelligent stand out for a specialty, an expertise, or rare skills. But all of them form a society distinct in its habit, its appearance, its language. "This is a people apart, without faith or law, without fire or home (*sans foi ni loi, sans feu ni lieu*)," writes Maxime du Camp, "perverted beings who, repudiating any constraint, stripped of any shame, live outside society and only touch it in order to harm it."[105] This is the reason they have populated the stories of outcasts since the end of the Middle Ages, and in which their "ruses, finesses, and skillful ploys," described by a menu, are untiringly retold.

A companion of fortune encountered in the lower depths of the East End confided to Jack London that here there are no women in real need—those who lack time, money, or even desire.[106] He should have stated that there are no "honest" women because the lower depths are engorged with—and literally disgorge—women "living the bad life." Prostitution is everywhere. Girls who are "bare-chested, lolling, ignoble; a fluttering of pale flesh, red sweaters, pink corsets, red hair; sometimes the little face is pretty, even fresh, but always the lewd mouth and the obscene gestures."[107] Except for young girls and old women—though vice has no age and the worst is always possible—all the women could be considered to be prostitutes. Where else could sexuality lead when it is decoupled from its reproductive function? This is the flesh of the lower depths, the incarnation of its constitutive debauchery. In contrast to other forbidden kinds of sexuality (inversion, sophism, sodomy, incest, bestiality, and so on) that are all highly euphemized, prostitution is omnipresent and literally saturates representations. The inversion of norms that characterizes the lower depths makes selling one's body an ordinary and usual activity, all the more scandalous because it incites other crimes ("macabre secrets," "perversions," abortion, infanticide); it engenders sickness and death. Even more structurally, in the composite and even improbable universe of the lower depths, the society of girls is the only one to maintain a form of social link, just as it is the only one to provide for the economic survival of the group. But despite her crucial role, the prostitute is badly paid in return for the physical and moral domination that is her daily bread. And when age and decline wither her charms, she is thrown out on the street or into the asylum, reduced to the state of a vile body as a beggar or vagrant woman.

However, not all the forms of prostitution are equal in the imaginary of the lower depths. Representations of it are paralleled in another social dimension: the universe of the *grandes horizontales* and courtesans of the Parisian *demi-monde*, the "pretty horse-breakers" of Hyde Park or the "Skittles" of Regent Street, who do not experience the depths except at the twilight of their lives, when they are caught by the sickness that leads them to the hospice or to the pavement of the Rue Monjol, one of "these sordid alleys where 'emptied' girls from everywhere came to be washed up."[108] But prostitution's all-comers people the lower depths: the lost tramps, the streetwalkers, the women with flabby, soft flesh of those who have worked a long time. The women of Saint-Merri are "fat and bulging, they are no longer fresh, but customers are not lacking, particularly local butchers and tripe-merchants accustomed to kneading raw meat."[109] All are hideous figures, and degrees of horror lead to the madame, the ogress, the woman who pimps young girls. Their sordid flesh, which is naturally on display, gives these spaces their moral, physical, and sensory identity. In Buenos Aires, "la Boca perspires like a lovely girl who does not care for herself;" in Nantes the *Quai de la Fosse*—sometimes nicknamed *Quai de la Fesse* (Quay of the Ass)—"was heavy with the stench of syphilis."[110] As the major figure of the lower depths, the prostitute sexualizes space, makes it into "an immense, gaping, unique sexual organ. The alleys are its folds, the houses its bulges, perhaps its pimples, its blisters; and the lights its covering that glints with sweat. The comings-and-goings of men and the cries are the beating of the heart's blood, the large and strong pulse of the vulva of the terrain stretching to the port."[111]

The fourth group comprises prisoners, detainees, convicts, and those incarcerated. This might be the most heterogeneous group because it includes various types such as condemned men and convicts who are serving sentences imposed by the courts, but also beggars, indigents, and vagabonds who have been increasingly locked up and put to work since the Middle Ages. But there are also prostitutes, of whom many are held in "*maisons closes*," where the regulatory system that became dominant after 1800 places them permanently at the mercy of administrative internment. And mental patients were being increasingly interned, especially in France after an 1838 law, as well as undesirables of all kinds: idiots, epileptics, syphilitics, the incurable, the senile. In short, an immense cohort of the outcast that nothing seems to unite but the fact of being locked up. And perhaps the lower depths truly exist only here, in the frightful mélange and artificial combining of all the socially dammed. Governments invented locales for this terrible mélange, starting with the "Grand Imprisonment" in the middle of the seventeenth century. Here is Bicêtre at the gates of Paris. Built on the ruins of a château that was said to be haunted, it was first a military hospital, created by Louis XIII in 1632 to receive "old, crippled and obsolete soldiers." In 1656, the creation of a "General Hospital" gave it its true vocation: "simultaneously a hospice, a state prison, and an asylum for madmen."[112] At the end of the seventeenth century, venereal cases (who were now castigated) were added, plus scrofulous adults, and children who had been placed in correction. A register of 1716 takes a census: "epileptics, the insane, feeble minds, deaf-mutes, those with scrofula or scurvy, the blind, the crippled, those suffering from ringworm, the misshapen, the mangy, venereal, the Deserving Poor, paralytics, invalid soldiers, foundlings, orphans."[113] It was there during the Revolution that Dr. Guillotin experimented with his machine, and there that convicts were put in irons and the chain gang was yanked in the direction of Toulon or Brest. Here, too, those condemned to death awaited the day of their execution. For two whole centuries, Bicêtre was "the receptacle of all that society has that is most vile," wrote Sébastien Mercier in the *Tableau de Paris*; it was "the vast sewer into which flowed all the mud of the kingdom," added Lamartine.[114] The arrangement was somewhat relieved by the reforms of psychiatrist Philippe Pinel, then the opening in 1830 of a prison for children at the Petite Roquette, and finally, the suppression of the chain gang in 1836. After 1850, Bicêtre was only an asylum and a hospice for indigents. "The administration of hospitals," noted Paul Bru, "has finally achieved the separation of crime from misfortune."[115] But the journalists who described the hospice in the 1920s continued to describe terrifying scenes worthy of the paintings of Hieronymus Bosch. "Bicêtre is the sepulcher of the living," noted Elie Richard, "as an Apocalypse befitting an inferior humanity."[116]

If one needed a second example of what might be called legal lower depths, there is Blackwell's Island in the East River between Manhattan and Queens in New York (today Roosevelt Island), an extraordinary site of relegation that mixed criminals, vagabonds, prostitutes, the insane, the sick, and the homeless.[117] Bought by the City of New York from the Blackwell family in 1828, the island was devoted to charitable and punitive institutions. In 1832, a penitentiary was built on it, a massive and lugubrious building of four stories and five hundred cells. Seven years later, it inaugurated an insane asylum, the Octagon, which Charles Dickens visited in 1842. In 1852, a poorhouse of 220 cells was added to maintain drunken indigents or debtors, and in 1856 a hospital to care for smallpox was added, but to which were also sent paralytics, epileptics, idiots, the blind, prostitutes, syphilitics, and others afflicted with incurable diseases. The construction in 1860 of a hospice for the indigent completed the ensemble. In the 1870s, there were almost eight thousand people of all kinds shut up there,[118] living in horrible conditions, mistreated by unworthy or venal guards. Roosevelt was a veritable museum of horrors. After a report by Nellie Bly in 1888, the authorities tried to put an end to abuses, and in 1921, the island was renamed (without irony) Welfare Island. But it was almost half a century before it was definitively closed down, and only in 1935 were penitentiary detainees transferred to Rikers Island.

The gypsies form the last category, the most homogeneous because it tends to subsume all the others. Gypsies, abhorred as a "cursed race," concentrate in their persons all the traits of the lower depths: they are said to be dirty, vicious, bearers of contagious diseases, beggars, thieves, murderers, and members of an occult organization that certainly exists. In England, they were reputed to be horse swindlers and money counterfeiters.[119] What better place than a gypsy camp to incarnate the lower depths? In Paris at the end of the nineteenth century, about two thousand of them camped near the Portes de Levallois in Montreuil, and especially in the south, between Montrouge, Kremlin-Bicêtre, and Ivry. This was the "country of the *gueux*" (now meaning rogues), the title given by *La vie illustrée* (December 4, 1908) to a mass of shacks, huts, caravans, garbage, and excrement, in which there lived in sickening promiscuity women, men, children, and animals of all kinds—"dogs, pigs, goats, donkeys, horses and even bears"[120]—all of them thieves and criminals.

COUNTERSOCIETIES

Paradoxically, this sordid, violent, and vicious universe is often described as a powerful and hierarchized countersociety. From the Kingdom of Argot at the end of the Middle Ages up to the contemporary mafia, this countersociety is a distinctive trait of the underworld—and perhaps the only one capable of giving identity and coherence to the improbable union of all sorts of marginal people. The whole imaginary of the underworld rests on this belief in the existence of a nation, a people, "a world apart that has its history, its traditions, its customs, its manners, its concepts, its needs, its morality, its vanity, its heroes, its glories, its language, even its literature, art, and way of thinking."[121]

Thieves and criminals, who are always depicted as belonging to vast organized gangs, were best placed to give currency to this idea. "It must be recognized that at this time there exists among us an organized society of crime. All members of this society help each other, and they rely on one another; each day they combine to disturb the public peace. They form a small nation inside the large one," noted Tocqueville in 1843.[122] It is a brotherhood, added Moreau-Christophe, united by the invisible ties of criminal solidarity.[123] And when M. Claude visited London a few years later, he described a "vast and cosmopolitan corporation of crooks and murderers."[124] This is a constant theme in representations dating back to the first descriptions of a society of thieves. Since the fifteenth century, thieves and murderers have been presented as redoubtable companies and as counterkingdoms (more on this in chapter 2).

In London in 1750, novelist Henry Fielding stated that villains "are incorporated in one Body [and have] officers and a Treasury"; and "have reduced theft and robbery to a regular system."[125] Such representations were reinforced in the nineteenth and twentieth centuries. The mafia and camorra claim to be secret societies with strict rules and rites even though they are criminal associations. In Berlin at the beginning of the 1930s, Kessel explored the Unterwelt, describing it as a formidable organization, "'a State within the State' in its implacable hierarchy and discipline."[126] As the natural companions of crooks, prostitutes are fully incorporated into this society. Then the observation of detainees, which discovered solid structures in prisons and penal colonies, gave even more weight to these countersocietal representations.

But belief in the existence of a parallel brotherhood involved not just the world of crime; from the start it was associated with beggars, vagabonds, and bohemians. Pitiable foot soldiers in the army of crime, all of them shared a mysterious link, an occult affection that undoubtedly attached them to "the great rebel and vagabond tribe for whom everything that is social is alien."[127] This seemed to go without saying for gypsies, presented since their arrival in France at the beginning of the fifteenth century as a homogenous nation led by the Count of Little Egypt.[128] Broadsheets and popular literature were pleased to spread the idea of a bohemian counterkingdom. Ponson du Terrail published *The King of the Bohemians* in 1867 and *The Queen of the Gypsies* in 1871. Later, Blaise Cendrars, in his autobiography *L'homme foudroyé* (the Astonished Man), recounts the election of the king at the Bicêtre Kremlin. Such an idea was shared by the authorities, especially the police, and this suspicion justified measures of surveillance and inspection, the census of

1895, and the very discriminatory law of 1912 that required nomads to possess an anthropometric identity card. But all kinds of vagabonds supposedly belonged to this rolling army. Here is how the journalist André Charpentier describes this improbable association in 1930:

> As extraordinary as this might appear, the wandering strays, the vagabonds, the ragged and shoeless of the underworld are all part of a mysterious and redoubtable association and they possess a common language that is transmitted from generation to generation among the "poor buggers" ever since the *Cour des miracles.*[129]

There is a system of signaling among them, a veritable outcast code that ensures communications among the members of this dispersed horde.[130] "All those affiliated with the lower depths are united by this enigmatic link that they faithfully transmit without changing anything, and which facilitates their miserable existence on the margins of a society that hunts them down and whom they hate."[131]

The most obvious sign of this organization lies in the existence of a language common to all marginal people. *Argot* (slang), "the vile language," gives the group a foundation and assures its identity. "What is slang?" asks Hugo in *Les misérables*. "It is at one and the same time the nation and the dialect; it is theft in its two kinds, people and language."[132] As soon as the figure of the outcast appeared, there was a strong conviction that it was by language that the group prospered, that it was structured by language.[133] Henri Estienne in 1556 denounced the "jargon by means of which the robbers look after each other and their bands can communicate."[134] And from *La vie généreuse* (published in 1596) to the *Mystères de Paris*, to journalistic reports between the two World Wars, all texts describing the lower depths are like lexicons that reveal to the reader the secrets of this "infamous vocabulary."[135] The function of slang is complex. In part it is a language that is picturesque, exotic, often tinged with notes that are burlesque or comic, and therefore it has a clearly playful function. But slang is also an instrument of duplicity that makes the lower depths a coded universe. "The ignoble and disgusting classes of human societies have composed *argot* to dissimulate the secrets of debauchery and crime," writes Charles Nodier.[136] Thus it is also the language of threat, a lingo that is gradually criminalized and becomes the "atrocious" language of prisons and penal colonies, and also the language of dissidence, of those who want to destroy civilization.

The underworld is not a universe in itself. It is always the inverse of the society above, of which it counterfeits and perverts the how that society functions. This is the reason it must necessarily be organized, hierarchized, and coded. From its popular roots, it has conserved the carnivalesque dimension of the world turned upside down. One is struck by how often descriptions in any given historical period can be traced over legitimate institutions or structures as their inverse. During the *ancien régime*, the lower depths functioned like an inverted monarchy—the "Kingdom" of Argot—with its sovereign, its ranks and levels, its corporations with well-defined duties. During the Revolution, they were seeking a new model: in the history of *chauffeurs* (thieves who burned the feet of their victims to find out where money was hidden) published by P. Leclair in 1799, the bandits assembled in council and decided to imitate the new organization of revolutionary France, divided into *départements*, into *arrondissements*, into cantons: "The Revolution that had taken place in France inspired Fleur d'Épine (the head of the gang) with the grand design for modifying its political system and mimicking the respectable establishments of the new régime, by regenerating its very own."[137] When the nineteenth century was seeking a new lens for reading social realities, it invented the concept of class, and so here were now the "criminal classes," "predatory classes," "dangerous classes." In revanchist France of the 1870s, the underworld was presented as the "army of crime." Later on, in the interwar era, it was conceived of as the "syndicate," "cartels," *Konzern*. In this organizational roundabout, the lower depths revealed their true nature: the inverted double, a counterfeit and caricatured version of orderly society.

These lower depths are not immutable. Profound changes affect them too, as you will see in the following chapters. However, they can be recognized as an incontestable transnational reality. Nothing resembles a Polish outcast more than an English vagabond or an Italian beggar. The iconography shows the same deformed bodies, the same grimacing faces, the same repugnant rags. At a time when the construction of national types was accelerating, poverty and crime proclaimed their transversal dimension. The circulation of texts, images, and motifs (at least in the Western world) contributed strongly to this phenomenon, to the point that we might consider the imaginary of the lower depths as the prime grand fact of cultural globalization. The fifteenth and sixteenth centuries were foundational, but the new resources of printing, networks for spreading rumors, and an extended readership's lively interest in these questions all increased the imaginary's circulation, exchanges, and transfers.[138] Distinctions and nuances appeared, but a Europe of *gueuserie* (roguery) indisputably emerged. The middle of the nineteenth century sees a clear acceleration due to the appearance of the serial novel, which accounted for the phenomenon of "urban mysteries." The novel by Eugène Sue was in itself a "world novel" (it evoked Germany, England, Algeria, and the question of slavery), but its extraordinary dissemination in the form of translations, imitations, adaptations, and appropriations constituted an exceptional phenomenon, which the mystery cycles that followed all endeavored to reproduce. The turning point of the nineteenth to the twentieth century marked a new enlargement. The explosion of international migrations brought about soaring trafficking of all sorts, principally of the prostitution market, which very rapidly globalized the system of representations. The colonial empires, China, and Latin America again became points of fixation. Major international ports were promoted at the heart of a trade system described as cosmopolitan. Hamburg, for example, "the Chicago over the Rhine," offered an "extraordinary mélange of every race, a veritable society of nations united by vice, where the drunken Peruvian fraternizes with the drunken Portuguese, where the Swede drinks beer mixed with cognac from the same glass as the Japanese, and the Italian succeeds the Brazilian in the arms of a girl from Berlin, from Cairo, or even from Paris."[139] All the major cities are now capitals of crime, and new figures emerge, such as the international pimp. One example will suffice; the sinister Raquedalle, "a repugnant product of the Parisian sidewalks," was dramatized by Aristide Bruant in *Les bas-fonds de Paris*. But very quickly, thanks to prostitution, he becomes the "universal man":

He is today in the Faubourg Montmartre; the next day takes his absinthe in Monaco or at the Café Royal in London's Regent Street; he then sails to New York; after a time, he is found in Cairo, Constantinople, Berlin, Vienna . . . the spiffing man—a genius, sir, a true genius!—fingers in everything, in all the tricks and all the possible and unimaginable treasures.[140]

2

Courts of Miracles

The nineteenth century gave the lower depths their name and their modern configuration, but many of their motifs are rooted in the more distant past, from which they draw a large part of their force. What they present is both immemorial and terribly present, which is why the underworld is so disturbing and so fascinating. In this chapter, I examine these traces in a discursive archeology that highlights the oldest strata, which continued to work upon this imaginary for a long time. This decisive sequence developed in the years of crisis at the hinge between the Middle Ages and modern times; on both the ideological and narrative planes, a fundamental matrix was set up, of which the *cour des miracles* (court of miracles) constitutes its high point and its icon. But it also borrows from many previous images, biblical and ancient principally, that gave rise to the vanishing lines from which this imaginary would burgeon in the eighteenth and nineteenth centuries.

SODOM, ROME, BABYLON

Western culture, to which this book confines itself, is ancient, drawing its sources from the Judeo-Christian tradition as much as from Greek and Roman antiquity. The Bible and the classical "humanities" have been the cultural manuals of our world. They forged the references from which our predecessors have thought and reacted, so we should not be surprised at the continual presence of these sources in stories of the underworld. In fact, the intrinsically "moral" and normalizing dimension of this imaginary accentuates the recourse to religious attestations, making the Bible more present than the founding texts of ancient culture, which are often considered to be more transgressive or more permissive.

Of the three cities that served as the urban armature of this imaginary, the biblical cities are the most significant, beginning with Sodom (Gomorrah is often forgotten), references to which nourish representations of the underworld down to the present day. The sinful city of Sodom incarnates vice—homosexuality as much as debauchery and lust—as practiced in a collective mode and, in this sense, inaugurates the antiurban discourse that is consubstantial with the imaginary of the bas-fonds. Let us briefly recall the content of the chapters of Genesis (18–19) that relate this event: God finds that "very great sin" is being committed by the inhabitants of Sodom, and he sends two angels there, who lodge with Lot, the nephew of Abraham. These two strangers, handsome and rich, attract the desire of the city's inhabitants, who demand that Lot deliver the new arrivals to them. Lot refuses and offers them his two daughters instead, an offer that is not accepted. Then the angels tell Lot and his household to leave and never return. Convinced of the crimes of Sodom (and also the guilt of the neighboring city of Gomorrah), "the Lord rained down fire and brimstone from the skies on Sodom and Gomorrah" that destroyed these cities and everyone living there (Genesis 19:24). But in their flight, Lot's wife turned to look back at the spectacle of destruction, and she was turned into a pillar of salt.

This story, recounted a thousand times, is foundational. In this instance, we want to retain the association of the city with collective lust, with the refusal of hospitality (a crime in societies of nomadic shepherds), as well as the ban on representing vice. Sodom henceforth became the absolute symbol of sexual perversion; there is scarcely any urban underworld that is not associated with it. For example, Paris is a "city that one might believe grafted onto Sodom and Gomorrah," we read in *Les mystères du Palais-Royal*.[1] But the expression is especially valid for London. Puritanical and obsessed by the idea of sexual debauchery, British culture trained its eyes on the sinful city. The Rose Tavern, a famous den in Covent Garden, was known as "the black hole of Sodom,"[2] and the area around nearby St. Giles was a "modern Sodom," as John Duncombe wrote in 1835.[3] The reference to the biblical city is obligatory both as a cliché, an imprecation, and as a suitable way of evoking "unspeakable" vice. Its name was splashed across the pages of newspapers during the Cleveland Street scandal in 1889 with the discovery of the existence of a bordello for men frequented by the best of London society, including Prince Albert Victor.[4] These usages carried over into the twentieth century, especially when depicting the situation in penitentiaries. Describing the universe of houses of correction in 1932, reporter Henri Danjou evoked at length the "bacchanals of Sodom over which reigned" young kingpins, as well as the "lamentable Gomorrahs" where the females were located.[5]

Babylon was another great biblical reference, even more important than Sodom. The symbol of the earthly city as contrasted with the celestial city of Jerusalem, Babylon was the great prostitute, "the Mother of the shameless and of the Earth's abominations." Everything about her was repulsive: she incarnated corruption, decadence, and dehumanized and perverted mercantilism. She was the dissolute city that practiced sacred prostitution. Each woman, reports Herodotus, had to couple at least once in her life with a stranger in the Temple of Ishtar and give money to the goddess. Babylon was also, says the book of Daniel, the site of political power, meaning of men who governed—instead of (and in the place of) God. But the city is complex, and it is one of the mysteries in the book of Revelation, where the apocalyptic meaning of Babylon remains hidden from human comprehension.[6] The accursed city, both in temporal and spiritual terms, long conserved an immense power of fascination. Protestants reactivated its image to describe Rome, and Victorians used it to depict London. Its shadow weighed heavily on antiurban discourse, which has been constant in modern civilizations. In the eighteenth century, urban growth and Romanticism revived the specter of Babylon.

As the antithesis of values underlying Western society, Babylon is the space of the ugly, of vice, of the spirit of lucre, of morbid passions. And Babylon became the usual term to describe the pathologies, the apocalyptic visions, and the anxieties of the city. London, especially, "the modern Babylon,"[7] the great black Babylon, is invested with an immense corrupting influence, in which immorality, irreligion, vice, crime, and class conflicts are mingled. In 1885 journalist William Stead published what became the most monumental scoop of the century (how he bought from her mother a young virgin for five pounds sterling), and his story in the *Pall-Mall Gazette* was titled "The Maiden Tribute to Modern Babylon." But Paris was not left out, Vidocq and Bruant frequently employed the Babylon expression. *Les mystères du Palais-Royal* makes Paris the "quintessence of the modern Babylon." Paris is the "source and international headquarters of the white slave trade," American missionaries wrote in 1909, concluding that the city had become the "Modern Babylon."[8] Indeed, the gradual internationalization of the lower depths multiplied the incarnations of Babylon. In 1864 the French serial writers Henri-Émile Chevalier and Théodore Labourieu published a book titled *Les Trois Babylones: Paris, Londres, New York.*[9]

Due to the strong impregnation of the culture of the time by the humanities, Greco-Latin history and mythology were morally less mobilized. Yet they did supply a repertoire of examples, figures, and texts (think of Petronius's *Satyricon* or Apuleius's *The Golden Ass*) that provided many representations of disreputable milieux. From slave markets offering young children in Alexandria's neighborhoods of prostitution to "the whorehouse of Canopus," from gambling taverns to the company of gladiators, antiquity was not viewed as particularly moral.[10] Rome, especially, with its crowded and ill-famed quarters of Suburra, Janiculum, or Velabrum, concentrated debauchery in areas where "little people" coexisted—the marginals, the destitute, thieves, prostitutes, runaway slaves, and street children. Plautus mentions beggars meeting at the Trigeminal Gate. Singular figures emerge, such as the *leno*—a pimp, slave trader, and go-between, an odious personage stigmatized by writers—or the Suburra girls, as well as participants in high society orgies on the Aventine Hill, symbolized by Messalina, the wife of Emperor Claudius. These representations only slightly nourish later tales of the lower depths, but some attempts do appear, such as that of the novelist Félix Deriège who at the height of the vogue for "urban mysteries" in 1847 tried to import the genre into Roman antiquity. Although he does describe some dens, his *Mystères de Rome* is in fact a historical novel more concerned with conjuring Catilina than with exploring the city's underworld.[11] Sometimes figures and places do appear: the Minotaur, the pirates of Sicily, or the city of Corinth, famous for its sacred prostitution and its high concentration of brothels. In 1906 Maurice Talmeyr described certain Paris quarters as "the current Corinth."[12] But unlike Sodom or Babylon, these references remain isolated and do not amount to a representational system.

INVENTION OF THE "UNDESERVING POOR"

The distinction between "good" and "bad" poor people, which soon corresponded to a distinction between the true and false poor, was one of the principal force lines that structured representations of the lower depths. The idea that countless indigents were fully responsible for a state that they had chosen out of vice, laziness, or aptitude commanded a major share of the representations. By permitting a linkage of poverty with immorality, of indigence with crime, this combination can be found at the very source of the phenomenon. The history of the poor in Europe is the subject of an immense bibliography that highlights the principal inflexions in the theme. Until the thirteenth century (more or less) the dominant opinion valorized poverty (even sometimes exalted it) as a sanctifying virtue. Relying on the example of Christ, but also of Job and Lazarus—plus the very positive figure of the Greek philosopher Diogenes—the poor man was seen as the "poor of God," the "poor of Christ," the "poor with Peter." He was a worthy and meritorious individual, a bearer of virtue, the "elect of God and the image of Christ." His example inspired the vow of poverty in the mendicant religious orders, whose model was Christ abandoning all wealth. It was a Christian duty to give alms to the poor. Therefore, the church fathers (and the authority that emanated from them) did not consider begging to be infamous. Doubts might arise (stories circulated about the trickery and dissimulation of some beggars), but they were not sufficient to challenge church doctrine.

The decisive rupture took place between the end of the twelfth and the middle of the thirteenth centuries, dictated in part by economic and social evolutions. Until then poverty had been collective and universal; precariousness was widespread and affected a large majority of the population, and it could be attenuated by charity from the village, the parish, the seigneury. But then the context changed: demographic growth, transformations in agrarian structures, urban growth, and the spread of the money economy all tended to complicate and to stratify society. The rising merchant capitalists did not want to be encumbered with people who were "useless to the world," and they insisted on the cardinal value of "work." In France and in England, the thirteenth century saw the appearance of the terms *vagabond* and *vagrant*,[13] a tendency to move from general and collective (hence acceptable) poverty to individual poverty. The poor were no longer the mass of the population and did not incarnate the body social. Now they were only a portion, so they could be gradually stigmatized. Poverty ceased being a positive value and became the product of degradation. First in Italian communes and then rapidly spreading throughout Christian Europe, the figure of the "shameful poor" emerged,[14] someone who did not exhibit him- or herself, and certainly did not beg. In counterpoint, this figure highlighted the rise of another antithetical category, the "undeserving" poor, who were beginning to be described as ugly, dirty, infirm, nasty, ragged, contemptible, and rootless. This was a decisive moment. The dichotomy it produced unleashed the prime labeling process in the history of representations of the social margins. There, at the beginning of the fourteenth century, according to Michel Mollat, was born the category of the "dangerous class."[15] The series of crises at the time—wars, the Black Death, famines—accentuated this phenomenon. This change in perception had major consequences for the world of indigents, who were now facing increasing stigmatization and repression and soon had to face society's temptation to lock them up.

Starting from this split, we witness a continuous and irreversible decline of the "good poor," who became less and less numerous, in favor of the "bad poor," who were more and more often rejected. Reformation beliefs in predestination and the valorization of work accentuated these trends. Concerned with banishing "good works" in favor of "faith alone," Protestants no longer glorified poverty but instead wanted to eradicate it. Innumerable representations now associated the indigent with all kinds of transgressive and deviant behavior, insisting on the laziness, duplicity, and trickery with which a "cloud of maleficent insects" attacked the peasantry:[16]

they were "pirates,"[17] rubbish and detritus, social parasites. "Poverty itself is no longer, as it was in the Middle Ages, the sign of transcendence, the image of Christ on earth," stated a publicist at the end of the nineteenth century, "it is the sign of degeneration, the image of the animalistic that threatens humanity."[18] The increasingly rare "good poor" were reduced to a remnant consisting of the infirm, invalids, old people, and orphans—even so, they were still suspect. Because any truly poor person was necessarily full of shame, all those who could be seen as poor were a priori the "*misérables*."

In parallel, an initial process of racialization occurred. The emergence of spurious indigence coincided with the arrival in Europe of the gypsies, and the synchrony with which the two themes progressed at the end of the Middle Ages is striking. In France in 1419, in a city in the east of France, occurs the first mention of a troupe led by the Count of Little Egypt, the mythical gypsy leader.[19] Paris was confronted by this "foreign population" eight years later, in August 1427, as narrated in the *Journal d'un bourgeois de Paris*: one hundred individuals who inspire a mixture of curiosity and fear are nevertheless welcomed, thanks to their Christian faith and to their persecution by the Saracens.[20] But the tone changed rapidly; gypsies were soon accused of theft and sorcery, and the hostility became general by the beginning of the sixteenth century. In 1560, the Orléans Ordinance enjoins them to quit the kingdom under pain of being sent to the galleys.[21] From then on, the edicts of interdiction and banishment multiply in an attempt to purge the kingdom of an "evil mob." The stigmatization of gypsies goes hand in hand with that of rogues. In England, their arrival is mentioned at the beginning of the reign of King Henry VIII in the early sixteenth century, and the quickly signaled presence of "dark strangers" played a major role in the definition of roguery.[22]

Disparagement, labeling, and repression marched along in concert. The first known nomenclatures of begging come from the Germanic world and from institutional texts. In 1342, for example, the city of Augsburg closed its gates to five categories of mendicants; the following year it increased the list to nine (presenting themselves as Jews, pilgrims, the sick, the infirm, the blind, and so forth, all corresponding to imaginary states that were simulated in order to beg more effectively).[23] Shortly afterward, around 1360, the register of Dithmar of Meckebach, the chancellor to the King of Bohemia

Charles IV, presented a nomenclature of eleven categories of thieves and criminals (thieves of horses or silver, counterfeiters, purse-cuts, and so forth). These texts of a legal and political nature resulted from a concern for social control (unmasking imposters)—and also from the desire to decode a universe conceived as forbidden.

These descriptions swelled in the fifteenth century. From 1430 to 1444, the city of Basel published a long list enumerating twenty-six categories of beggars and vagabonds who were falsely infirm, with a very precise description of the tricks and procedures designed to arouse commiseration and alms-giving. The list stressed the case of the pretend-blind, who covered their eyes with bloody rags or even punctured the eyes of their children. Thus it was as much a matter of unmasking shameful and criminal tactics as of preserving citizens from being duped by them. Legal institutions also issued such documents, as in the middle of the fifteenth century, during the trial in Dijon of the band of *Coquillards* (who wore the false "scallop shells" of pilgrims to St. James of Compostella) that was investigated by the magistrate Jean Robustel. The document contains a long enumeration of sixty-two types of crooks (*crocheteur, pipeur, vendangeur, desgobischeur, blanc coulon*, and so on) along with an explanation of each activity and the jargon surrounding it.

Stigmatization soon gave way to the desire for detention. In the mid-fifteenth century, almost everywhere measures were taken again vagabonds and the poor, who had to be "set to work." In 1349, King Edward III of England promulgated a *Statute of Labourers*, which was designed to repress professional begging.[24] In January 1350, an edict from the King of France, John the Good, banned the able-bodied from begging, and the King of Castile, Pedro I, did the same the following year.[25] All these measures, which were responding to each other, were in full accord with new representations that desacralized the poor. An ordinance of 1367 declared that those who could work—but chose not to—would be imprisoned. The alternative was simple: either work or be punished; and some, including Jean de Gerson (theologian and Chancellor of Paris University), proposed "enclosures for the poor."[26] But the various monarchies did not have the means to apply this principle, which was being discussed everywhere in Europe by the end of the Middle Ages. Experiments in detention took place in Flanders in

1525, and in London dangerous indigents were incarcerated in the Bridewell house of correction starting in 1553. In France, those picked up on the major roads were sent to the galleys. A Parisian order of 1545 prescribed that merchant provosts and magistrates should open forced labor workhouses for able-bodied beggars, but this order had scarcely any effect. In Lyon in 1614, the Rectors of Charity decided to detain the poor in a general almshouse that had been created in 1534. They were soon imitated by the Charity of Marseille.[27] A massive movement was at work in Europe in these years of crisis, to which Louis XIV's absolutist state gave decisive impetus with creation of the *Hôpital Général*.

The context was difficult in the "somber seventeenth" century of multiform crises, which was marked by a rapid rise in the numbers of indigents and vagabonds. The conflation of poverty, delinquency, and sin progressed quickly. In his famous *Civil and Criminal Trials*, whose first version appeared in Lyon in 1607, Claude Le Brun de la Rochette associated laziness with poverty and lust. Consequently, the temptation was growing stronger to imprison the poor in hospitals, which was inspired by the English and Dutch systems of forced labor. Most "good people" in France shared this sentiment: "Indigence is despised everywhere these days," wrote François de la Mothe Le Vayer in 1643 in *Des richesses et de la pauvreté* (On Riches and Poverty).[28] The creation of Paris's Hôpital Général in April 1656 belongs in this favorable context. Until then a hospital had been a "house of charity established to receive and treat without pay the indigent sick," as Pierre Larousse wrote. It offered hospitality to pilgrims, to travelers, to the infirm, and to the sick. These "hospitals" were religious establishments destined to receive and help the deprived. But the new institution had quite another function, offering an obligatory and normalized form of assistance in which the able-bodied poor were put into forced labor. Its goal was to prevent begging and laziness: the "sources of all disorder." Targeted were the poor "of all sexes, places, ages, of whatever quality and birth, and of whatever estate they may be, able-bodied or invalid, sick or convalescent, curable or incurable." Paris's Hôpital Général was formed by gathering together five preexisting institutions: La Pitié and the Savonnerie for children, the Salpêtrière and the House of Refuge (the future St. Pelagius) for women, and finally Bicêtre, where men, old beggars, and undesirables had been lodged.

We know little about how the institution functioned, but it was a mixture of convent, prison, asylum, and manufactory.

In 1662, this system was extended to the whole kingdom. In effect, an edict prescribed the creation of such a hospital for the poor and beggars in every town, and it encouraged these institutions to appoint retainers or guards to make inquiries about beggars. "All of these poor will be instructed in piety and the Christian religion, and in trades in which they can make themselves capable, without their being permitted to wander, nor to go from town to town under any pretext whatsoever, nor to come into our good city of Paris, and in which the inhabitants of cities and big towns will be constrained by all due and reasonable means."[29] These were by no means structures of care but, instead, of imprisonment. If the detainee's state of health required it, he or she was sent to the Hôtel-Dieu: on-site infirmaries were not installed until 1781.[30]

We know that this arrangement was a subject of *Madness and Civilization* by Michel Foucault, who saw it as the expression of a normative power proper to a monarchical order that was being asserted at the time, the centerpiece of an absolutist arrangement suitable to the classical age. "Hence the Hôpital does not have the appearance of a mere refuge for those whom age, infirmity, or sickness have kept from laboring; it will have not only the aspect of a forced labor camp, but also that of a moral institution responsible for punishing, for correcting a certain moral 'abeyance' which does not merit the tribunal of men, but cannot be corrected by the severity of penance alone. The *Hôpital Général* has an ethical status."[31] This was for Foucault the sign of the growing hold of the state over individuals that inaugurated modern systems of discipline. A whole network of institutions for imprisonment was thrown across Europe, which the British investigator John Howard would soon visit and describe in *The State of Prisons in England and Wales* in 1777.

Foucault's analysis was much criticized by historians for its overly general formulas and for its description of provisions as they were conceived without reference to their actual application. In truth, the Hôpital Général idea was seldom put into effect, first for financial reasons, and then due to the many local conflicts and rivalries that it aroused. By 1663, it had gathered only six thousand people in Paris, half of them able-bodied, and the other half composed of old people, children, the infirm, or crippled. Therefore, it affected only a minority of the crowd of vagabonds and destitute in Paris at the time. Many historians have relativized the scope of the 1656 edict, recalling that many other edicts had preceded it and that others would follow.[32] The system was expensive, not very productive, detested by the people, and functioned badly,[33] and many attempts were made to reform it. Throughout the eighteenth century many ideas were put forward regarding ways of interning able-bodied beggars and putting them to work. A repressive turning point occurred in August 1764, when it was decided to send beggars to the galleys and to reserve the hospital for the aged, the women, and the sick, and to place children in "specialized" structures such as foundlings' homes or the Hôtel-Dieu. But the desire to intern vagabonds and mendicants persisted, and 1764 saw the creation of mendicity depositories, which a decree from the State Council made mandatory in October 1767. By 1768 there were eighty of them, but they also took in the mentally ill, prostitutes, even pilgrims, and therefore were scarcely different from the hospital. An ordinance of July 1777 invited internment in a "house of force" of "any beggar found either in the streets of Paris, or at the doors of houses, in public places, or in churches."[34] These "begging depots" were just as negatively viewed as the old Hôpital Général. Sébastien Mercier depicted those of Paris as places of degradation and corruption, which entrained its guests "down the path of the low-life and debauchery."[35] But the French revolutionaries were just as repressive with respect to idleness and did not want to close them.[36] They even considered transporting the bad poor to Madagascar, but in July 1791 they came back to the depot solution (renamed "receiving houses"), which now was supposed to include rehabilitation. However, they continued to serve simultaneously as hospice, prison, and asylum, in which violence, sickness, and promiscuity remained the rule. Other sites played an analogous role, such as Marseilles's convent for the repentant, which "welcomed" all possible sorts of radical women: prostitutes, adulterous women, concubines, seduced girls, delinquents, criminals. This place became key to the popular imaginary of Marseilles, at once prison, hospital, and refuge.[37]

It is quite probable that the "Great Confinement" functioned badly or only partially. Nevertheless, this was a decisive moment. Not only was there a desire to gather into the same space of relegation all the detectable figures of social exclusion but actual sites now were being used, even imperfectly, to realize the plan. This was the case with Bicêtre, which from the middle of the seventeenth to the middle of the nineteenth century housed within its walls a diverse population of old people, beggars, the insane, the sick, and criminals (see chapter 1). "Vice, crime, misfortune, infirmities, the most disgusting and disparate maladies, were all mixed up together," declared Doctor Pariset.[38] Bicêtre's infected premises, with fetid walls and floors strewn with rubbish, was a major fixation point in this imaginary. Diderot, Mirabeau, Malesherbes, Howard, and many other eighteenth-century writers had gazed aghast at what (in the expression of Sébastien Mercier) was a "terrible ulcer on the body politic, a wide and deep ulcer, that could not be envisaged without averting the gaze." Those in the nineteenth century—Appert, Michelet, Hugo, and Lamartine, for example—did likewise, being incapable of turning their gaze away from this belly of misery. "Bicêtre . . . the name alone has a sinister aspect and resonates on the ear like a death-knell," concluded the novelist Pierre Zaccone a little later.[39]

KINGDOM OF ROGUERY

One of the principal effects of these changing representations was to create an ample European library on "roguery" whose motifs and themes would durably structure the imaginary of transgression. Texts that relied on lists of false beggars and people pretending to be poor dating back to the end of the Middle Ages now gradually enlarged their nature and scope. There was a shift from inventories drawn up by magistrates or chancelleries to the literary treatise, from the judiciary to fiction and the imaginary, which was a sign of growing public interest in these descriptions. Bronislaw Geremek has minutely established the cartography of this production and underlined its principal traits.[40] From the end of the fifteenth century, enumerations of charlatans and false beggars and false pilgrims, and other marginals, were exploited out of a concern that was now more ethnographic and literary. This was the case notably with the *Speculum crematorium*, a treatise composed by an Urbino ecclesiastic denouncing the art of trickery that he said had been developed by the inhabitants of Cerreto, a small village in Umbria. This was also the case with the famous *Liber vagatorum*, a book describing German rogues that also dates from the end of the fifteenth century, and Martin Luther wrote a preface for one edition. The same sort of description is found in the contemporary *La nef des fous* (*Ship of Fools*) by the German humanist and theologian Sebastian Brant. The audience for these texts was enormous. Benefiting from the new resources now enabled by printing, they were taken up and distributed via new networks of cheap printing and peddling. They soon became fixed in a quasi genre, "the literature of beggars and rogues," which spread throughout Europe in the sixteenth and seventeenth centuries[41] and displayed two traits: the revelation of ruses, frauds, or supplication tricks, and the presentation of strong hierarchies thought to govern this world. In England, *The Fraternitye of Vacabondes* by John Awdeley, published in 1561, distinguished nineteen categories of vagabonds and twenty-five of crooks. The hierarchies seemed less rigid in Spain, but the *Ordenanzas mendicativas* of Guzman ascribed an order to the society of mendicants. Productions within this genre quickly became widespread throughout Europe: picaresque literature in Spain, tales of roguery in France, vagabond books or pamphlets in England, *Schelmenroman* in the Germanic countries. Of course, each country developed specific traits, but the unity of the genre was demonstrated by the circulation and incessant transfers between countries.

In France, such works occupied a privileged place in the fixing of this imaginary: *La vie généreuse des mercelots, gueux et boesmiens contenant leur façon de vivre, sublitez et gergon.* . . . (The eventful lives of knaves, rogues and bohemians with their way of life, ruses and jargon . . .) published in Lyon in 1596, and *Le jargon, ou langage de l'argot reformé, comme il est à présent en usage parmi les bons pauvres* (Jargon, or language of argot as it is presently used among the good poor), a celebrated text attributed to a certain Olivier Chéreau and published around 1630. *La vie généreuse*, a sort of picaresque autobiography, traces the initiation into the rogues' life of a Breton squire. This text, like its predecessors, enumerated various "estates" that are combined with the ruses and trickery they use. But its innovation was to describe the organization of the "monarchy" of rogues as a veritable counterkingdom ruled by the *Grand Coësre* (this chief was also called *Dasbuche* or the King of *Thunes*), who distributed his provinces to the many affiliates—the *cagoux*—who served as his lieutenants. *Le jargon* also evoked the king of rogues and described how he was elected, then dramatized the Estates-General of the Monarchy of Argot, consisting of eighteen corporations that each paid tribute to the king. In these two texts we find many of the elements that had been circulating in Europe since the end of the fifteenth century, notably the detailed taxonomy of the various ways of begging and stealing. But the description of the rogues' monarchy is pushed to the extreme. It seems to form a state within the state, a countermonarchy that is precisely organized and ruled. The *Argotiers* "are so numerous that they compose a huge kingdom: they have a King, Laws, Officers, Estates, and a very particular language."[42] The idea was of a society below taking root as the inverted double of the society above, in both its structuring and its hierarchies. "Beggars have their magnificences and delights, as well as do the rich, and, 'tis said, their dignities and polities," noted Montaigne in his *Essays*.[43]

These texts are foundational. Continuity with the nomenclature used at the end of the Middle Ages is obviously very strong: it is still a matter of describing by enumeration the organization of the mysterious world of marginal people, of unveiling their procedures and the language community that unites them. The latent concern for social control remains essential, but three principal innovations appear.[44] The first concerns new attention paid to biography. The formerly very collective society of beggars and crooks gradually allows a few personalities or singular figures to emerge, whose entry onto the stage calls for spotlights on individuals. And when attached to individual destinies, this subgenre tends to become more empathic. This is significantly the case with Spanish picaresque stories that in an autobiographical mode try to narrate the often-facetious adventures—punctuated with jokes—of a *picaro*, the marginal but sympathetic hero. Living on expedients and vagabonding between various social classes, the picaro incarnates a way of life that refuses integration and socialization, yet does not descend into degradation or vile depths. Masterworks such as the "lives" of *Lazarillo de Tormès* (1544), *Guzman de Alfarache* (1599), and *Buscon* (1626) all enjoyed immense success.

The second innovation is directly related to the first and concerns the mischievous, recreational, and sometimes even antic character of these tales. No doubt some earlier texts that tried to convey the most elaborate maneuvers used by the crooks or to lift the veil on forbidden universes had already possessed such a dimension, but now it gave rise to an ironic reading of such fictions. In the sixteenth century, this extension assumed a clearly burlesque accent that corresponded to the carnivalesque tradition that characterized the popular culture of the time. This displacement was particularly noticeable in Germanic "puckish" literature, the *Schelmenroman*, marked by the figures of Simplicissimus and especially Till Eulenspiegel, the latter the son of peasants who is taken for a simpleton but who reveals himself to be very clever and mischievous. This figure also flowered in the Spanish picaresque works, whose imprint marks all of European literature. Consequently, the view of marginal types was inflected, becoming lighter, more astute, and also more entertaining, even to the point of offering discrete approval of transgression. Henceforth this descriptive mode lies at the heart of the system of representation of the lower depths.

The last innovation, no doubt the most decisive with respect to our argument, concerns the emergence of specific topographies explicitly devoted to the underworld of the rogues and the marginal types. This is the motif of the courts of miracles as it was born in Paris in the middle of the seventeenth century: a secret and dangerous place where, when night falls and as if by a miracle, the blind recover their sight, the armless *manchots* their arms, and the legless *culs-de-jatte* their legs. The oldest mention dates from 1547. In the *Propos rustiques* of Nöel du Fail, Tailleboudin described the existence in the city of Bourges of a "street of miracles" where blind beggars miraculously recover their sight. At the start of the seventeenth century, David Ferrand spoke of a "cave of miracles," this time in Rouen, and about the same time there was mention of a Parisian courtyard in the *Nouvelles et plaisantes imaginations de Bruscambille* (1613).[45] In Paris, a memoir of 1617 alludes to the "place vulgarly called the *Cour des Miracles* behind the convent of the Filles-Dieu, at the bottom of a rampart between the gate of Saint-Denis and Montmartre, where one usually saw in the evening throughout the summer people dancing, playing, acting or laughing, and having a good time."[46] In 1630, *Le jargon* by Chéreau gave a more precise description:

> This place is called in Jargon the *Cour des Miracles*, or *piolle franche* (free zone) [...] the place where all sorts of maladies find their cure: here is where the blind find clarity, the deaf-and-dumb hear and speak, the place where those who are frenetic & twisted in their head come back to their senses, where the paralytics receive a complete and healthy disposition of their body, the one with dropsy is eased of his swelling, the violent ardor of fever is extinguished, the flow of blood is staunched, & where even the cripples recover complete use of all their members.[47]

But we did not have a more precise description until the appearance of the famous (and a thousand times copied) text by Henri Sauval, *Histoire et recherches des antiquités de the ville de Paris*, published in 1724 but written around 1660.[48] An advocate at the *Parlement de Paris*, erudite and a historian of the capital, Sauval was the author of many "scandalous chronicles" that detailed the life of courtesans and prostitutes and covered the brothels of Paris.[49] Thus he was in his element evoking the famous Court of Miracles. Just when it was being crossed off the map of Paris by the new police service under La Reynie, Sauval offered an enclave of beggars as sort of lawless space that becomes the effective kingdom of thieves and rogues. In the elaboration of the underworld motif, we understand the importance of a representation that confers territorial materiality on the theme of the counterkingdom. Sauval detected several courts of miracles in Paris, but he especially described the largest, whose main entrance was situated in the Rue Neuve-Saint-Sauveur, "a place of both considerable size and a very large stinking, muddy, and irregular unpaved cul-de-sac." This venue was stocked with several characters who also became formidably prominent in the underworld universe. To reach this labyrinthine space, you have to wander down "little ugly streets, stinking and winding; to enter you have to descend a rather long slope, twisted and uneven in plane." This was the lair of dirtiness, where dwellings are "low, sunken, dark and deformed, shaped of earth and mud." Five hundred families lived there, in generalized poverty and promiscuity, all laden with an infinity of little children, legitimate and illegitimate and stolen, or a total population estimated at close to 30,000 persons. Vice, theft, and irreligion reigned there in absolute mastery, "nobody has faith or law there, they know not baptism, marriage, or any sacrament." This was the capital of the rogues' kingdom. Seated on a barrel, with a plaster bonnet in the shape of a crown on his head, dressed in the Harlequin's robe, armed with a pitchfork from which was suspended a carcass, the grand Coësre reigned over the "people of argot" who paid him homage and tribute.

Almost two hundred years after it was written, this is the text that Victor Hugo would adopt in his *Notre-Dame de Paris* in 1831.[50] And, of course, it was Hugo who gave the Court of Miracles its decisive impetus, which turned it into an almost universal motif. Departing from Sauval's account, Hugo was content to transpose the action to 1482, but he modified neither the places nor the main characters. Hugo's Court of Miracles was a narrative stage, ensuring the link (against the backdrop of Romanticism) between the old roguery that had never been truly disarmed, and the new lower depths that groaned underneath the Paris of the July monarchy. The entry of the poet Gringoire into the Court of Miracles inspired illustrators such as Gustave Dore:

> Where no honest man had ever penetrated at such an hour [...] the thieves' city, a hideous wen on the face of Paris; a sewer from which there seeped every morning and to which returned every night to stagnate that gutter stream of vice, beggary, and vagrancy which is always overflowing in the streets of capital cities; a monstrous hive to which all the hornets of the social order bring back their booty every evening; a counterfeit hospital where the gypsy, the unfrocked monk, the ruined students, the dregs of every nation [...] of every religion, Jews, Christians, Muslims, idolaters, covered in simulated sores, were beggars by day and at night transformed themselves into robbers; an immense changing room, in a word, where at that time all the actors dressed and undressed for the endless drama of robbery, prostitution and murder played out in the Paris streets.[51]

BANDITS AND BRIGANDS

The accounts and forms born at the start of modern times would not disappear, even with the Enlightenment. The eighteenth century witnessed a blaze of Argotic literature, marked by a vogue for the *poissard* (the vulgar), the Bacchic, the burlesque, and incessant editions of stories like *La vie généreuse* or *le jargon*. But profound variations are noticeable. In the first place, print production multiplied considerably. To traditional forms were added *canards* (broadsides detailing spectacular crimes or accidents), *feuilles volantes* (broadsheets), broadsides, chapbooks, diatribes, *causes célèbres* (famous court cases), court verdicts, last dying speeches, and so on. An immense print culture developed that made deviance and crime its principal themes. The content was also transformed in the wake of what the picaresque genre inaugurated in Spain. The biographical approach tended increasingly to replace collective portraits, and the figure of the brigand or bandit took the place of beggars and vagabonds, now fated to be just supporting players. Two specific forms resulted, each articulated and differing in intention.

The first was so-called scaffold literature, which in diverse forms—broadsheets, gallows literature, execution accounts, or sermons and pamphlets—detailed the misdeeds of famous criminals at the end of their lives. These texts, strongly normative, were most precocious and popular in Protestant countries due to the importance they gave to collective confession and to last testaments. In Switzerland, for example, the Zurich pastor Johann Jakob Wick compiled nine hundred of them in the second half of the sixteenth century.[52] They were also numerous in England[53] where they expanded into a subgenre. Collections of "last dying speeches—" the words of the condemned just before their execution—appeared in innumerable *occasionels* (ephemerals) and other products of pulp literature hawked at fairs and markets. Their popularity may be attributed to public fascination with the spectacle of punishment and capital execution. The accounts given by the chaplain of the famous Newgate prison in London included confessions gathered by the chaplain just before people were executed and often they were transformed into the romanticized biographies of criminals. Other texts, such as the *Newgate Calendar*, or register of wrongdoers, were collections of booklets devoted to famous trials, often aimed at middle-class readers.[54] A similar output developed in France, principally in the form of *canards* (broadsheets) or tales of execution, such as that of Dame Lescombat in 1755, who had her husband murdered by her lover, or that of the poisoner Desrues in 1777. These texts, which dramatized transgressive acts or milieux, obeyed an obvious moralizing intention. Again, the normative design was paramount: it is always a question of reinforcing political authority, religious allegiance, familial and social hierarchies. But national or cultural nuances are also perceptible: the Germans and Swiss concentrate on the victims, the English and the French more on the criminals.[55] Sometimes there was a search for contradictory sensations and ambivalent emotions that could arouse a paradoxical admiration for transgressors.

The second principal form that developed was the biography of brigands. Of course, the genre already existed: for a long time, rural bandits and brigands (actual realities in the countryside) had been the subject of stories. In France, the *Histoire de la vie, grandes voleries et subtilités de Guilleri et de ses compagnons* (History of the life, grand thefts, and tricks of Guilleri and his companions) told the early seventeenth-century story of the misdeeds of a band of thieves from Poitou whose chief, *Compère* (old fellow) Guilleri, was executed in 1608. In this text are all the classic motifs of roguery: a repertoire of ruses and deceits, the description of a countersociety, and the unveiling of a secret language. Nevertheless, the figure of a more generous bandit emerges from this biography. This is even clearer in the version of the Guilleri affair offered by Francis de Rosset in his *Histoires mémorables et tragiques de notre temps* in 1685. We find the same evolution in England with the figure of James Hind, a highway robber who was drawn and quartered in Worcester in 1652; and Claude Du Vall, "the gallant highwayman" who was executed in 1670 at Tyburn. But this movement became widespread in the eighteenth century. Gradually bandits quit the archaic universe of roguery, of farcical courts of miracles, and became invested with their own representational spaces. Focused on a "master criminal," these tales draw on ambiguous forms in which explicit condemnation intersects with implicit glorification. Some biographies flirt with touches of political and social contestation: a brigand who attacks the powerful, tax agents, and state functionaries gratifies the expectations of ordinary folk, and they tended to make him a hero. In France, such an evolution is noticeable in the figures of Cartouche, a cooper's son who became the chief of a band of thieves in Regency Paris; and Mandrin, "an honest man" ruined by the tax collectors who is transformed into a smuggler and champion of the antitax protest in the Dauphiné region.

Of course, tales of these ambiguous figures cannot totally idealize them: they remain "guilty men" who issue from a "contemptible" world. Certain texts, such as the *Histoire de la vie et du procès de Cartouche*, published in 1722, were even instigated by a disinformation (and manipulative) campaign designed to turn excessive public sympathy away from the bandit.[56] Most of these tales, however, offered more positive images: receptive to current political and social affairs, they presented themselves as "reversible" texts that offered glimpses of both legitimate violence and the illegitimate kind. Sometimes the bandit is close to a figure who redresses wrongs, such as the socially conscious bandit synthesized by the British historian Eric Hobsbawm.[57] In fact, this phenomenon was more noticeable in England, where it derived from the medieval tradition of Robin Hood. The partially antithetical figures of Jack Sheppard (a highwayman) and Jonathan Wild (at once a master thief and bounty hunter) lie at the source of an immense bibliography that feeds the theme of the honorable bandit. Both men were the subject of innumerable biographies—including one written by Daniel Defoe—and are found (under transposed identities) in John Gay's famous *Beggar's Opera* in 1728, now in a tone of comedy and social satire that breaks with traditional representations.

A whole pantheon of famous brigands was established in Europe (marked in Spain by Diego Corrientes, in Germany by Schinderhannes), which testifies to the emergence of a different sensibility of transgression, of a new genre that mixes legalism and fiction, condemnation and glorification. French Romanticism and then the Revolution accentuated this evolution. Schiller's drama *The Brigands* (1781) was a key work that made the bandit the prototype of the romantic hero, the man in revolt, the tragic incarnation of individual freedom.[58] By now the bandit had escaped from the lower depths.

Indeed, such works that nourished a whole culture did not disappear with the ancien régime that had given birth to them centuries before. Now printed at low cost, usually accompanied with engravings and laments, such texts were transmitted by networks of printers and booksellers, whose editorial apogee came in the middle of the nineteenth century. For example, *Le jargon* was one of the best sellers of the *Bibliothèque Bleue* in Troyes, where it went through thirty editions. Most of these tales were also reissued, adapted, and reutilized by the popular press in pamphlets and chapbooks, and in various serialized print forms that took over from them. At the beginning of the nineteenth century, these stories enjoyed their widest dissemination. In 1817, Walter Scott gave new life to a Scottish bandit of honor called Rob Roy. The novelist William Ainsworth, son of a reputable Manchester lawyer, acquired celebrity in 1834 with his novel *Rookwood*, which recounted the life of Dick Turpin, another highwayman who had been hanged a century earlier. The success was even greater for his *Jack Sheppard*, published in *Bentley's Miscellany* in 1839. The novel detailed all the bandit's travels and adventures but aroused unanimous hostility to him (among both the educated and working classes) due to the grave moral danger he posed—but the novel enjoyed extraordinary success. The edition in three volumes that followed its magazine serialization sold more than three thousand copies in its first week, and many adaptations were made, especially in the popular theater and the *penny gaffs*.[59] In the agitated and turbulent England of the 1830s, there was no real distinction between the twilight of the Newgate literature, the start of the social novel (*Oliver Twist* also appeared in *Bentley's* in 1837 and 1839), serials in the manner of Reynolds's *Mysteries of London*. Invariably they described the same atrocious sites, the same miserable fates, the same social plagues. The oldest ones gesture toward enduring modern worries about crime, and publication of the *History of Crime in England* by Luke Pike (1873) and many others periodically reactivated the country's notorious cases.[60] In France, biographies of Cartouche ("prince of thieves") and Mandrin were reissued as serials or recycled in more contemporary series.

In parallel, representations of the cour des miracles enjoyed an extraordinary boom after publication of Hugo's *Notre-Dame de Paris*. To be fair, some writers had been ahead of Hugo: in *Raoul*, published in 1826, and in *The Duelist* of the following year, G. de la Baume and Théophile Dinocourt had already dramatized the *cour des miracles*, that "frightful cesspit of poverty, vice, and libertinage, an asylum for beggars, crooks, thieves, and all kinds of bad types."[61] The theme was manifestly in season, at the crossroads of contemporary worries about poverty and crime and of Romanticism's fascination with the Middle Ages. But Hugo's novel propelled it to the heart of the abundant production of historical novels that flowered during the July Monarchy. In 1832, in *La cour des miracles*, Théophile Dinocourt proposed to study the "character and manners of this interesting tribe." The same year, Paul Lacroix published *La danse macabre* and lingered over "this muck of the population" that had forever banished morality and religion: "There, with no concern for the future, each person enjoyed the present; they lived there with the greatest license, knew neither baptism nor sacrament." The following year, in 1833, Charles d'Arlincourt, in *Les écorcheurs* (Swindlers), described contemporary Paris as a "place of infection of all kinds, center of all species of corruption." In *Marie de Mancini*, Marie Aycard counted forty thousand as "the number of these *misérables* [...] divided among the seven or eight *cours des miracles* that infested Paris." Philippon de la Madelaine went further in 1834 in *Le justicier du roi*, in which his own court of miracles was in the hands of a "totally separate population whose instincts were for disorder, whose customs were pillage, whose life was spent in rapine." In *Le chevalier de Saint-Pont*, also from 1834, Théodore Muret was interested in these swarms of "children who at age twelve were already trained in corruption and debauchery."[62]

Hugo, as we see, was not short of heirs. In romantic Paris of the 1830s, the cour des miracles became an obsessive motif, and its hold over the invention of the underworld seemed decisive. *Les mystères de Paris* itself belongs to the lineage of Hugo's novel, whose opening pages are about a "mystery."[63] In 1843, Jules Janin again lingered over this "horrible nation, whose various names were just as horrible as the language they spoke: *cul-de-jatte, bossus, boiteux, manchots, béquillards, coquillards, cagots, lépreux avec leurs plaies, beuglements, glapissements, hurlements, fourmilière d'ordures vivantes* [the legless, humpbacked, armless, crutches, the Coquillard gang, pharisees, lepers with wounds, bellowing, squealing, shouting, a hive of living garbage]—in short, the whole cast of the *Cour des Miracles*."[64] And the vein continued untiringly. In 1845, Maurice Alhoy, famous author of dramas and essays about prisons, published *Les brigands et bandits célèbres*, a succession of anecdotes and life stories drawn from the tradition of roguery, and he devoted a lot of space to the cour des miracles. Octave Féré goes from his *Cour des Miracles Sous Charles VI* to *Les mystères de Rouen* in 1860, which was still being published by Fayard in 1889.

In Dijon, the memory of the Coquillards of regional glory gave rise to the publication of many titles including *Compagnons de la Coquille*, written by a curator at the city's archives, which in 1842 traced the history of bands of evildoers, swindlers, and deserters who had been assembled in the winter of 1455 by a powerful "King of the Coquille." Thieves, assassins, and counterfeiters, these bandits who use a language inaccessible to common people, implement a "plan of general pillage of the city, with the help of Coquillards who turned up on all sides."[65] The *cour des miracles* and its inhabitants passed very quickly into the common vocabulary as a synonym for "lower depths." "A new *cour des miracles* is being established in Dijon under the benevolent eye of the police," the editor of *Bourguignon Salé* wrote at the end of the century to express discontent with the urban reorganization of the city.[66] "Here is a fine revival of the *cour des miracles*, a population of truands,[67] false cripples, and cadgers, amongst whom a Sheep will be the *Grand-Coërce*," he said.

There was another resurgence of this animosity during Paris's Universal Exhibition because it was now a *lieu de mémoire* (site of memory) before the term came along. In 1889, in the fifteenth arrondissement, a Tour de Nesle was erected, 26 meters high. In 1900, the main Cour des Miracles itself was reconstructed on the Avenue de Suffren, with its maze "of dark and picturesque streets, a town belonging to the era of Notre-Dame de Paris."[68] Use of the term did not fade away. Albert London saw the penal colony as "a new kingdom" nicknamed the New Cour des Miracles Camp: "There were about 400 men, of whom a good hundred were infirm. Some lacked an arm, other were victims of elephantiasis or were blind or hunchbacked."[69] Henri Danjou in 1932 was still talking about "people of argot" and "escapees from the *Cour des Miracles*."[70] In Paris, old streets such as Brisemiche and Pierre-au-Lard "exuded the *Cour des Miracles*."[71]

"Do you know why I attach so much importance to precise knowledge of the state of the criminal classes during this period of the fifteenth century?"

asked Marcel Schwob in 1892. "It is because I think it is the vestige of a moral situation that seems to me of capital value for historical science and for the history of humanity. During this period, for the first time the dangerous classes became aware of an autonomous life located outside the limits for regular society. They made a counterweight to the bourgeoisie that was grouped around the royalty. This was the substance that would nourish the movement against the authority of the Church and State, which began to be manifest at the start of the 16th century."[72] Schwob is perhaps pushing the point too far. For what does survive seems to point more to the anguish of elites and their desire to stigmatize than to express an (improbable) awareness of those excluded by society. No doubt, it is also difficult to consider associations of crooks and rogues as a revolutionary force. But Schwob's intuition and realization are no less remarkable. The end of the Middle Ages is indeed a major turning point in the appreciation of the world of transgressions. The attention paid for the previous two centuries to beggars and vagabonds gradually began to shift to the figure of the brigand. The universe that results is still conceived as miserable and corrupt, but it is also more structured, better organized, and peopled with individuals who occasionally demonstrate good qualities and even have distinctive personalities. The complex assemblage of anecdotes, warnings, and biographies that contains them does not renounce its normative and moralizing function, but it has also taken note of the spectacular potential lying within the world of roguery. As Hugo says of Quasimodo: "His people might be a collection of fools, cripples, thieves, and beggars—no matter! They were for all that a people, and he was their sovereign."[73]

3

"Dangerous Classes"

The social and moral realities covered by the term *bas-fonds* existed well before the nineteenth century, but the worst seemed to arrive at the heart of this century of progress and positivism. Hovels, cutthroats, and infamous houses of debauchery suddenly began to saturate the descriptions of cities. The "dangerous classes" appeared, peopled by all the outcasts who seemed to want to submerge society, and thus entire neighborhoods toppled into indigence and savagery. New words emerged to refer to these dens of horror: slums, the lower depths, *sottomondo*, the underworld. The language does not reveal everything, but there is nothing anodyne or insignificant about the almost simultaneous emergence throughout Europe of a new lexicon trying to depict identical social realities. From the evidence, we can see that something happened in the nineteenth century that "recharged" this imaginary, giving it unprecedented scope and causing it to evolve. A whole system of representations that had been erected at the end of the Middle Ages around outcasts and marginals was being reordered into a more coherent scheme, now clearly inscribed in a social dimension. New kinds of knowledge and new vectors of power took charge of it. A whole descriptive régime took shape that closely linked a sociographic summary, philanthropic or repressive motives, and a rhetoric of terror. In this chapter,

I describe the importance of the nineteenth century in the emergence and fixing of this imaginary; the weight of context is determinant. The social, political, religious, and cultural contexts explain the convergences, thresholds, inflexions, and chronologies to which the various motifs belong and how they were being reorganized.

SOCIAL MENACES

As a description of a social world, the underworld naturally maintains close ties with economic and social contexts; however, the relationship is rarely linear. In fact we know the distance that may exist between portraits of the lower depths, even the most "objective" ones, and the real life of the marginal and impoverished people who indeed could rarely be approached. But the grand phases of social history, especially abrupt crises and ruptures, undeniably demand strong inflexions in the order of representations. That the underworld emerged at the time of pauperism, urbanization, and the "social question' is obviously not by chance. In fact, two periods, two specific sequences, may be distinguished.

The first period, at the beginning of the nineteenth century (principally the years from 1820 to 1840), is the more decisive because the principal terms that interest us were being forged at that time. The beginning of this century was marked among the elites by a strong feeling of anxiety and by recognition of a radical mutation in the forms of social life. Two synchronous processes converged and exacerbated these sentiments: first, the shockwave of the French Revolution, which is blamed for having accelerated the decomposition of social ties and the traditional hierarchies that structured the social world; second, the shockwave of the "industrial revolution" (the term, first introduced in 1820, did make sense to contemporaries), which gradually came to be perceived as a decisive rupture. An acceleration in migratory flows, the transformation of frameworks of industrial labor, and the appearance of unprecedented forms of urban pathologies aroused unprecedented disquiet among many people. The feeling was that traditional standards were being blurred, society becoming unintelligible, combined with social panic brought about an intense movement of self-analysis and the desire to put order back into a society that had become unreadable.[1]

Faced with these anxieties, people tried to understand, to pierce the opacity, to decipher the social world. The first third of the century was marked by a rapid acceleration of the social inquiry and observation movement.[2] Beginning in the first decade of the 1800s, and even more in the 1830s, physicians, "economists," philanthropists, reformers, and all kinds of "observers" began publishing the results of their investigations. Most of these works explore the shadowy zones and highlight the figures of disorder, danger, and social darkness. It is principally the poor, the vagabonds, the ragpickers, the detainees, the prostitutes, and criminals who are pressed into serried ranks in the almost endless train of social inquiries that this period produced. What studies by Villermé, John Kay, Eugène Buret, Edwin Chadwick, Adolphe Blanqui, and so many others demonstrate are the terrible social and moral consequences that the economic transformations caused among the most vulnerable of workers. These are consequences that literature, which shares the same anxiety, is simultaneously taking up and enlarging. In Les misérables, Victor Hugo commented on the social realities of the 1830s: "Meanwhile within the country, pauperism, the proletariat, wages, education, the penal system, prostitution, the lot of woman, riches, misery, production, consumption, distribution, exchange, money, credit, rights of capital, rights of labor—all these questions hovering over society built up an awesome overhang."[3] The "lower depths" exposed in both these kinds of discourse are the illegitimate children of these protean worries. They signal real places that have been produced by rapid and brutal social change, but they also speak of the need to consolidate the contours of the real world by dramatizing its inverse. They are simultaneously a symptom, an antidote, and a spectacle.

The invention of pauperism and the debates it instigated is closely linked with the emergence of the lower depths. The term *pauperism*, in use in England after 1815, first appeared in France ten years later[4] and then spread quickly. It referred to a new form of poverty, a new social state produced by factory working conditions, one marked by low wages, structural unemployment, and the loss of complementary traditional income. It is a scandalous kind of poverty—far from the customary conception of the idle and lazy paupers—that instead refers to the condition of men and women who are actually working. In an 1806 treatise on the police, the British magistrate

Patrick Colquhoun defined poverty as the condition of someone who does not have any goods in reserve: "it is the condition of all those who must work in order to subsist."[5] In France, Villeneuve-Bargemont made the same point by distinguishing traditional poverty, "isolated, circumscribed, and passing," from the new pauperism, which is "no longer an accident, but the forced condition of a large portion of the members of society."[6] Hence the anxiety among most of the elites—social, religious, philanthropic, and political—who saw this phenomenon as an unbearable regression and so their own analyses, discourses, and critical theories proliferated.

The situation became more complicated when poverty (often extreme poverty) affected the growing contingent of workers whose recompense for their labor left them to congregate in rundown and insalubrious neighborhoods, with insufficient nutrition, and prey to insecurity about tomorrow. Obtuse observers were quick to see these pauperized workers as savages, the new "barbarians" camped on the margins of society. Their rags and scrawny appearance raised fear; their poverty was literally horrifying. In December 1831, Saint-Marc Girardin's phrase was a commentary on the insurrection of Lyon silk workers: "The barbarians who threaten society are not in the Caucasus or on the Tartar steppes, but in the *faubourgs* of our manufacturing cities."[7] Romanticism's current fascination with barbarian invasions, with the Middle Ages, and with the American savages that the novels of Fennimore Cooper had just popularized, merely strengthened these hostile convictions—and the resulting alarmism.[8] The perceived risk was great that a "demoralization" of these new proletarians would spill over into the ranks of the bad poor, and that the former would become targets of choice for delinquency, prostitution, debauchery, and crime. Therefore, a dual phenomenon took shape in the decades from 1820 to 1850: harsh poverty, which until then had been conceived of as a *moral* perversion, now became a *social* reality, capable of swallowing whole contingents of impoverished workers, even entire cohorts of migrants that urbanization was attracting to the new factories in cities. In this way, the working classes and the dangerous classes tended to be confused with each other, or to be conflated in both their recruitment and future evolution. This was the source of a tenacious amalgam that Louis Chevalier had once uncovered.[9] "The criminal class," wrote British publicist Thomas Pint, "lives and, as it were, melts into the working classes; it constitutes a point of vicious contact with these classes."[10] The lower depths that appear in 1840 are the products of this dual realization.

This phenomenon is particularly clear in France and England, which were the two principal points of fixation. In France, it resulted from fear of riots, barricades, and revolution, all conceived as the natural companions of pauperism. In England the rumble of insurrection also disturbed people, but it was fear of social dissolution that was most frightful. Industrialization had come earlier and more vigorously to England than to the Continent, attracting toward manufacturing zones constantly growing contingents of uprooted rural folk, small farmers who were expelled from the Highlands or regions of landholding concentration, and battalions of starving and despised Irish migrants, itinerant workers, and so forth. The extreme poverty suffered by the proletariat, the atrocious living conditions (especially during the "Hungry Forties"), and the resulting social agitation made the elites feel they were living in a society brutally split into two enemy camps that would definitely collapse if polarization continued. In 1845 in *Sybil, or the Two Nations*, the young Benjamin Disraeli described the menace of a working population in an imaginary Lancashire city that had become brutal, vicious, and degenerate. The pace differed according to the situation elsewhere in Europe, but these worries affected most societies. In Madrid in the 1860s, urban growth and industrialization provoked the emergence of alarmist stories and press reports on the *barrios negros* to the south of the city.[11]

The second stage, still more intense, arose at the end of the century, beginning in the 1880s and lasting until 1900. The Great Depression that hit the Western world brought a terrible realization: all the efforts at integration and economic prosperity of the middle of the century had not rescued the poverty-stricken classes, whose extent and immense suffering were now rediscovered. In Great Britain, where this phenomenon was most pronounced,[12] a new wave of inquiries by missionaries, reporters, and philanthropists uncovered intolerable living conditions. Whether the focus fell on the extreme indigence that had developed in the new industrial zones, on the sexual debauchery that seemed to accompany it, or the delinquency that turned working-class areas into gangrenous slums, a veritable shock wave gripped British society. Although it had been thought that all the moralizing efforts of triumphant Victorianism had borne fruit, the opposite was discovered: the nation was sunk in poverty and vice. Now, in these British years also marked by rising social agitation and by the combativeness of the "new syndicalism," the issue of the underworld assumed its full significance. While new social inquirers such as Charles Booth tried to demarcate the scope of the phenomenon with the help of statistics, hundreds of missionaries (representing all the country's churches) plus journalists, novelists, and touristic "slummers" traversed the bad quarters in search of a *residuum* that needed to be publicly exhibited and then reduced. London's population reached five million inhabitants in 1881, and its cartography also changed: the focus of concern was no longer just on Covent Garden, Drury Lane, and St. Giles. New zones of concern arose in the East End, which extended the length of the Thames, offering unknown territories named Whitechapel, Bethnal Green, Limehouse, or the Nichol. These neighborhoods were even more alarming because they were peopled by new migrants: Jews coming from Poland or Bessarabia who established a new ghetto depicted by Israel Zangwill in 1892,[13] but also Greeks, Poles, and Romanians.

The acceleration of international migrations produced the same effect in American cities, principally in New York. Certainly Five Points and southern Manhattan had been perceived as zones of poverty and crime since 1830, but the vertiginous rise in migration beginning in the 1880s gave the phenomenon unprecedented scope due to the origin of the new arrivals, who mostly came from eastern and southern Europe or from China, which aroused strong ethnic prejudice. As in London, the end of the century was marked by a massive investment by churches, journalists, and novelists in explorations of the underworlds. The U.S. census of 1890 officially proclaimed that the "western frontier" had disappeared, and the verticality of cities was being accentuated by skyscrapers, so the plunge into the underworlds could even appear to be a new adventure.[14]

RIOTS, OR THE VOMITING OF THE UNDERWORLD

These social fears were closely combined with political worries and were, in fact, inseparable from them. Workers, proletarians, and the barbarians of the big cities aroused so much dread largely because of the political role ascribed to them. The eruption of ragged people onto the political scene was hardly an unprecedented phenomenon or source of anxiety. From the Roman plebes to medieval peasant revolts, the emergence of the popular element had always aroused the anxiety of elites, but the French Revolution exacerbated this phenomenon. The "populace," the "mob," the *sans-culottes*, because they had once constituted a possible social alternative, thereafter figured as horrible and politically unacceptable. An intense "social fear" resulted, which in nineteenth-century France reactivated the incessant replay of revolutionary events (1830, 1831, 1832, 1834, February 1848, June 1848, 1871), which welded the propertied classes into a defensive reflex. Analogous fears animated the British elites in the first half of the nineteenth century. They were frightened by the activity of the "radicals," the threats of insurrection, and the social troubles from 1836 to 1848 that culminated in the Chartist agitation.

Now people were certain about the "natural links" between hovels, dives, and vice, on one hand, and the barricades, on the other. "There are two natural sisters in the world," wrote Alphonse Esquiros in 1840, "and they are the prostitute and the riot. These smoky hovels and these suspicious alleys, when the alarm sounds, vomit combatants onto the street."[15] For many contemporaries, insurrection and riot were nothing more than the overflowing or vomiting of the underworld. Did a riot by ragpickers in April 1832 not precede the barricades in June?[16] In the 1840s, the conspiratorial figure shifted from being described as a fervid royalist or republican to becoming a creature of the underworld who plots schemes in dives, the back rooms of taverns, or the hovels of the big cities.[17] For example, the Austrian ambassador recounted a meeting of the *carbonari* in Paris: "Imagine a narrow and dirty street, in the middle of which flows a muddy and fetid stream. In this street, there is one house even filthier than the others. Its entry is blocked by vegetable debris, rags, greasy paper, rotten straw, smashed pots and plates, oyster shells, broken bottles, and other garbage."[18] In England in the 1840s, social and political agitation was explicitly identified as the activity of criminal hordes emanating from the underworld. "Degradation, debauchery, sensuality, and criminality gain ground with unprecedented rapidity in the manufacturing regions and among the dangerous classes who are heaped there," explained Archibald Allison in an article in *Blackwood's Edinburgh Magazine*. They even "gather every three or four years in a General Strike or a dangerous insurrection that provokes universal terror as long as it lasts."[19] In the eyes of many observers, revolution was the plague that would arise if excited by a few unscrupulous demagogues. The Parisian insurgents of June 1848 were merely the "moral and physical scum of society." Venal souls, motivated by cowardice or the prospect of pillage, "live off low-level prostitutes and are mostly former vagabonds, convicts, or thieves."[20] *The People's Representative*, a Proudhonist organ, went on in the same vein, describing "beings without principle or flag, the rejects from the penal colony and prison of society, of which they are the irreconcilable enemies."[21] Other witnesses swore that the *filles de joie* (loose women) were the principal actors in such events.[22] This is the "same infernal population that haunts the cabarets, who form the army of rioters in the days of upheaval, men totally prepared to respond to the call of assassins coming from abroad,"[23] noted a Lyon magistrate in 1859. The Paris Commune carried these stereotypical representations to their paroxysm. The Commune, wrote Gustave Chaudey in the *Century* on March 20, 1871, is the work of bandits, the downgraded, "the dregs of the convicts and prosecuted criminals," all of them moved by vengeance, alcohol, madness, bestiality, all of them exhibiting "horrible aspects" and "vicious, bilious, and scowling" faces.[24] For Gabriel Tarde, the Commune was the product of a "hideous troop," a "drunken multitude" that takes the form of an orgy, mixed with insanity, drunkenness, and sexual debauchery.[25]

Paris was not the only city to witness a convergence between the fear of riots and the fear of the underworld. In London during the troubles of the winter of 1885–86, "the West End for several hours was in the hands of the populace," noted *The Times* on February 9, 1896, and the panic continued for several days as shops were pillaged by the mob and "classes of disorder."[26] The same images were used to depict the syndicalists and anarchists at the end of the century: all of them criminals, madmen, or amoral. Again in 1928, a police report depicted the "individualists" as people "without scruples, most of them given to exaggerated sexual appetites, using every kind of subterfuge to live, shrinking from no method liable to make them money." Five years later, a second report explained that the anarchist circles "are especially frequented by the sick, the unbalanced, the miscreants, the idle in search of schemes."[27]

This stigmatization of the "inferior classes" was not limited to the discourse of conservative elites. At the same time, Marx and Engels were forging the concept of the *Lumpenproletariat*, the ragged proletariat, defining a fringe of impoverished workers composed of downgraded elements who were without class consciousness and were easily put to use by the bourgeoisie, for whom they served as a backup force. During his stay in Manchester, where he settled in 1842, Engels discovered the realities of a subproletariat that he often identified with the Irish, whom he defined as "excess" and "superfluous" people. In 1846 in an homage to the poet Karl Beck, Engels was the first to use the expression *Lumpen* to depict the milieu of beggars and thieves.[28] In a passage from the *Communist Manifesto*, Marx similarly mentions "the passively rotting mass thrown off by the lowest layers of the old society,"[29] and he sees this as one of the keys to the repression of the European revolutions from 1848 to 1850. The "*Lumpenproletariat*, this scum of the depraved elements of all classes, which established headquarters in the big cities, is the worst of all possible allies. This rabble is absolutely venal and absolutely brazen,"[30] and so it serves as manpower for forces of reaction. Engels again returns to them in the 1870 preface to *The Peasant War in Germany*: "Every leader of the workers who uses these scoundrels as guards or relies on them for support proves himself by this action alone a traitor to the movement."[31] Marx, meanwhile, used the expression in a slightly different sense to depict the *déclassés* of all kinds who were found backing Napoléon III: "vagabonds, discharged soldiers, discharged jailbirds, escaped galley slaves, swindlers, mountebanks, *lazzaroni*, pickpockets, tricksters., gamblers, pimps, brothel keepers, porters, literati, organ-grinders, rag-pickers, knife grinders, tinkers, beggars—in short, the whole indefinite, disintegrated mass, thrown hither and thither, which the French term *la bohème*."[32] What is striking about this enumeration is its similarity to the ones filling the newspapers or the "physiologies of reprobates."[33] It must be the sign of social reality in a mid-nineteenth-century Europe that was in the full throes of an economic crisis and undergoing the effects of unfettered liberalism. But this sign also speaks to the force of dominant representations. In any case, we understand why the advent of the underworld is inseparable from the fears (or hopes) of a radical overthrow of the political order.

THE DARK CONTINENT

The association of the poor and marginals with the peoples from remote worlds is an old reflex. Beggars and vagabonds were long described as savages, barbarians, and ferocious beasts, and the previous chapter recalled the links made between vagabonds and the nomadic tribes that came from Egypt and Bohemia. But the resumption of colonial expansion that marked the nineteenth century lent considerable strength to this theme. The emergence of the bas-fonds in France was contemporaneous with the conquest of Algeria, along with the rise of worker insurrections that shook major cities such as Paris and Lyon. The phenomenon was felt in all Western cultures, which often used terms borrowed from the colonial vocabulary to depict the underworld, linking exoticism and discovery, but also anxiety and sometimes horror, with the desire for conquest. By the end of the century, the descriptions tended to be "racialized" due to the anthropological theories that were circulating at the time.

"I feel myself surrounded with Robinson Crusoe's cannibals," exclaimed Hippolyte Raynal when, in 1829, he encountered detainees of the La Force prison.[34] Since the eighteenth century, a tribal lexicon had been used to signal both the savagery and the radical otherness of these peoples. "These men have their own customs, their own women, their own language," confirmed Eugène Sue. The ragpickers, noted Frégier, lead a life that is "totally nomadic and almost savage"; the "tribes of rag-pickers who sort through the rubbish of Paris" were endlessly discussed.[35] In London at mid-century, Henry Mayhew, who defined himself as a "voyager to the unknown country of the poor," began his tale by evoking the explorer George Pritchard and making the notion of wandering tribes the theme of his book. The "street-folks," he writes, are a race apart, a wandering race, a race of nomads who are distinguished from "civilized tribes" by the repugnance they feel for work, their lack of foresightedness, their passion for drugs and libidinous dances, the absence of religiosity in them, and the lack of chastity among the women. Around this dichotomy a whole social anthropology was erected. For other observers, many of them nineteenth-century Britons, a large part of the horror of the underworld was ascribed to the Irish, who were described as a savage and repugnant people, accustomed to muck, to violence, and to the company of animals.

In France, the assimilation of menacing proletarians to American Indians was a recurrent motif, explained in part by the immense success of the novels of Fennimore Cooper. The American novelist lived in Paris from 1826 to 1833 and enjoyed enormous success. Everyone the country counted as belonging to the "thinking class"—Balzac, Sainte-Beuve, Dumas, George Sand, Maxime du Camp, Eugène Sue, Béranger—was passionate about the "Walter Scott of the savages."[36] Balzac, in the *Père Goriot*, mentions the Huron and Illinois Indians; "everybody was interested in the Sioux, the Pawnees, and the Delawares," remembers Henri Cauvain.[37] The association between the savages of the Old and New Worlds seemed quite natural, and the first pages of the *Mystères de Paris* ratified this analogy: "We are going to attempt to depict some episodes from the lives of French savages who are as far removed from civilization as the Indians that Cooper so vividly depicts."[38] A few years later, Dumas transplanted the Mohicans to Paris, and an abundant French literature about the Western USA developed during the Second Empire. Such a phenomenon left traces: by the beginning of the twentieth century, all the crooks of Paris would be called *apaches*.[39] The British also had their "Indian moment," but it had taken place a century earlier due to their own colonial history. At the beginning of the eighteenth century, a gang of "Mohawks" was described in London, a violent band led by a chief with repulsive tattoos who attacked passers-by and disfigured them with a knife, and who did not hesitate to rape and murder. In 1712 John Gay (author of *The Beggar's Opera*) had traced their misdeeds in a play called *The Mohocks*. In the nineteenth century, however, inspiration was sought instead in the East Indies, heart and jewel of the British Empire, especially after publication of *Ramaseeana* by William Sleeman in 1836 and the *Confession of a Thug* by Meadows Taylor in 1839 that popularized the "diabolical and insane system" of the Thugs.[40] Presented as a fraternity of criminal convicts, the stranglers of Kali fascinated romantic England. In London (as in the United States, which quickly followed the movement), Thugs were labeled crooks and bad boys. Other borrowings were made from India: in Manchester, a band of young crooks was called the "Bengal Tigers," some were referred to as Dacoits, and James Greenwood spoke of the Dayaks of Borneo.[41] The term *outcast*, although of older origin, had another surge in the 1880s to describe the Indian untouchables. A little later, the term *Arabs* was used for street children and for young vagabonds roaming the cities.

Many contemporaries felt that impoverished peoples formed a "race" that could be described by physical anthropology. Moreau-Christophe devoted a large part of his *Monde des coquins* (World of rascals) to evoking the physical characteristics of those he was studying: of course, skulls in the enduring phrenological tradition, but also facial traits, the shape of hands, and both plastic and mimetic gestures.[42] Maxime du Camp saw a filiation between primitive races and the later (and despised) race of *bohémiens* (gypsies). The argot of truands, he explained, comes from *calo*, the language of "the wandering Roma."[43] In Germany in 1858, the criminologist and magistrate Friedrich Avé-Lallement published a panorama of the Germanic lower depths, which he depicted as hereditary and contaminated by Jews and gypsies.[44] Criminal anthropology was soon flourishing, and it conferred a theoretical and scientific framework on these analogies. The celebrated *Criminal Man*, published by Cesare Lombroso in 1876, endeavored to demonstrate the structural links that tied the criminal to the savage, both of whom were regressive products of evolution. "The difference is quite small—sometimes nil—between the criminal, the uneducated man of the people, and the savage," which also explains, Lombroso said, the fascination with thieves and assassins among the popular classes.[45] Criminals must form a "particular ethnic group," writers such as Émile Gautier crudely concluded.[46] And is it not because they are savages that society can easily transplant them to colonial penitentiaries?

Beginning in the 1880s, the African metaphor predominated. In *Bleak House* (1852–53), Dickens had already drawn a ferocious portrait of Mrs. Jellyby, whose charitable activity is split between the indigents of her parish and those of Boriobollla-Gha. But the beginnings of the penetration into the interior of the African continent enabled an assimilation between the investigator and the explorer, and between poverty-stricken people and the savages of the African continent. James Greenwood, in *Low-Life Deeps* (1881), thought he was in another country looking at another race.[47] The expression the "Dark Continent" soon served to designate both the underbellies of British towns and the heart of Africa. "In these pages, I propose to record the result of a journey into a region which lies at our own doors,"

wrote journalist Georges Sims in *How the Poor Live* (1883), "[a journey] into
a dark continent that is within easy walking distance of the General Post
Office. This continent will, I hope, be found as interesting as any of those
newly-explored lands which engage the attention of the Royal Geographic
Society—the wild races who inhabit it will, I trust, gain public sympathy
as easily as those savage tribes for whose benefit the Missionary Societies
never cease to appeal for funds."[48] William Booth, the founder of the Salvation Army, published *In Darkest England and the Way Out* in 1890, which
was explicitly presented as an echo of the famous book by Henry Morton
Stanley, *In Darkest Africa*, that appeared the same year. Moreover, Booth
begins his first chapter with an homage—and a question—to the illustrious
explorer: "As there is a darkest Africa, is there not also a darkest England?
[...] The stony streets of London, if they could but speak, would tell of tragedies as awful, of ruin as complete, of ravishments as horrible, as if we were
in Central Africa."[49] The following year, feminist journalist Margaret Hark-
ness extended the metaphor by publishing (under the pseudonym John
Law) *In Darkest London*. On the threshold of the 1890s, when England was
rediscovering with dread the extent of the poverty that festered at home
and when the carving up of Africa was accelerating, these analogies reached
the height of their influence. London missionaries, journalists, and novelists made the East End a dark and colonial land, peopled by individuals
without history or culture. So this is a land that must be reconquered too.[50]

For many, interest in the underworld was ethnographic, corresponding
to the fascination with distant voyages and peoples. "The people, the rabble
if you will, has for me the attraction of unknown and undiscovered populations, something 'exotic' that travelers go to seek with a thousand sufferings
in distant lands," explained Jules de Goncourt.[51] In England there was often
a similar interest: "the majority of the inhabitants of the west and south of
London know as much about things in the East End as about the Hindu
Kush or the southern Territories of Australia," a journalist for the *Daily
Telegraph* wrote in 1888.[52] Many of these metaphors derive more from curiosity or from simple rhetorical conventions than from racist thinking.[53] In
Le Havre or in Nantes, bad areas in Brittany were said to be those that had
long been peopled by homegrown "miserable Bretons."[54] But these remarks
tended to become harsher and more "racialized," particularly in societies

confronted with significant foreign immigration. Rejection and stigmatization were now strongly tinged with racism. In the United States, once the
Irish danger was passed, the threat was clearly associated with blacks, with
Jews, Italians, and Chinese. The latter, explained journalist Thomas Knox
in 1878, had definitively taken control of the San Francisco underworld.[55]

HELL IN THE HEADLINES

The third context for the European underworld was religious and cultural
developments. The former relates to the religious changes that affected all
nineteenth-century European societies. Despite disparities linked to different religious and political traditions, a single movement was altering the
sensibilities of the Christian world. Under the influence of redemptive and
"Italianate" piety, little by little religious sensibilities and representations
began moving away from preaching based on fear of damnation and toward
worship of a "Good Lord," a theology that endeavored to save the greatest
number of the chosen. There was a gradual decline in preaching about Hell
and a rise in less fearful prospects, especially those associated with Purga-
tory, which enjoyed a resurgence in the Catholic world.[56] First apparent
in the 1830s, this trend to "dis-hellification" accelerated in the second half
of the century. There was a countervailing spread of Satanism and various
forms of devil worship, and Max Milner has situated their golden age in this
same period from 1830 to 1850, as evidenced by the proliferation of popular works including *Memoirs of the Devil* by Frédéric Soulié (1837–38), *The
Devil in Paris* (1844), and *The Hells of Paris* (1853).[57] But it is clear that these
new uses of hell often derive from figurative and distanciated approaches.

Secular metaphors were developing simultaneously, especially newly
minted ones related to social and urban hells, which quickly spread. The
association of the underworld with hell emerged almost naturally as a commonplace representation. In a society that was still very religious yet marked
by strong secularization, the underworld offered a relevant symbolic alternative. From Granville to the Cruikshank brothers to Gustave Doré, engrav-
ers and illustrators powerfully developed this motif, bathing the nameless
misery of the sinful quarters in a sepulchral light. In 1868, in *Asmodée à
New York*, which Ferdinand Longchamps published simultaneously in

France and the United States, the reader is led by the devil himself on a tour of the Five Points. Georges Sims, author of *How the Poor Live* (1883), quickly earned the epithet "Dante of the Underworld." Certain areas or specific places such as labor camps and prisons were even raised to the rank of Pandemonium (the capital of Hell as imagined by John Milton in 1667 in *Paradise Lost*). Their residents are depicted as devils. "The convict is a reprobate, damned by society, for whom there can be neither remission nor mercy," wrote a journalist in 1844.[58] "*Dante didn't see anything*" was the title chosen by publisher editor Albin Michel for the 1924 reportage by Albert Londres about the French Army's military prisons. And often the atmosphere was even worse in asylums, hospices, and hospitals, populated by "sick people screaming, shouting, and loudly demanding their release."[59] People remembered that the old Bicêtre—simultaneously prison, hospice, and insane asylum—had been that "place where in the evening the damned came back to dance the funereal *danse macabre*, where the phantoms promenaded freely, celebrating the profane Sabbaths, and inmates indulged in diabolical orgies."[60] This infernal dimension of the underworld was even more prominent in Protestant societies due to the strong investment by pastors and ministers in the "reconquest" of neighborhoods plagued with poverty and vice.

After changing religious views, the second phenomenon was the emergence of a new cultural system based on the commodification and mass production of culture. Everything converged to make the decade from 1830 to 1840 that of the Underworld—and 1836 was "Year One of its Media Era."[61] Newspapers, books, images, and stage shows were gradually absorbed into modes of production that tried to make them consumables destined to be sold at the highest number and at the lowest price.[62] So, of course, the underworld lay at the heart of this mass culture enterprise. The revolution of the serialized novel (or stories "at the bottom of the page") that many saw as a "swamp" (that is, the press had its own underworld) favored texts that exploited the world of social outcasts. The extraordinary success—and more important, the seminal influence—of *Les mystères de Paris* (serialized in 1842–43) remains undisputed.[63] Eugène Sue certainly borrowed a lot from the Gothic imaginary, but also from Vidocq, the former criminal who founded the French investigation bureau, whose 1828

Memoirs shifted tales of bandits to the locales of prisons and penal colonies, and from Hugo's early works, *Last Day of a Condemned Man* (1829), *Notre-Dame de Paris* (1831), and the short story "Claude Gueux" (1834), and from many other works, including Jules Janin's *The Dead Donkey and the Guillotined Woman* published in 1829. But Sue was the first to incorporate these themes in the new fictional dynamic of the serial novel, which gave them a rhythm, a breath of life, and a totally unprecedented reach. He was also the first to closely combine the three registers of the imaginary of the underworld: an uncompromising description of horror and evil; a preventive concern to understand in order to be protected; and, finally, a heroic dimension that mixed (sometimes contradictorily) philanthropic commitment, democratic aspiration, and media sensationalism. This is why *Les mystères de Paris* was a phenomenal success and gave rise to a quasi genre of "urban mysteries" whose dimensions are only now being appreciated. Hundreds of renditions appeared, set in nearly every city in the world. London was the first: Anténor Joly, literary editor at the *Courrier Français*, asked Paul Féval (who had never been to the British capital) to dash off the first series of *Mysteries of London*, which appeared in 1844 under the pseudonym Sir Francis Trolopp. That same year, the English serial novelist and radical activist George Reynolds began writing his own *Mysteries of London*, whose first installments began to appear the following year (1845) and whose serialization lasted until 1856. A whole movement had begun. In France, all provincial towns quickly acquired their own *Mysteries*—Rouen, Lyon, Marseille, Nancy, Lille, Belfort—and the trend soon spread to the rest of the world: the *Mysteries* of New York (1845), Hamburg (1845), Barcelona, Berlin, Vienna, Boston, Naples (1847), Brussels (1850), Mexico City (1851), Stockholm (1852), Florence (1854), Lisbon (1854), Rio de Janeiro (1866), Chicago (1891), and Buenos Aires (1897).[64] This list is unending and carries on into the twentieth century, an extraordinary volume of production that sometimes bears no relation to Sue's novel other than the desire to capitalize on the sensational charge carried by the title. The *Mysteries* no doubt constituted the first great phenomenon of cultural globalization.

Into this breach leapt thousands of other serials and popular novels, over which the shadow of the *Mysteries* permanently hung. Whether crime, sentimental, or historical novels, most of the great popular cycles offered a prime place to representations of the underworld, indispensable to their dose of "sensation." The same is true of the detective novels that emerged in the 1860s, and all of the serial novels and pulp fiction that flourished in its wake. Soon all fiction was in thrall to the representation of society's shadowy zones. After the wave of novels about pre-Haussmann Paris, of which *Les misérables* was the apogee in 1862, and the British social-problem novels that proliferated in the wake of Dickens and Disraeli, came an output of more naturalistic fiction that also plunged into the lower depths, the lower classes and their sordid realities. "There is a common bias in all young literature: studying the underbelly of society," Albert Wolff accused in *Le Figaro* on July 21, 1882. He was outraged to observe novelists' exclusive interest in "studying only prostitutes and drunks, whom this literature so graciously calls sluts and dastards." Maupassant, who answered Wolff a few days later in the columns of the *Gaulois* (July 28), recognized that a "lower depths mania was indeed rampant" in literature, but he saw it as merely a temporary reaction, a corrective to "the secular theory of poetic things." Still, the "true crime" movement lingered, and even conquered the theater thanks to Oscar Méténier, secretary to the police commission and inspirer of cabaret impresario Aristide Bruant, whose show *Him!* played at the Grand Guignol in November 1897 and created a scandal. Violette, a prostitute, receives a client who has just committed a crime and is about to commit another one, and she only manages to escape him thanks to Madame Briquet, the brothel-keeper.[65]

And we know that the media success of the underworld was not confined to literature. It delighted the daily papers, whose *faits divers* (sensational stories) brought each day a horrible crop of crimes and heart-rending scenes, but it also proliferated in specialist magazines such as *The National Police Gazette*, created in New York in 1845, and the *Illustrated Police News*, which followed in London in 1864, or like their innumerable followers, whose number literally exploded between the two twentieth-century wars. "True crime" accounts prospered in the theater, cabarets, and *café-concerts*, the main venues for songs about "girls and gangsters." Tourist guides and handbooks were devoted to them. The cinema, the decisive invention of the late nineteenth century, seized upon them from its inception. Ferdinand Zecca, the powerhouse of Pathé studios, led the way in 1901 with the

Histoire d'un crime, which portrayed (using flashbacks) the destiny of a murderer from the hovel (where he plans his crime) to the scaffold where he pays for it. Zecca went on to set many films in the Parisian underworld, including *Les Apaches de Paris* in 1907, and that same year his assistant Lucien Nonguet shot *The Underbelly of Paris*. The vogue for films with sequels (the *Nick Carter* films, then Jasset's *Zigomar* films, the *Fantômas* series, and Feuillade's *Les Vampires*) plumbed the vast depths of the Parisian underworld.[66] The phenomenon was simultaneous in the United States. Edwin Porter shot *How They Do Things on the Bowery* (1902), in which we witness a rube getting rolled by a streetwalker. Four years later, in 1906, *The Silver Wedding* depicted the running combat between "underworld" figures and the New York City police, and *The Black Hand* explained how a gang of crooks used newly arrived immigrants to sow social contamination.[67] Needless to say, such themes have continued to pervade the cinema ever since.

The underworld was at the heart of mass culture as it arose in the nineteenth century and as it grew from there. This prominence also largely explains the mammoth expansion of the theme. The reasons for its centrality are numerous. Whatever the type of plot or narrative device, most "media stories"[68] love to dramatize a sociology of extremes that are strongly polarized. Opposite the pole of high society, aristocratic, and social elite figures who were traditionally the characters of fiction, the gangster and other inhabitants of the underworld appeared to play the obvious counterpoint role. "We believe in the efficacy of contrasts," Sue had noted at the beginning of the *Mystères de Paris*. And now in these scenarios, the underworld acquired a decisive function: to accentuate the social gap, but also to blur ordinary certainties by showing that pure as well as perverse beings exist in *both* worlds, and to produce, by tales of a fall and decline (or conversely by a social ascension), a strong fictional dynamic. A second series of reasons emanates from the conditions of production of these tales, governed by the desire to standardize characters and situations, to serialize plots—in short, "rehashing,"[69] which tries to wring something new from the old. To do this, creators must draw from a limited stock of models and schemes,[70] and prominent among them were the gangster and the underworld: a setting used a thousand times, characters seen a thousand times, plots known inside and out—but which creators always try to present as new. "To beat well-trodden paths, to recommence a study in which it seems there is noth-ing novel to be found, to make something new out of the old (the very old), like mischievous navigators who want to discover America a second time or the fools who try to invent gunpowder but a little late"—this is the thankless task awaiting reporters of the underworld, admitted Jean Kolb and Raymond Robert in 1933.[71] Ultimately, the novelist and academician Joseph Kessel, in *Hollywood, ville mirage* (1936), said he was "tired of the underworld," which he knew "down to the bare bones."[72] A final reason relates to the need for "sensation"—for horror, spine-tingling emotion, and thrills—which the media values for both dramatic reasons and commercial ones. We know that the underworld—the ideal backdrop for incest, rape, murder, vice, material and moral filth, obscenity, and pornography—is a reliable purveyor of these representations. This becomes even more valid as the consumer's standard of living rises above actual poverty, encouraging him or her to experience social fears in the form of spectacle. This explains why, despite long-standing criticism of the unhealthy exploitation of the audience's "base instincts," the plunge into the underbelly of society was—and remains—a major theme of the culture industries.

The nineteenth century exacerbated all the issues to do with outcasts and their social transgressions, and there was a need to forge new terms and expressions explaining them. Among the many shifts that could be per-ceived, two appear decisive. The first is that the working world is now over-shadowed by the representation of poverty and vice; the working classes are equated with the dangerous classes. Unlike the truands of tradition, the underworld now clearly assumes a social dimension. This change of para-digm, indicated by Louis Chevalier in his famous book *Laboring Classes and Dangerous Classes: In Paris During the First Half of the Nineteenth Cen-tury* (1958), overthrew the classic representation of the undeserving poor who refused to work and chose instead the path of vice. Now, as Eugène Buret wrote, there was a "floating population in the big cities, that mass of men whom industry calls around her, which she cannot constantly employ, which she holds in reserve, as if at her mercy," from which the hordes of criminals that threaten civilization are recruited.[73] For many observers, the erosion of morals occurs no longer due to vice but to deteriorating social conditions. As Engels stated in 1844, "if the influences demoralizing to the working-man act more powerfully, more concentratedly than usual, he becomes an offender as certainly as water abandons the fluid for the vaporous state at 80 degrees Réaumur."[74] There lies the specificity of the underworld, the social swamp with its communal fate and circumstances that link crime, vice, and poverty—the world of the "*misérables*."

Although the observation was widespread, and incontestably associated the vicious classes (felons, thieves, prostitutes, and so on) with the working-class world, the analysis was rarely made in such objective terms. Ultimately, the emphasis was placed on the "naturally" vicious character of many workers. Yes, the world of delinquents was indeed peopled by workers. "The [worker's] smock reigns and resists, in this terrible region that reeks of spilled blood,"[75] declared the photographer Nadar in *quartiers* south of Paris. Yet many writers refused to make such clear connections between poverty and delinquency. Moreau-Christophe even made this rejection the central argument of his *World of Rascals*, which is explicitly presented as a refutation of Victor Hugo's themes. And he was not the only one to think that way. If there were so many factory workers among the dangerous classes, explained Octave Féré, it was not because "work cannot give them the means to live better, but because vice has stupefied them, because the passion for alcohol dominates them and they drink away two weeks' wages as soon as they get them, before going home."[76] Even Victor Hugo, whose *Les misérables* is still the alpha and omega of social Romanticism, was sometimes prey to this confusion. Quite at the bottom of the lower depths, in the "deepest pit" where the "light goes out" as it gives "onto the abyss," there is no longer any question of poverty and ignorance. In this lowest level, in this world "without any connection with the upper galleries," lurk the "blind Inferni. [. . .] The demon is dimly present; every man for himself." "Under the dark vault of their cave, they are forever reproduced from the seepage of society. [. . .] From beggar to prowler, the race preserves its purity."[77]

Although the nineteenth century indisputably took poverty and crime as social facts, the celebrated observation of Louis Chevalier deserves to be examined. He pointed out that this had less to do with the shift to social description (from the traditional one that emphasized the insular and colorful, the immoral and vicious, the world of roguery) than with the converse, the extension of these traditional images to include all the "lower classes." It was as if the characteristic traits of beggars, mendicants, and predators of old—vice, drunkenness, debauchery, improvidence, violence, and so on—had now come to affect almost all the working classes. In the last third of the century, when the policy strategy was to try to integrate the working world by making it more responsible, its unassimilable elements— its *residuum*, whether thugs or apaches—would still maintain the habitual characteristics of the insular and professional world of vice and corruption.

The second great innovation of the century was integration of the underworld into the channels and practices of mass culture. No doubt the stories of beggars and brigands had always sought the widest public, which had enabled European networks to peddle fiction. But the change in scale that took place in the nineteenth century altered the very structure and nature of the stories.

PART II

Scenarios of Society's Underside

4

Empire of Lists

"A series is never 'found,' but always constructed," wrote Franco Moretti in *The Atlas of the European Novel*.[1] Yet it is around the series and its many auxiliaries (lists, inventories, classifications, nomenclatures, and so forth) that the natural sciences were erected, and in their wake, the social sciences too. Taxonomy, and sometimes even "taxo-mania," has governed the production of knowledge in the West since the Middle Ages. Beginning with the eighth-century scholar Alcuin, enumeration has been a teaching tool at all stages of the learning process. Michel Foucault has shown how the ordering of the world is organized according to the logic of the classificatory table, which alone can articulate the ensemble of representations into some coherence and thus give them continuity.[2] The world of the lower depths obeys this imperative too; the most common organizing principle of its representations is indeed the inventory or the classification. From the first lists of medieval "truands" to feature stories in contemporary magazines, classifying is at the root of all representations of the underworld. This enables us to find continuity in profoundly heterogeneous situations, and to give an order to them. Static and dynamic at the same time, nomenclatures follow and resemble each other, constituting a sort of evolving "gallery" of the underworld and its history, which have been in constant movement.

THE POLICE *HABITUS*

Thus it is in the form of "lists" that beggars, truands, and vagabonds make their entry into history. These inventories were developed in the mid-fourteenth century and first emanated from Germanic cities such as Augsburg, Breslau, Basel, and Konstanz—followed closely by Italy, France, and England. They illustrate the cohorts of suspect individuals: false pilgrims, fake blind persons, thieves of horses or money, converted Jews, counterfeiters, pretend lepers, and so on. By the same token, these texts have a policing function, recording a collection of very different individuals, giving them consistency and coherence. They are an instrument of power that institutes collective identity. The number of these categories has regularly increased over time as better knowledge and expertise (on the part of the police and later in ethnographies and linguistics) enabled more accurate identification of marginal populations. The trial of the Coquillards in 1455—a band of "bad boys" who passed themselves off as pilgrims with the shell insignia, hence the name—named sixty-two types of thief, most of the terms abstruse nowadays: *crocheteur, pipeur, vendangeur, desgobischeur, blanc coulon*, and so on. In the same manner, the *Liber vagatorum* at the end of the fifteenth century enumerated in its first section twenty-eight categories of imposters and deviants, from "trickster" beggars to false monks, blind musicians, those feigning madness, women pretending to be pregnant, or beggars simulating jaundice. In England around 1560, *The Fraternitye of Vacabondes* by John Awdelay distinguished nineteen categories of vagabonds and twenty-five sorts of rogues. Similarly, various "children of trickery" were represented throughout modern Europe. The institutional and police dimension governs these representations, which testifies to the importance of "lists" in the creation of state knowledge in which indices are used as political instruments.

Later changes in these nomenclatures, especially in the seventeenth century, showed a dual evolution. First, the lists tended to become denser and more complex, and the various types became more specialized and more numerous. They also tended to be structured around vocational trades, "estates," and corporations. When these were gathered into a kingdom, a countersociety was formed that was crisscrossed by subtle internal hierarchies based on the principle of the "division of labor." For example, we have seen how the medieval *Jargon* and its imitators in seventeenth-century France portrayed the annual "estates-general," during which the estates within the monarchy of Argot paid tribute to their monarch, the *Grand Coësre*, featuring "eighteen old and now incomprehensible types of crooks, bastards and ruffians such as *'millars,' 'malingreux,' 'sabouleux,'* and *'polissons.'*" Thieves especially gave rise to interminable classifications. The first book to be devoted to them, the *Histoire générale des larrons* (thieves) by François de Calvi, published in 1666, detailed in three very dense volumes the ruses, subtleties, finesses, trickery, and stratagems used by thieves. Supported by anecdotes, it exposed the thousand of ways of stealing, justifying itself by society's need to be forewarned.[3] These distinctions may rely on other divisions, for example pertaining to different degrees of stigmatization. In German society in modern times, the category of *vagabonds* became differentiated from that of "infamous" professions (such as executioners, prostitutes, tanners, butchers, Jews) and from the category of criminals, even the though categories interpenetrated.[4]

Such classifications proliferated and found renewed justification in "police" texts that emerged at the turning point between the eighteenth and nineteenth centuries. In his *Treatise on the Police of the Metropolis* (1797), Patrick Colquhoun divided the 115,000 thieves, prostitutes, tricksters, gamblers, vagabonds, beggars, and so forth that he identified in the city of London into twenty-four categories. But it is especially in Eugène François Vidocq's *Memoirs* (1828), the foundational text of modern policing, that this practice achieved its full scope. Not only did Vidocq construct a large portion of his story around this principle, but he specifically justified its existence. "I will present the original features of several classes of society that are still hidden from civilization," he explained in chapter 30 of his *Memoirs*, "I will faithfully reproduce the physiognomy of these castes of pariahs." The result is the structuring framework of his tale, whose rules he explicitly sets. "I will classify the various species of villains, from the assassin to the crook, and shape them into useful categories."[5]

Vidocq wanted to establish a subtle taxonomy of the lower depths that would be able to categorize individuals—but also their activities, behavior, language, and locales—with the help of a learned nomenclature.

These classifications explicitly functioned on the naturalist model that predominated at the time and they referred to such scholars as Cuvier, Gall, and Spurzheim. Vidocq thus boasted of having adopted "the Linnaean method" in order to classify thieves: "By this series of comparisons, which the reader will not expect, I managed to reach the borders of natural history." Mentioning the physical monstrosities of Geoffroy-Saint-Hilaire, Vidocq strived in his entries to draw on more scholarly terminology, turning burglars into "*sulodomates*" and swindlers into "*balantiotomistes*." In the end he gave up, explaining in an unusually modest aside: "I have found baptized thieves, but I will not be their godfather, since it is enough to be their historiographer." The series opened with the *cambrioleurs* (burglars) or those who break into the *cambriole* (little chamber)—and this is the sole appellation that has passed into current usage. Vidocq—or one of his "*teinturiers*" ("black" or ghostwriters)—then weaves in several adventures, and offers a complete tale in the story of Adèle Escars (who forcefully enters the book at this point), but then he goes back to nomenclature. The last fourteen chapters of the book (64 to 77) devote long passages to each of these types of villain, such as *boucardiers, floueurs, emporteurs,* and *grecs* (the latter synonymous with "cardsharps"!).

What is original about this immensely influential book is that it breaks with the old typologies of beggars and rogues to concentrate solely on criminals and thieves, and along with them on the world of prisons and penal colonies, which henceforth acquire prominence in structuring the underworld. Another result is an abrupt break in the argots that appear in the text: the traditional lingo of truands and rag-and-bone men and gypsies is now superseded by the slang of convicts.[6]

It is an understatement to say that Vidocq's book was copied. Abundantly distributed and soon translated into English and many other languages, it gave birth to a genre whose fortunes have not yet waned: policemen's memoirs.[7] From Canler to Faralicq and Borniche in France, from the *Recollections of a Detective Police-Officer* to Chief Constable Chadwick or Superintendent Bent in England, and from Cappa to Bondi in Italy, the resulting library has not ceased to adapt—if not downright copy—the nomenclatures inherited from Vidocq. Most of these reminiscences are organized in an analogous way: after recalling the circumstances that made them enter the police and after evoking their first feats, the writers begin in the second half of the memoir to list the "different categories of wrongdoers, stacked into so many levels," as Commissioner Guillaume wrote almost a hundred years after Vidocq.[8] Circulating from book to book, these taxonomies comprise an interminable litany located somewhere between obligatory scenes and morsels of bravura, but they are also a marker of the memoir's generic fabrication. The high narrative productivity of taxonomy encouraged prolix authors such as the former Parisian police superintendent Gustave Macé to extend interminable lists in every direction: the typologies of revelers and prostitutes, of dives and gambling dens and the hangouts of cutthroats, of prisons and penal colonies.

Deeper reasons are also at work. These nomenclatures, files, and dossiers constitute the customary reflex of the legal professions,[9] especially in the ordinary *habitus* of the police officer, for whom they provide the usual categories for understanding and interpreting transgressions. As Canler (who directed the Paris detective force from 1849 to 1851) explained at length, a good policeman is one who manages to identify the type of misdeed—and hence the type of person, belonging to what group, and finally the individual who committed the deed.[10] Dividing delinquents into compartments meant assigning each act to a category of individuals at a time when identification of any perpetrator remained chancy. This was explained to Charles Dickens, too, by his friend Inspector Fields of Scotland Yard, who claimed he could recognize a thousand varieties of robbers.[11] Thus a sort of ideal categorization governed the police imaginary, which explains why some regulation of prostitution was always favored by police professionals.

But beyond these technical imperatives, nomenclatures also testify to a concern to order the world, to rationally distribute social roles, so that each person occupies his or her assigned category. They also provide warnings about the procedures used by villains and "tricksters," which thus confers on police labor an obvious public utility and uplifts their tales thanks to scientific claims deriving from "criminology." Nomenclatures enable police writers to explore the world of vice and to deliver often complacent descriptions of various "social plagues" without risking the moral disavowal ascribed to novelists.

A policeman relishes case files, he thinks in alphabetical order, and often his classifications serve in lieu of reasoning. Witness the very picturesque handbook for police administration written in 1884 by Superintendent Adolphe Gronfier, son and grandson of police officers, serving at the time in the Parisian *quartier* of Grenelle. His book is a mélange of notes, anecdotes, and circulars that are put into alphabetical order from *Affiches* to *Voleurs de magasins*, via *Aliénés*, *Bateaux à vapeur*, *Champignons*, *Duel*, *Foires*, *Hospices*, *Falsification* (of olive oil), and *Mendiants*. But the real interest lies elsewhere: in the extraordinary manuscript composed by Gonfrier who, in the fine and regular handwriting of a civil servant, originally wrote his text as annotations in the margins of two volumes of the *Dictionnaire général de police administrative et judiciaire* (General dictionary of police and legal administration), which was then in use among the police. The result is a sort of clandestine book that runs in the margins of an official volume, that is interleaved into its structure and its alphabetical order, as if no proper police thinking could do without this kind of classification.[12]

These practices testify to Gonfrier's evident cultivation and to his validation of police expertise: classifying people from the shadows seemed to be the sole means of illuminating their destinies. For example, what could be done to identify troublemakers in a city such as Buenos Aires, which was so turbulent in the last third of the nineteenth century due to unprecedented growth? Six million Europeans arrived in Argentina between 1870 and 1914, and Buenos Aires went from two hundred thousand to one and half million inhabitants.[13] How could the forces of law and order detect these contingents of immigrants, prostitutes, and individuals with no definite profession who were swarming on the outskirts of the city? The police response took the form of lists and dictionaries:[14] lists to record the name, number, and activity of all the miscreants; and dictionaries to decode their language. The two operations were superimposed, moreover, because the same term, *lunfardo*, served in Argentina to refer both to professional thieves and to their argot. The newspaper *La Nación* started things off by publishing the first nomenclatures of the "urban Bedouins" in 1879. In 1887, Superintendent José Alvarez published a long *Galería de ladrones de la capital* (Gallery of the capital's thieves) as the only means of shedding light on the lowest underworld, the occult network that he detected in the swarming underbelly of Buenos Aires. Thereafter typologies of thieves and pickpockets multiplied. Some took the form of complex and erudite lexicons, such as the one published by the legal scholar Antonio Dellapiane in 1894; others were conceived as encyclopedias, manuals, or chronicles, such as Detective Barres's 1934 book *El hampa y sus secretos* (The underworld and its secrets), which expounded upon, in the most rational order, the tricks and tactics conceived by thieves, the transatlantic routes that had taken them to the New World, and the infinite diversity of the society of undesirables.

In Buenos Aires, as in Paris, police culture was a print culture,[15] a formalized culture of the *fiche* (index card), the compilation of facts, the archive. It offered an ethnography of marginals and delinquents processed as types, photo galleries, and illustration plates. It is fundamentally a "criminography."[16] In the second half of the century, these lists were complemented by anthropological drawings (and later mug shots) that pigeon-holed delinquents into their discipline's categories and detected even more "types." Here the image replaced the text, but the same taxonomic logic governed this rational inventory of the deviances that Lombroso and his criminalist colleagues tried to engrave into scientific marble. The plates became photographic, fixing for the first time the actual faces in the galleries of the underworld. Now the types seemed to multiply to infinity, losing themselves in countless albums. But doesn't a profusion of classification risk obliterating its efficacy and its ability to assign categories? By superimposing all the faces of criminals in "composite" images, Francis Galton tried to get around this difficulty.[17] But don't the resulting "illustrated statistics" amount to the portrait of *a type*, and in this sense, of *the absolute type*?

FROM PHILANTHROPY TO LITERATURE

Originally a police habitus, taxonomy also became indispensable to philanthropic practices. The dichotomy between the true poor and the false poor, which we recall emerged in the thirteenth century, was the usual way of apprehending poverty, and so it came to govern all charitable practices. The issue was crucial to philanthropists, who believed that not being able to recognize the poor person who was shamming—who did not merit any aid— meant running the risk of perverting alms and charity, which would imperil the whole charitable arrangement as well as its religious foundation. The just "distribution of aid" depended on identification and classification of the poor.

In the 1820s, a former member of the famous French "Society of Observers of Man," Baron de Gérando, advocated the practice of the "home visit," an extraordinary method of investigation designed to "unmask shams," that is, distinguish between false and true indigence. One had to enter the poor person's home, explained Gérando, attentively observe the interior (the family's furniture and clothing), and analyze the family's language, reconstruct its use of time, interrogate its neighbors, and, finally, "penetrate into the most intimate secrets" in order to "sort out all the traces of this suspect life." The ultimate goal was the classification of poverty, which for Gérando amounted to "the great art of charity." This classification was to be the "fundamental basis" of assistance, the only means of establishing the "actual degree" of poverty. Therefore, elaborating "nomenclatures" was the duty of every philanthropist.[18] Such practices were carried to an extreme by the missionaries of the London City Mission, for example, who scoured the working-class neighborhoods of Victorian England and filled their reports with thousands of pieces of information.[19] By the end of the 1860s, investigators from the Charity Organization Society were able to conduct meticulous inquiries, at the end of which they could divide those requesting assistance into three categories: those whom it was suitable to help, those who might be recommended for aid, and those who had to be rejected. The result was a veritable science of poverty—a "pauperology."[20] Based on moral types, it transformed the poor into suspects, and even offenders, who were being asked to justify themselves morally as much as socially.

This knowledge, this very need for classifications and typologies, nourished a great number of social inquiries. In London, such a taxonomic enterprise was undertaken in the middle of the century by Henry Mayhew and his "investigators." The avowed goal of the four volumes of *London Labour and the London Poor* (1851–1862) was to distinguish between "those that *will* work," "those that *cannot* work," and "those that *will not* work," and to note all the distinctions separating the various "wandering tribes" (vagabonds, idlers, petty jobbers) from civilized people. Mayhew's approach referred explicitly to the naturalist model: he wanted "to enunciate for the first time the natural history, as it were, of the industry and the idleness of Great Britain in the nineteenth century." A concern for exhaustiveness required setting out a clear inductive method that could draw "concrete laws" from particular situations. An admirer of John Stuart Mill's *System of Logic* (1843), Mayhew began his methodological chapter by specifying what he means by induction:

> We may either proceed from principles to facts, or recede from facts to principles. The one explains, the other investigates; the former applies known general rules to the comprehension of particular phenomena, and the latter classifies the particular phenomena, so that we may ultimately come to comprehend their unknown general rules. The deductive method is the mode of *using* knowledge, and the inductive method the mode of *acquiring* it.[21]

Thus the book takes the form of a naturalist treatise. The classifications that organize it lead to the establishment of a long gallery of types: forty-two grand categories of "street-folks" parade before our eyes, comprising a whole universe, complex and hierarchical. There are two volumes on traders (costermongers, street sellers of everything from fish to lucifer matches) and then petty jobs (dock laborers, porters, coal heavers, chimney sweeps, ballast men, destroyers of vermin), almost all accompanied by engravings that record the physiques of this picturesque population and provide information on their earnings. The final volume ("those who *will not* work") is devoted to "prostitutes, thieves, swindlers, and beggars" and completes what Mayhew presents as the "cyclopedia of the industry, the want, and the vice of the great Metropolis" (Preface to volume 1). The information that has been gathered is indeed exceptional, and the careful classification is particularly impressive. Compared to the *Physiologies* and works such as Curmer's *Les Français peints par eux-mêmes* (The French depicted by themselves), Mayhew's work stands out for his seriousness and concern for documentary exhaustiveness. With the help of John Binny, one of the *London Labour* informants, Mayhew then launched into an ethnological study of those detained in the prisons of London that similarly tried to elaborate a scientific classification of the criminal classes.[22] But here, too, the result was limited to a simple succession of types, bearers of signs of depravity proper to each category, marked by the influence of the institutions where they are studied. The book functions in the manner of an "anthropo-zoological garden."

Therefore, although original in its scope, Mayhew's endeavor was less novel in its approach and organization. The classificatory model derives from the naturalist paradigm that dominated the era's epistemology and organized all sociographic thinking. "I have applied to the study of human societies rules analogous to those that trained my mind in the observation of minerals and plants," wrote Le Play in 1846.[23] Thinking in terms of "types" and their assembly into "galleries" or into "plates" is the most classical mode of social description. Not until Charles Booth's study at the end of the century did a different organization emerge. Breaking with the moral tyranny of types, Booth suggested other modes of classification, one that could be grasped quantifiably, which profoundly redefined the customary nomenclatures.[24] But taxonomies did not disappear. In 1923, and then again in 1940, Nels Anderson enumerated forty-seven categories of the homeless among the hobos of Chicago.[25]

In the tight circulation of models and expertise that linked nineteenth-century social observation to philanthropy and literature, it is not surprising to find the same principle at work in fiction, which likewise is trying to speak the truth about the social world. The same classificatory model with its tableaux and physiologies fed the "panoramic" literature of the 1840s; it marked the great novelistic efforts to elucidate a whole society that was inaugurated by Balzac and pursued by so many other novelists. Tales of the underworld were not immune from this rule. If novelistic necessities required them to have lots of action, a driving forward of the plot, the novels were indeed peopled by types: the *escarpe* (assassin), *ogresse* (brothel madame), *ange déchue* (fallen angel), *gamin des rues* (street kid or Arab), and so on. This is what the *Mystères de Paris* and all those that follow were offering readers. The iconography that accompanied the mid-century illustrated editions is not mistaken either; there are few scenes of action or exploits and few group portraits but instead engravings mostly devoted to stereotypical figures, from the *Artiste* to the Policeman, from the Caretaker to the Streetwalker.

It seemed difficult for a writer who might want to "demonstrate" something to escape this mode of representation. Moreau-Christophe's famous *Monde des coquins* (World of rascals), which wanted to be a "realistic" response to Victor Hugo's *Les misérables*, is an exhaustive census of the capital's crooks (thieves, swindlers, assassins, and so on), giving each variety its share of examples and memorable anecdotes.[26] The virtues of such a classification are immense: it buttresses a claim to incontestable rationality, even to scientificness (after all, the author has "constructed" an analytic grid), and confers on the result the semblance of a commonplace that everyone should be able to verify. Despite technological advances, the iconography of the underworld barely dispensed with these procedures. This iconography was found again in the (half-tone) photographs that accompanied the first great reportage in New York in the 1890s, Jacob Riis's *How the Other Half Lives*. Riis was undoubtedly the first reporter to make photography the prime element in the journalistic story and an instrument of social ethnography. Thanks to the cumbersome flash and a new type of dry-plate camera, which eliminated long posing time, he could photograph at night and in the course of his perambulations around dark slums. However, his photographs did not escape the recourse to typologies, if not stereotypes: "The Tramp," "The Boy in a gang," "Typical toughs," "Street Arabs," "Immigrant in a sweatshop," and "Bohemian cigar-makers at work," among others.[27]

DOCUMENTARIES

Such documentary processes were obviously encouraged by mass publishing's production (and profit) requirements. Whether writing novels, magazines articles, or "documents," one had to write a lot, to write quickly, and to make something new, but without upsetting the reader's expectations. Thus the keys to "popular" writing were to trot out the same stuff, to standardize, and to serialize. Consequently, resorting to inventories and taxonomies was an obvious shortcut, both on the documentary level (it sufficed to draw on a ready-made stock of motifs and themes, and then adapt, readapt, or simply recopy them) as well as on the narrative level, since many authors were content to follow well-trodden paths for their plots. The extreme productivity that resulted explains the continuous rise (beginning at the end of the nineteenth century) of innumerable "inquiries," novels, and "documentary novels" about the underworld. The naturalist model had, in fact, come under challenge from literature and the young science of sociology. But newspaper and serial editors were not embarrassed by such scruples, especially because the growing demand would flood a pulp fiction market that more or less recounted the same story over and over.

The very abundant production of picturesque works about Paris that appeared in the wake of Baron Haussmann's urban renewal—along the lines of *Paris étrange, Paris oublié, Paris ignoré, Paris-escarpe, Paris horrible et Paris original, Paris qui passe*[28]—endeavored to reveal an older and mysterious Paris that had survived the transformations, but they employed the same taxonomic procedure. Louis Barron's *Paris étrange*, centered on the description of the bas-fonds, used a juxtaposition of quartiers—Maubert, Les Halles, the faubourg Saint-Antoine, Croix Nivert, Batignolles-Clichy—and then, within each quartier, specified the types of places (dives, squalid cabarets, asylums) and types of colorful figures found in them. At the same time, on the other side of the Atlantic, Edward Crapsey, a reporter who covered lower Manhattan from 1868 to 1871, offered in *The Nether Side of New York* (1872) an unsurprising exploration of crime, vice, and poverty in the city. The twenty chapters are all constructed around the presentation of a particular type of deviant—pickpockets, "skinners," "fences," outcast children.[29] Stories about thieves continued to inspire hundreds of books. Whether they insisted on the picturesque and creative aspects of thieving activity, or offered themselves as guides to be used by honest people, these works were legion and usually based on an enumeration of the various ways of being robbed. The facile French list included "*à la tire*" (the English term *pickpocket* arrived in France in 1876), "*à l'étalage*," "*au bonjour*," "*au rendez-moi*," "*à la détourne*," "*à l'américaine*," "*à la roulette*," "*au poivrier*." The practice turned quickly into a routine, in which each type of theft became a simple type case that the author defined and then illustrated with anecdotes. In the early twentieth century, this method was used by Eugène Villiod in *Comment on nous vole, comment on nous tue* (How they rob us, how they kill us), by Louis Thinet in his *Histoires de voleurs* (Thieves' stories), and even by the former director of the Paris Police Alfred Morain in *The Underworld of Paris*.[30]

The stories of prisons and penitentiaries also proved particularly propitious for this kind of arrangement. Without much extra effort, writers could give successive descriptions of types of jails and then types of prisoners, generally combined with a few colorful anecdotes. The classifications of detainees that filled books about penitentiaries were derived from the same principle, first distinguishing the "good" from the "bad" prisoners, then dividing the latter into "types" based on the degree of vice or immorality. Maurice Alhoy, a playwright and publicist who was in vogue, carved his study of penal colonies into fifty installments: *Histoire, types, mœurs,* and *mystères* appeared in 1845, which did not prevent him from publishing in the same year his *Les brigands et bandits célèbres,* and the following year (helped now by his collaborator Louis Lourine) *Les prisons de Paris: Histoire, types, mœurs, mystères,* also in installments.[31] This principle reached its paroxysm in the tales of penal colonies that proliferated between the two World Wars, composed by journalists who made the journey to Cayenne in French Guiana, by doctors and philanthropists who protested about detention conditions, and by those few convicts who escaped or were liberated and could market their own accounts. First, all of them describe the sea crossing, then the arrival at Saint-Laurent, then how the prison camp is organized; most of the remaining material is spread across endless typologies: the type of camp (the transport camp in Saint-Laurent, the Godeberg camp, Nouveau-Camp, Charvein, Passoura, Annamites camp, Malgaches camp, and so on), then the type of labor (from the hell of building the first colonial road to the sought-after roles of turnkey, medical orderly, cook), and especially of the type of convict, the most anticipated of all these inventories (all usually illustrated by a portrait of a famous convict and colorful details that personalized the list). "It is impossible to exhaust in this work all the various types of convicts," wrote Dieudonné, one of the accomplices of the famous French anarchist Bandit Jules Bonnot.[32] "There would be a lot to write on each particular case."[33]

Beginning in the 1910s, the immense harvest of tales that described the world of the "white slave trade" organized that subgenre organized. However, the taxonomy of the various "traffickers of women" described was more detailed because it covered a fresh activity. Daniel Parker, member of the French League to raise public morality, structured his story by examining the following:

> *Rabatteurs*: charged with recruiting women into prostitution; *Placiers* and *courtiers*: assemble the victims into small groups for exchange or sale; *Faussaires*: who forge identity papers; *Indicateurs*: spies who keep tabs on the Police; *Souteneurs*: pimps who each exploit several women; *Tenanciers*: who manage brothels either "tolerated" by the municipality or clandestine ones; *Grands patrons*: usually an important figure who owns several establishments; *Trafiquants internationaux*: very powerful personalities who pull the strings.[34]

Most of the "inquiries" and journalistic features on the underworld functioned similarly, and their number exploded in the 1920s and 1930s. The chronicles of criminal gangs regularly served up by newspapers and magazines were all based on a reiteration of the same typologies of the "special world," and they used the same categories ("those who steal," "those who kill")[35] that a sensational story about a fresh crime could merely reactivate. When the press had exhausted covering the actors, nothing was simpler than to move on to the locales and offer enumerative cartographies of the dives, shacks, and "hot streets," such as the never-ending list given by Jean Bazal in 1935: the Bois de Boulogne, the Champs-Élysées, Montparnasse, Les Halles, and many more.

This method proved so productive that it governed not only the organization of the text but became an editorial strategy, giving rise to series and collections that the French editors of *"petits livres"* (pulp fiction) such as Fayard, Tallandier, Ferenczi, and others could market in the interwar period. The installments of Henry de la Bruyère's *La pègre démasquée* (The mob revealed), published in 1925 in the collection "Popular reportages," were presented as "the most complete and most truthful investigation that has ever been undertaken until now on all kinds of villains, from the *surineur de barriers* (gate cutters) to the high-society swindlers of salons and palaces. Never has the underworld of Paris and the great cities been dug up with such precision." And Guy de Téramond's "admirable" series *Les bas-fonds*, published by Ferenczi in 1929, was presented as a "dramatic, powerful, and complete study of the criminal underworld," devoting its ten volumes (at the rate of one a month) to ten key figures: the trafficker in women (No. 1, *Sold, a novel of the white slave trade*); the drug trafficker (No. 2, *Dramas of cocaine*); professional gamblers (No. 3, *Gambling dens: A novel*); blackmailers (No. 4, *Exploits of gamblers*); society dancers (No. 5, *Dancing !... novel of the exploits and crimes of dancers*); prostitutes (No. 6, *The Queen of hookers*); foreigners (No. 7, *Vices of Paris, a novel about aliens*); prisoners (No. 8, *Women's prisons, a novel of modern manners*); street children (No. 9, *Pariahs, novel of miserable childhoods*); and, finally, indigents (No. 10, *Hovels and tramps, novel of the lowest depths*). "Each novel," promised the editor, "is a special and complete study, and the collection will form the most sensational library that has ever been written on crime and criminals." However, the series was original only due to the author's (or editor's) very Balzacian concern for an exhaustive sociology of the lower depths. For historians, though, this bespeaks the heuristic interest of such nomenclatures when they are considered in series or over a long period of time: to the traditional actors (the indigent, the prostitutes, the prisoners, the street children), Téramond added a few emerging types—the cocaine addict, the *métèque* (dago), and especially the society dancer, a new figure "born from the war"[36]—that enjoyed sudden success in the 1920s.

Another form of enumeration prized by reporters between the World Wars collected "surprising stories" (Kessel's phrase in *Montmartre Nights*)— a series of anecdotes set in typical locales and often incarnated in remarkable individuals: Barbou, the Corsican who cut out the tongue of the man who turned him in to the police; Berthe, the provincial woman who left her family to follow the Cossack Stiopa; Fred, the hotel manager who supplies society women with cocaine; and so on. The fates of these figures were briefly sketched (often with the help of dialogue) and formed the kernel of each chapter. "I love people and places for the rêveries they give me," wrote Kessel, as if to justify himself.[37] Maryse Choisy, in *A Month Among Women* (1928),[38] explored brothels; her study was constructed, too, as a successions of portraits focused on the fates of prostitutes (and sometimes their clients) and descriptions of establishments, and comprised a sort of Grand Tour in print. Henry Danjou, in *Place Maubert*, was even more explicit: "Find me men and women, whomever you want," he asked his guide Maurice at the beginning of the reportage. "As long as they have a story, I am opening you a credit line. Find me *lives!*"[39] These lives and locales were the substance of each of the chapters that followed. There was hardly any tale of the underworld that truly avoided this expository mode, which was the heir of long medieval nomenclatures. Albert Londres himself, who tried to be distinctive by crafting a more composite story told in a more distanciated tone, did not always manage to escape from the hold of taxonomies. *Au bagne* (In the penal colony), which in 1923 made him famous, also offered a gallery of convicts. In *Marseille, port du sud*, which he published in *Le Petit Parisien* in 1926 and as a book the following year, he toured the locales to describe classic local types: "sellers of women, night-time guides (extra for foreign women), jewelry receivers and fences, pickpocket ringleaders, burglars, mobsters, girl-tamers, fleecers of drunkards, trembling informants, and prosperous upstarts."[40]

Victor Hugo's expression had been "enumerations that would make Homer weary," and from the beginning these lists and nomenclatures were at the heart of representations of the lower depths. And they continued to feed many later works, including some historical fiction that resorted to reproducing medieval taxonomies, or followed those of Vidocq or Canler.[41] Whatever intentions underpinned them—policing, philanthropic, or editorial—all proved to be very effective instruments for labeling "deviancy" in the sense that Howard Becker has given this term.[42] Not only did they assign individuals to pigeonholes, but they turned these slots into a commodious framework for their exposition, rationally constructed and informed, and suitable for mass dissemination. The lists were active agents of normalization. However, they have proved rather paradoxical: in effect they mingled (contradictorily) a distinctive logic that aimed to singularize each of the represented types and categories with a cohesive and centrifugal logic that aimed inversely to unify them in a homogenous universe. A strange "social world" resulted. No doubt one of the major functions of these classifications lay in combining such different types and gathering them into natural families, into "social species." They effectively fabricated a society that did not exist in reality. Within the system of representations, the lists played a role analogous to that played by institutions of detention—prisons, asylums, hospices, and others—within the order of practices: to assemble heterogeneous populations in the same place. Therefore, a classification *orders*, but it also *institutes*. In the underworld, it ultimately conferred a dynamic and a narrative because authors loved to animate their tableaux, to make them move. By insisting on recurrences, but also by periodically adding some new figure, classification bespoke the slow evolution of this "natural" world. These galleries were a sort of printed cinema, a magic lantern show of the most ancient scenario, but also the most effective one in the imaginary of the underworld.

5

The Disguised Prince

The "disguised prince"—behind this enigmatic expression that seems to refer to some masked ball in high society, is hidden one of the most productive scenarios in the imaginary of the underworld. It can be summarized in a few words: unrecognizable underneath his disguise, an individual of exemplary character immerses himself in the low life in order to render immanent justice there. One of the sources of this figure is the famous Harun-al-Rashid, the caliph who is one of the main characters of *The Thousand and One Nights* (or *The Arabian Nights*). Disguised as a merchant, he roams at night about the streets of Baghdad in the company of his faithful vizier Giafar. Another association is with Prince Rudolph, the hero of *Mystères de Paris*, or maybe one of his many avatars. In truth, the model easily could be extended to all those who are committed "to the good cause"—philanthropists, reporters, or agitators—and who make an incognito plunge into the "bad places" that were multiplying in the last third of the nineteenth century. Like Rudolph and the caliph of Baghdad, they were trying to reestablish righteousness, truth, or justice. So let us follow this disguised prince in his nocturnal peregrinations, let us penetrate alongside him into the shacks and nighttime refuges, and let us listen to him justifying his strange venture.

THE PRINCE AND THE PHILANTHROPISTS

The nocturnal and anonymous rambling by a kingly righter of wrongs in the urban underworld is anchored in a long tradition. This particular practice of power has been ascribed notably to King Louis XI of France and to King James V of Scotland, who traveled his kingdom disguised as Gudeman of Ballangeich.[1] But it was only with the introduction into Europe of *The Arabian Nights* at the beginning of the eighteenth century that this figure acquired notoriety. Antoine Galland provided the first French translation of this composite ensemble of tales from India, Persia, Arabia, and Egypt: stories of love and adventure, of crimes and thefts and prostitution, encased in the framing story of the Princess Scheherazade telling a story each night to fend off execution. Galand's *Ali Baba* version enjoyed an extraordinary success. The story ensemble was quickly translated into English, then into most European languages, and spread rapidly in an astonishing to-and-fro movement of multiple versions, often very distant from the originals.[2] Galland adapted them a great deal, largely eliding the erotic dimension of the tales, and placing at their center the figure of the caliph of Bagdad, thereby inaugurating the modern motif of the disguised prince.[3]

Contemporaneous with Charlemagne (who reigned at the turn of the eighth to the ninth century), Harun-al-Rashid as portrayed in Galland's text incarnates the good king who wants to see things for himself: when night comes, in the guise of a merchant, he walks through the streets of Baghdad. He observes someone and follows him, and so he is witness to crimes, miseries, and clandestine affairs. The next day, he summons to his palace the figures of the previous night in order to punish the guilty and to reward the virtuous. His venture is dictated by a concern for justice and charity, but the caliph is also a gloomy insomniac. His nocturnal quest aims to quench his melancholy; he is searching for adventure, distraction, pleasure. Everything is entangled in his personality: a concern to know the reality of the lower depths, a desire to enjoy their spectacle, a power to render justice. Thus we should not be surprised that a nineteenth century obsessed by the issues of pauperism and crime should make this figure a sort of icon and the precursor of the great explorers of the bas-fonds. "Mr. Rudolph indulges in charity and extravagance like the caliph of

Baghdad in the Arabian Nights," noted Karl Marx in 1845 in *The Holy Family*, stressing the parallel between the hero of *Mystères de Paris* and Harun-al-Rashid.[4] The allusion quickly spilled beyond erudite circles. In the second half of the nineteenth century, Londoners often used the expression "to go Harun-al-Rashid" to refer to quasi-incognito trips through the capital's slums.[5] Robert Stevenson did not merely appropriate the metaphor but fully developed it in a series of stories beginning in 1877 that amounted to his first published fiction, and a few years later he assembled the series in *New Arabian Nights* (followed by *More New Arabian Nights*).[6] In "The Suicide Club" and the six stories that followed, Prince Florizel, the beloved sovereign of Bohemia, cruises the London underworld in various disguises accompanied by his friend Colonel Geraldine. He meets crazy people, criminals, adventurers, women in distress, and anarchists, and makes himself the instrument of a sovereign justice. In this London at century's end that had just dethroned Paris as capital of the underworld, Stevenson explicitly synthesized *A Thousand and One Nights* and the *Mystères de Paris*.

In fact, several types of figures share the inheritance of the caliph of Baghdad. All of them are shameless discoverers of the underworld, but they explore it with different styles, postures, and sometimes legitimacy. Just before the French Revolution, Restif de la Bretonne in the *Nuits de Paris*—which he once thought of titling the "French Thousand and One Nights"—featured a "nocturnal Spectator" called Le Hibou (the owl); the first twelve installments appeared in December 1788 (but the text had been written over the two previous years). Dressed in a "blue cloak" and carrying a pickax as well as concealed pistols, the narrator, alias Restif himself, wanders at night through the streets, often in the most sordid parts of Paris. He witnesses a thousand quaint or dangerous scenes: he meets beggars and people who cannot pay their rent, saves a girl from a stream near Les Halles, discovers the remains of a child's cadaver at the corner of the rue de la Huchette, and tracks "resurrectionist" body snatchers in the St. Séverin cemetery. All these adventures are recounted the next day to his mentor, a neurasthenic marquise called La Vaporeuse. In real life, Restif was a *mouche* (a police informant), as indicated by his blue cloak. The text brims with clues to his relations with the lieutenancy of the police (maybe the marquise?): he threatens those he questions with summoning the authorities and constantly visits the guardhouse. Some critics hypothesize that Restif used his information to pay for his freedom to write and publish.[7] Certainly this form of police voyeurism is less noble than stories inspired by the benevolent Harun-al-Rashid, but it is perhaps also one of the most realistic, actually the kind of police activity practiced by Vidocq and his followers. "Spies," trackers, detectives, informants—all of them plunge incognito into the underworld, or what is presumed to be such (in the United States, the Pinkerton agency penetrated labor unions). In return these agents were well paid, for there is scarcely any heroism attached to such shadowy figures.[8]

The second type of disguised hero is much more valorized: the bohemian philanthropist and righter of wrongs. The romantic bohemian figure who emerged on the heels of the underworld itself offered a range of night-owl adventurers, "divers into the Parisian ocean," in Alfred Delvau's expression,[9] whose nocturnal activity was inspired by that of the caliph of Baghdad. Gérard de Nerval's *Nuits du Rhamazan* was explicitly conceived as a variation on Galland; it was followed in 1852 by *October Nights*, in which the writer explored the principal Parisian bas-fonds. An indefatigable explorer of the Paris streets, Alexandre Privat d'Anglemont was one of the most accomplished types of these romantic prowlers of the city, but he lacked the disguise of any redemptive activity. Then along came Rodolphe de Gerolstein, a German prince we first discover one cold evening in December 1839 disguised in narrow city streets as a laborer. The all-powerful hero of the *Mystères de Paris*, Rodolphe is pursuing a personal quest. However, whenever this is possible, he tries to save innocent souls (Fleur-de-Marie, the Morels) and to punish the guilty (the Schoolmaster, the Owl, the notary Jacques Ferrand), sometimes in a particularly cruel way. For contemporaries, the analogy with the caliph was all the more obvious because it was paralleled with another resemblance (often noticed too) that linked the serial novel, still new in 1842, with the interminable logic of *The Arabian Nights*. In fact, behind the figure of Prince Rodolphe looms that of another righter of wrongs, Eugène Sue himself, who is reported by Félix Pyat to have explored the bas-fonds disguised as a painter, accompanied by a Herculean friend (Duflos) and a French boxing master (Charles Lacour). "I need to see, to touch," Sue writes to Marie d'Argoult.[10] It is said that this is how he was won over to philanthropy, then to socialist doctrine.

But perhaps another prince, Louis-Napoléon Bonaparte, actually inspired Eugène Sue. Monsieur Claude reports that around 1831 Prince Bonaparte dressed as a laborer to frequent the Lapin Blanc and other taverns to study "on the fly" the sensitive issue of pauperism and its effects "on the most debased classes."[11] The former head of the *Sûreté* was absolutely certain that the future Napoléon III served as a model for Rodolphe in the *Mystères de Paris*, but it is unlikely that Sue, who chose exile after the coup d'état in December 1851, would have accepted this connection. Nevertheless, the figure of Rodolphe is fundamental, joining together (like his creator) a romantic bohemianism, the philanthropic endeavor, and progressive reform. Other heroes quickly came along in his wake, beginning with Alexandre Dumas's Salvator, also a disguised prince (his real name was Conrad de Valgeneuse, a dispossessed marquis who had become an ordinary police agent), who pursued his vengeance while coming to the aid of all those who had been disinherited and other "Mohicans de Paris" in Alexander Dumas's serial of the same name.[12]

In Great Britain, many philanthropists and reformers engaged in the incognito exploration of the underworld. Their pathfinder was an investigative journalist, James Greenwood, who in 1866 dressed as a tramp and spent "A Night in the Workhouse," a deed that had an extraordinary impact, and which I discuss in detail later in the chapter. His initiative triggered many others.[13] The same year (1866), a poet known only as M.A. also introduced himself at night into a workhouse, about which he gave a long account in a verse play.[14] Also in 1866, Joshua Stallard, an eminent member of the Royal College of Medicine and an active partisan of reforming the British charity system, sought the means to reproduce Greenwood's exploit, but this time in a female workhouse. Convinced that no woman of the bourgeoisie could withstand this ordeal, he hired the widow of a worker who was presumed to be "used to" poverty. Under the successive names of Ellen Stanley and Jane Wood, she went into the workhouses of Stoke Newington, Lambeth, Whitechapel, and St-George-in-the-East, and described their often unbearable conditions. The tale was published from Stallard's point of view, and he constantly reframed and interpreted the widow's account.[15] This kind of immersion proliferated at the turn of the century. In 1904, for example, Mary

Higgs, the wife of a Congregational minister and friend of the journalist William Stead, spent three nights incognito in a home for women in Kedging and published an anonymous account. In 1910, it was the turn of Georges Edward, an Anglican rector, to spend four nights as a vagrant who slept in lodging houses.[16]

This practice was obviously tempting for social reformers who wanted to uncover and expose the abuses they thought were being perpetrated. Thus the British socialist John Robert Widdup, editor in chief of a militant paper in Lancashire, disguised himself as a vagabond to get himself admitted in 1894 to the Burnley poorhouse so he could denounce its atrocious conditions. The more restrained Beatrice Potter (the future Beatrice Webb) also felt the need to disguise herself when she participated in the investigation conducted by her cousin Charles Booth, which is described in *Life and Labour of the People of London*. It was as a young Jewish woman newly arrived in Britain that Potter got herself hired in a candy factory. Potter relates the experience in *Pages of a Work-Girl's Diary*, published in September 1888 in the magazine *Nineteenth Century*.

The most famous example of this exploit is certainly the American novelist Jack London, who used the subterfuge of disguise in 1901 to immerse himself in the slums of London's East End. Back in the United States, London became involved in radical movements (such as the march of the unemployed on Washington by Coxey's army in 1890), and he developed a theory of the hobo condition in "War of the Classes—The Tramp."[17] London thought of himself as a correspondent in a new social war: he wanted people to learn about the brutality of the experience of poverty as perceived from the inside. His own East End experience was offered as a series of vignettes, sort of dispatches from the front, and was given coherence by the indignation of the narrator-protagonist. The tale's ending is free of the traditional devices of the investigation, instead offering a veritable social analysis; like a prosecutor, London denounced the responsibility of "industrial society as it exists today." Of course, the text had a hard time finding a publisher and finally appeared in March 1903 under the title *The People of the Abyss* in the socialist monthly *Wilshire's*, and then it came out as a sensational book in October 1903 from the New York publisher MacMillan.

But the clandestine exploration of the abyss did not belong solely to progressive activists. It could also serve to demonstrate the plague of what some called "false poverty." This was the project of the Frenchman Louis Paulian, chief editor in the Legislative Chamber at the end of the nineteenth century and a recognized "penitentiary man" (he was secretary of the Prison Society). A friend of the ragpickers (whom he considered to be useful workers) but a resolute enemy of beggars, he devoted two landmark books to the contrast: *La hotte du chiffonnier* (The ragpicker's sack) in 1885, then *Paris qui mendie* (The beggars of Paris) with a first edition in 1893 (followed by many later ones).[18] In both books, Paulian signals the limits of a documentary approach: "This vast enquiry not having produced the result I expected, I decided to have recourse to personal experience, and just as I had before become a rag-picker in order to study the habits of rag-pickers, so one fine day I became a beggar to study the habits of the beggars."[19] Yet the two ventures were very different: the first consisted of accompanying ragpickers on their journeys, whereas the second is much more clearly related to the investigation and identification of fraud. Paulian fashions a disguise as a beggar, transforms himself into a paralytic, rents a (hideous) wig from a fancy dress shop, and repeatedly immerses himself in a beggar's Paris: the steps of the Madeleine, then of the Palais Bourbon, finally at the entrance to the Église Saint-Germain-des-Prés, where he is arrested by a police sergeant. "By turns a crawling cripple, a blind street-singer, carriage-door opener, mechanic out of work, unemployed professor, paralytic, deaf-and-dumb, I have had every kind of infirmity and have practiced every kind of deceit."[20] But the idea was not really original. In 1836, Marc Michel, a young playwright from Marseille who later worked with the famous French author of vaudevilles Eugène Labiche, had put on stage the local notable Dessulamarre, a man so scandalized by the growing number of beggars that he wants to build a workhouse in the English style.[21] To justify his plan, the philanthropist explores the city dressed as a pauper, begs in courtyards, in front of the church, and even in the Court of Miracles, the lair of truands of the old city. But Dessulamare became a character in a novel that was not very successful; in fact Paulian was a recognized publicist whose inquiry aimed to expose the existence of scandalously fraudulent begging that "feeds a man more easily than working does."[22]

"UNDERCOVER"

A third figure, the journalist, is the most modern and successful kind of disguised prince. Perhaps we should consider both *Les Mystères* and *Les Mohicans de Paris* series as early "media" creations, whose scope was inseparable from the newspapers that disseminated them, but the "new journalism" that developed in the last decade of the nineteenth century introduced pronounced innovations. The incognito descent to the darkest parts of the underworld was one of these.

The founding reporter was the Englishman James Greenwood. Brother of the editor of the famous *Pall Mall Gazette*, in January 1866 Greenwood published a sensational report titled "A Night in the Workhouse."[23] In England, visiting workhouses had become widespread among philanthropists who were "going slumming". In 1858, Louisa Twinning had even founded the Workhouse Visiting Society, and countless tales of such visits had been published. But nobody had tried "with no motive but to learn and make known the truth, how the night passes among those outcasts we have all seen crowding around the workhouse doors on cold and rainy nights," or had given an account of what "actually" happened there—that is, unvarnished. This was Greenwood's goal, and it connected traditional slumming to journalistic reportage. What Sue had prefigured in the novelistic realm, Greenwood performed in journalistic practice. In January 1866, under the name Joshua Mason, he presented himself in rags to be admitted into the workhouse of Lambeth, an impoverished area in south London, and he spent the whole night there. The article was published in three daily parts, from January 12 to 14; its success was phenomenal, and the tale quickly spread abroad. Louis Blanc reported in one of his "Letters from London" published in *Les Temps* on January 29: "This story is poignant; it is terrible; it reveals horrors that one barely dared to suspect." Greenwood's report was soon published as a serial, in both a cheap edition and a deluxe version, and it also gave rise to theatrical adaptations. Greenwood, then age thirty-five, had found his path. He became one of the principal specialists in the London underworld, to which he devoted many other accounts, including an equally memorable one about a fight organized in Hanley between a man and a dog, which was published in *The Daily Telegraph* on July 6, 1874. He also authored a dozen books on these matters.[24]

Greenwood's initiative founded a genre, that of incognito investigative reporting in the most inaccessible places of the underworld. The tense social context in England at the end of the nineteenth century was propitious for this kind of enterprise. Dozens of similar ventures took place in the wake of Greenwood's, encouraged by the ambitions and aggressive methods of the new journalism. Journalists rushed to gain entry into shelters for beggars: F. G. Wallace-Goodbody in January 1883, C. W. Craven in 1887, and Everard Wyral, whose story was published in the *Daily Express* in 1908, all stirred up public outrage.[25] In 1910, the journalist Walter Cranfield, covered in rags and with a four-day beard growth, immersed himself among the homeless of the British capital. He begged, sold matches, slept in a dosshouse, then in a hospital, took refuge in a church, and then described in minute detail the conditions of his companions in misery. He published the tale of his experience among the poor of London under the title *A Vicarious Vagrant*.[26]

But shelters for beggars and vagrants were not the only target of this new journalism. The most sensational affair was the one that shook England in July of 1885. On July 4, William Stead, editor in chief of the *Pall Mall Gazette*, began publishing what became the most famous series in the world of sensational investigations: "The Maiden Tribute of Modern Babylon." Under the guise of working for a secret commission, the journalist explained how he negotiated the purchase of a young virgin (age thirteen).[27] No detail was spared in describing the existence in London of a vast market of sex slaves in which poor girls were kidnapped or sold, then sequestered, drugged, and offered to lecherous clients. Stead described the manageresses and doctors who certified the virginity of young girls, the captivities and rapes. The purchase of Lily was presented from beginning to end. Thanks to a matron who acted as intermediary, Stead struck a deal with the little girl's mother: three pounds sterling payable immediately, two pounds more once the gynecological certificate was given. Lily was then taken to a midwife who guaranteed her virginity, then she was undressed and chloroformed. When she awakened, she was sent to France and handed to the Salvation Army. The reverberations of the reportage were unprecedented; sales of the *Pall Mall Gazette* literally exploded, and the story was quickly taken up and translated into many languages. In London, it led to a surge of puritanism that turned into moral panic. But it also led to a Royal Commission and to raising the age of consent to sixteen under the Stead Law, named after the reporter, who would go down on the *Titanic*.

The American newspapers gave a name to this kind of practice: the "stunt" was designed to provoke the actual event—"Nothing happens, [so] I make news"[28]—and reporters turned themselves into specialists in what they called "role (or exposure) reporting," or more often "undercover journalism." Here is how Frank Luther Mott, a well-known U.S. historian of journalism, defined it in 1941: "A clever and adventurous writer assumes a disguise or forges documents to gain admission to a hospital, jail or asylum, and then makes the narratives of this experience an exposé of the administration of the institution."[29] The icon of this type of journalism was Elizabeth Cochrane, known as Nellie Bly (she borrowed her pseudonym from a character in a popular song), the first of the "stunt girls." She started in 1885 at the *Pittsburgh Dispatch*, wrote a series on the Pittsburgh slums, then on those of Mexico. She then moved to Pulitzer's *New York World*, where in October 1887 she accomplished one of the most famous undercover reports in the world. Simulating madness, she got herself interned in Bellevue Hospital, an asylum on Blackwell's Island, and she remained there for ten days before being liberated when the newspaper intervened. The series of articles she published in the *New York World* (which were reprinted in a book titled *Ten Days in A Mad-House*) exposed the filth, the rats, the horrible food, the tainted water, the blows and bad treatment inflicted on patients, some of whom were tied up by the nurses. The scandal was such that a lawsuit was brought again the asylum's administration. For her part, Nellie Bly pursued this kind of reporting for several years, experiencing a woman's prison, a hospital for the destitute, and a Salvation Army shelter, and she became the bête noire of such institutions.[30] She was followed by other women journalists, who saw such undercover work as the means to winning a full place in the profession. For example, the American Elizabeth Banks got herself hired in some of the worst sweatshops of New York, then as a servant in London.[31]

In the 1880s in France, this was known as *journalisme à l'américaine* because this kind of reportage remained rather rare. In fact, it was mocked as a hare-brained idea from across the Channel. Here is how the daily

newspaper *Paris-Journal* (March 2, 1880) made fun of a journalist who
had tried it out:

> Imitating the famous British reporter, our colleague slept at a home-
> less shelter in the rue de Tocqueville, but something happened that
> exposed his ruse. Having forgotten his wallet under the bolster of his
> camp-bed, he returned to get it two days later. Imagine the stupefac-
> tion of the house-manager at seeing him descend from a carriage at
> the shelter door! So yesterday's beggar—registered under the pseud-
> onym "Casubiano"—had to reveal his quality as a gentleman. More-
> over, his wallet had been turned in to the office by the person who
> had found it, and so it was indeed returned to our colleague.

In 1882, Georges Grison, celebrated petty crime reporter and court chronicler (notably at the *Figaro*), viewed such subterfuge as how a mere beginner
might proceed:

> I did not need the classic disguise that naïfs think they have to adopt
> in order to penetrate into their lairs: a cap, a smock, down-at-heel
> shoes. . . . No! Even under the rags, *especially* under the rags, their
> expert eye can spot someone who is not one of their own, and this
> runs the risk of being taken for a spy and treated accordingly. So I
> always go to them in a frock coat and high hat, without disguising or
> hiding myself, and tell them frankly what I desire to know.[32]

In fact, this journalistic practice was slow to be adopted in France, no doubt
due to the hybrid character of the French press, which long preferred a
strong literary dimension.

Nevertheless, in April 1885, a journalist from *Gagne-Petit* went undercover to investigate "the poverty of Paris." A little later, Séverine (pen
name of a French anarchist and feminist) disguised herself as a sugar factory worker to investigate a strike. And Andrée Viollis got herself hired as
a nurse to investigate a hospital, then she assumed the identity of a delinquent just released from prison to find out about the support system for
former prisoners.[33] But neither Jacques Duhr nor Albert London, the two

tutelary figures of French "*grand reportage*," ever made use of undercover work. In fact, an opposite technique—estrangement—was advocated by Albert London in order to truly enter into a situation or a state of mind. In 1918, France's "Charter of the Journalist's Professional Duties" banned the use of imaginary appearances in order to obtain information. "Camouflage is not very useful to insert yourself among the truly authentic," noted reporter Georges de Lavarenne as late as 1932, "since to recognize each other within the neighborhood's freemasonry the latter have precise signs, their own vocabulary, of which outsiders are ignorant."[34]

Yet within less than a decade (the 1920s), undercover reporting would become durably implanted in France. On November 16, 1923, *Paris-Soir* published "La Jungle de Paris," a series in which the journalist René Daix disguised himself as a vagrant and wandered the capital's streets without a coin in his pocket. He posed himself the question: "Can an able-bodied man die of hunger in the capital?" For three days he chased about finding the "tiny resources of the big city." He distributed leaflets, washed cars, cleaned graves in a cemetery, washed dishes in restaurants, and scalped tickets in theater queues or at the Opera. His conclusion on November 21 was categorical: "I have finished the three days of poverty I assigned myself. During this span of time, I lived among frustrated and often crude men by performing crude tasks, sometimes painful, but always easy to do. I lived roughly and coldly, but I lived." The translation into French of Jack London's *People of the Abyss*, which was serialized in *Le Quotidien* in March 1926, encouraged the movement.[35] In 1928, Maryse Choisy, one of the rare women engaged in this profession, published her report about brothels, *Un mois chez les filles* (A month with the girls [prostitutes]).[36] The prefecture of police had refused to give her official authorization, so she decided to get herself hired as a cleaning maid in a brothel listed in one of the many "pleasure guides" to the capital. Then we follow her to a number of other establishments: to Ginette's, to the *institut de beauté* of Margaret Fairy (who prostituted teenagers), to the Cosy-bar, the Fétiche (a lesbian house), to a whorehouse in Le Havre, then to the Ace of Hearts in the "Sébasto" (the boulevard Sébastopol, a Parisian street devoted to prostitution). By the end of her reportage, we forget about her disguise (the author barely escapes from a pimp on the rue des Vertus) and focus instead on her portraits and her general reflections on prostitution and brothels. The following year Maryse Choisy went on to use undercover reporting (cross-dressed as a young monk) to enter one of the monasteries of the celebrated Mount Athos in Greece (where even today no women are permitted) for *Un mois chez les hommes* (A month with the men).[37]

In June 1929, Georges Le Fèvre, a star reporter who had just joined the editorial board of the *Journal*, which he wanted to turn around, performed the now classic immersion in the world of vagrants and simpletons. "Je suis un gueux" (I am a beggar) was a series of fourteen articles published between June 9 and June 22, 1920, an anonymous two-week dive into the thirteenth *arrondissement*, one of the poorest in Paris. He described a world that was harsh (and harshly exploited)—a society of rejects and "*vieux pilons*" (old codgers) who could expect nothing from the modern world. Complemented by similar experiences in Berlin and London (how these missions were carried out is nowhere mentioned), the reportage was published as a book on the very day after the final episode appeared.[38] Now such stories reached the climax of their history in France. In Marseille, Jean Dorian put on makeup in order to explore the old city's underworld, but he was unmasked by the sector's police chief. Armand-Henry Flassch got himself arrested while disguised as a down-and-outer, a jug of wine in his hand, to write a "living report" on the prefecture's lockup, which he published in *Détective*. This was obviously a prime subject, because five years later (in May 1934), under the pseudonym "M. Froment," the journalist Maurice Aubenas also got himself arrested in order to spend a night in the holding cell. He published photos of the judicial anthropometrics and of the round loaf of bread he carried away when he got out.[39]

Despite the proliferation of such stories, which were often flat and vapid, undercover journalism gradually won honor. Undertaken by a few prestigious figures such as Nellie Bly, it appeared as both an ordeal and an exploit in which the reporter could truly give the best of him- or herself and also serve society. The movement continued in the second half of the twentieth century, especially for penetrating the reputedly forbidden worlds of the poor and the marginal.[40] But such a practice had its limits and required a clear ethics. In *Shock Corridor*, a rather brutal film by Samuel Fuller released in 1963, the main character, a cynical and ambitious journalist, immerses himself in an insane asylum to investigate a murder. Certain of winning a Pulitzer Prize for this, he is capable of doing anything to reach his goal. Gradually caught in his own trap, he ends up losing his mind.

THE POWER OF NARRATIVE

Whether social reformer, missionary, or reporter, all those who immersed themselves incognito in the underworld felt the need to justify their action. Yet the context was favorable to these extreme forms of exploration. Poverty (especially in Great Britain where the movement began) was reassuming an intensity that people thought had disappeared, which struck fear into Victorian consciousness and called for the application of energetic solutions to eradicate it. At the same time, the "new journalism," trying to play a growing role in social issues, was determined to employ "combative methods." Nevertheless, to assume the place of the poor in a workhouse or to simulate the purchase of a young virgin was considered by many to be exaggerated, if not frankly scandalous. Had not Lot's wife been transformed into a statue of salt for wanting to view the destruction of Sodom? Therefore, it was felt necessary to legitimize a practice that many would define as a provocation doubled with shameful voyeurism.

Its defenders responded that this was the sole means to flush out the real situation, to see and to show realities that often remain inaccessible. They went on that occasional public visits or inspections of these "total" institutions—workhouses, hospitals, or prisons—could not teach us anything. Such formal visits were prepared and prearranged, rigged. The only means of knowing and making known "what a homeless shelter is actually like," explained James Greenwood in 1866, was to enter one anonymously and secretly. Only then could the dirt, vermin, rats, inedible gruel, snickers and monstrous looks that inmates were given become apparent. Only this first-hand knowledge, the validation of the investigator's "I saw," enabled lifting the veil on these sordid realities.

For Beatrice Webb, a disguise was an artifact that allowed one to get into the necessary state, to prepare oneself psychologically for the experience one was going to share with the poor. Yet she recognized a little later that this was only an illusion.[41] For others, "cross-dressing" disguise was the only way to gain access to the speech of the poor, to obtain their trust, confidences, and testimony. Immersed in the underworld of Whitechapel, Jack London tried to admit to his companions in misery that he was an investigator wanting to understand how the other half lived. "At once they shut up like clams. I was not of their kind, my speech had changed, the tones of my voice were different, in short, I was a superior, and they were superbly class conscious."[42] In these conditions, camouflage appeared to be the only possibility for acquiring the experience of an insider, of permitting effective exchanges, of acceding to the realities of the underworld. According to Restif de la Bretonne in the eighteenth century, this was the principal virtue of *inconussion* (unknowability): "this unknowability makes each person an Individual, whose affairs, relations, faults and weaknesses are unknown, who can act with freedom and total human dignity."[43]

But such justifications were not unanimously accepted. Herbert Spencer, for example, denied any validity to this method, which he thought blurred the lines separating the investigator from the investigated, mixing observation and imagination. It is impossible, he wrote to Beatrice Webb, to see society as it is when one adopts this posture, one merely projects one's expectations onto it.[44] The sociologist Alexandre Vexliard, who studied the milieu of Parisian vagrants in the 1950s, experimented personally with subterfuge: "Several times, we mixed into the life of vagrants, we shared their existence by wearing suitable dress." But he thought the results were very disappointing because the type of discussion he wanted did not suit the marginals: "Vagrants do not usually ask each other about their past. It was impossible for us by this means to obtain individual biographical information, and even less so, to pursue any indications methodically."[45] Thus they returned to the more classic social science method of the individual interview.

In participant observation, the boundary between observation and identification often proved fragile. The Chicago school of sociology, whose ties to a certain kind of investigative journalism were apparent, had from the start concentrated on personal experiences.[46] Josiah Flynt spent several years living the vagabond's life in the United States of the 1890s before offering an analysis of this experience in *Tramping with Tramps* in 1899. The same was true of the famous study of hobos by Nels Anderson, published in

1923, also in Chicago. This tradition of a sociology of identification continues to mark much of the work in Chicago today. Sudhir Venkatesh recently immersed himself for five years in the Robert Taylor Homes, one of the worst ghettos of Chicago, sharing the life and sometimes even the activities of the Black Gangster Disciples, an African American gang specializing in selling crack cocaine.[47]

Georges Orwell, who had spent several years *Down and Out in Paris and London* at the end of the 1920s, had early on drawn very pessimistic conclusions about the identification strategy.[48] His initial ambition had been clear: not to seek to show to others—he was constantly criticizing journalists for this—but to understand for himself, to see from within, to live inside. "I wanted to submerge myself, to get right down among the oppressed, to be one of them and on their side against their tyrants," he wrote a little later.[49] What he sought in the experience of the vagabond and the tramp was a personal decentering. But he did not achieve this, always feeling himself caught in the position of an observer, and the experiment ended with his realizing it had failed. "Unfortunately, you do not solve the class problem by making friends with tramps. At most you get rid of some of your own class-prejudice by doing so."[50]

The philanthropists and reporters who roamed the underworld were not generally encumbered by such considerations. On the contrary, they often evoked what an ordeal the experience was. The cultural distance that separated some of these observers from the realities they were exploring should not be minimized. In fact, we know about the sensory shock, even profound repulsion, felt by some philanthropists (male and female) upon contact with these "degraded souls," whom nothing in their culture or history had prepared them to encounter. The new journalism took account of these transformations, and its ethos required taking a risk. You had to pay with your person, engage your body and your senses. Emerging from the ordeal, James Greenwood explained the humiliation he had felt in taking off his ragged clothes and slipping naked under the bed cover, the anguish of dipping into a filthy tub in which floated all the shelter's grime. He describes the disgust of having to eat the foul *skilley* (a mush made of water and oat flour) and of lying on a repugnant straw mattress. William Stead, for his part, had to defend himself in court after the publication of "The Maiden

Tribute." The mother of little Lily denied that she had sold her daughter and accused the journalist of kidnapping and sequestering the child. At the close of a twelve-day trial, Stead was condemned to three months forced labor, which he spent in the Holloway Prison, a conviction he turned into a trophy and about which he felt proud his whole life. But we should also qualify the scope of the risks run by reporters. Most stays in the underworld were relatively brief and the immersion was limited—what was one night in a workhouse or even ten days in an insane asylum compared with the destinies that were encountered there? Those like Jack London or Georges Le Fèvre, who remained submerged much longer, kept the possibility of arranging pauses. Newspaper editors had the means necessary to put an end to the experiment if a serious problem arose for the journalist. Finally, the dive into the underworld was not always made solo. James Greenwood did not go alone into the workhouse but was accompanied by someone named Bittlestone, whose presence he took the precaution of erasing from the published account.[51] Le Fèvre possessed guides in London and Berlin. This may explain why these "explorers," unlike other social observers such as Charles Booth, Seebom Rowntree, or even Henry Mayhew, were never considered as proto-sociologists and have been the subjects of only literary or journalistic analyses.[52]

In contrast to other approaches to and representations of the under-world, these narrators were never content with a purely descriptive or "revelatory" approach. Immersion always involved some kind of action and was intended to have practical effects. Most of these narratives contain: an empathic dimension with respect to the miserable that was accentuated by the process of identification, a desire to denounce the causes of that misery that was evident among reporters and social reformers, and finally, a dramatization that highlights the spectacle of horror. Here we recognize the three "topics" (morality, media, and politics) whose articulation, according to Luc Boltanski, prepares a path toward action.[53]

The initial motivation arises from a sense of justice: to relieve poverty, to save the innocent, to punish the guilty—indeed the intentions of the caliph of Baghdad. Some of his followers were more ambitious. Restif de la Bretonne's nocturnal Spectator, apart from the aid he gave to ruined families or to young girls ripe for prostitution, did not hesitate to give society practical advice, to suggest reforms, to risk positing utopian solutions. The character Rodolphe and his author Eugène Sue (whose voices intermingle) fit together to propose some structural reforms: a Poor Bank, prison reform, social-democratic engagement. And such a perspective becomes evident in the case of reporters such as William Stead or Nellie Blye, who indeed wanted their articles to bear fruit in precise reforms, which sometimes did result. But merely stressing the obvious malfunctioning of institutions—shelters for the poor and asylums for the insane—was the most frequent motive. Here we find the infamous gruel served to inmates, there the coarse nurses who strike and harass patients, some of whom are there because they were caught in a veritable human rattrap, and further along, the mind-numbing labor after a night in the asylum when you have to "pay the reckoning" by breaking rocks or spinning flax. But behind the factual denunciations there sometimes lurked less humanitarian intentions. With Greenwood, the prime cause of dysfunction came from the fact that the workhouses never really distinguished between the meritorious poor and those who were less so, which meant they received too many drunks and crooks who sullied the establishment. The needy, the poor buggers who ought to find a bit of comfort there, were unfortunately treated in the same way as the mass of underserving poor who took up too much space. For Greenwood, a solution would come from a more rigorous system of classification, capable of identifying the true unfortunates and of abandoning the residue of beggars and vagabonds to their sad fates. Curiously, Louis Blanc echoed this representation in his article for *Le Temps*, when he described a workhouse that has turned gangrenous due to the inclusion of the "worst kind of derelicts" who created an atmosphere of obscene debauchery.

In France between the World Wars, several undercover reportages tried to demonstrate that work *did* exist for whoever wanted to find it. In 1923, René Daix claimed that an able-bodied man does not die of hunger in Paris. Georges Le Fèvre developed an analogous idea in *Je suis un gueux* (I am a beggar): unemployment does not appear in his series, which was trying to demonstrate the omnipresence of work. Le Fèvre was successively an unloader, a sandwich-board man, an acrobat, a poster sticker, and a *carbi* (coal shoveler). A job can always be found, asserted the reporter. The problem was that the work, by the constraints it imposes—schedules, outfit, different forms of socialization—prevented odd-jobbers from getting access to traditional assistance. You arrive too late at the night shelter and it is full, so you are sent on to the Salvation Army, a reject even from the solidarity of the underworld. Work, concluded Le Fèvre, thus becomes a handicap that the intelligent vagrant quickly abandons.

Other motivations appeared less disinterested, however. Reporters in the era of the new journalism found obvious professional compensations. A well-executed feature series could turn a big profit. "A Night in the Workhouse" earns James Greenwood the tidy sum of "30 pounds sterling, and more if the affair turns out well."[54] When skillfully conducted, such operations were also evident career accelerators. It was really only after the Lily affair that William Stead gained the status of a great press boss. Nellie Bly, marginalized by being a woman, was primarily seeking to break into the profession, and it is not by chance that so many undercover reports were undertaken by women (Elizabeth Banks, Andrée Viollis, Maryse Choisy). The effects on the newspaper industry were just as decisive. The *Pall Mall Gazette*, founded in 1865, had difficult beginnings and scarcely exceeded a circulation of a thousand in the first year, but the Greenwood and Stead affairs enabled it to increase its sales tenfold in less than a decade.[55] The model of such reportages proved particularly productive. On top of the suspense of the plot, the narration easily accommodated dialogue, anecdotes, and picturesque portraits. The dailies frequently relied on the flavors of a serial often attached to such features. Here is how *Le Journal* presented Georges Le Fèvre's venture in 1929:

> To better understand the lower depths of Paris and those who live there, Georges Le Fèvre adopted the costume of the destitute. He lived several weeks in poverty, with no support or money, going so far as to make the sacrifice of not ever entering his residence, though it lay nearby. *Le Journal* in a few days will begin the publication of the tough investigation that Georges Le Fèvre conducted in these milieus.

The spectacular dimension of these narratives and their scandalous odor were determining factors. We should not forget that the caliph of Baghdad became bored indoors and this was the reason he went out at night. The vogue for undercover stories began in the 1860s, at the very time that England witnessed a surge of "sensation novels" such as the works of Wilkie Collins and Mary Elizabeth Braddon. We saw that the founding tale, Greenwood's "A Night in the Workhouse," sold thousands of pamphlets for a shilling and vastly more as a "penny dreadful"; a month after its publication, it was adapted for the stage of the Theater Royal in Marylebone, then went on to other London theaters.[56] What stands out is the number of "effects" and exaggerations and dramatic twists with which these texts were filled. The bath, the disinfection of rags, the vermin, and persecution by guardians or nurses were the stock bravura scenes that circulated and were reprised from text to script. The erotic and sexual dimension of these tales was also undeniable. Transvestism had long been a homosexual practice; now behind the philanthropic or journalistic slumming came a variety of "queer" slumming.[57] And the eroticism of poverty sometimes gave way to less figurative scenes. Even if it was told in a roundabout way, Greenwood's story exposed the hypocrisy of separating the sexes in poorhouses, allowing the reader to glimpse the homosexual orgy that unfolded at night. And the phenomenal success of *The Maiden Tribute of Modern Babylon* owed as much to its erotic charge as to the indignation it aroused. Stead recycled scenes from the pornographic repertoire, reproduced sadistic scenarios: young and innocent virgins are sequestered, tied up, tortured, deflowered, and raped. In one installment, a madam explains how thanks to the padded rooms in her establishment, one never heard the cries.

More than any other case, Stead's testified to the structural ambiguity of this type of narrative that mingled philanthropic goals and reforming militancy. (Stead mounted his operation in partnership with both feminist Josephine Butler's movement to abolish the sex trade in young girls and with the Salvation Army, and he was supported in radical circles.) The media could exploit an event already told in the register of melodrama, of pornography and the unhealthiest voyeurism. But the normative function of these narratives continued to predominate. Disguised prince? Perhaps the expression is more suggestive than it appears. It signals the observer's absolute exteriority very clearly: the social chasm between the prince and the underworld is an insurmountable barrier between disjointed worlds.

If disguise allows them to be brought together temporarily, this is due to duplicity and the false complicity of cross-dressing. The expression also perfectly connotes the power invested in the explorer. The disguised prince denounces abuses, relieves poverty, renders justice—but always by using a superiority that is simultaneously social, political, financial, and ceremonial, factors of domination that are actually being reinforced in the exercise. Marx wrote of Rudolph, "He cannot lead that kind of life without sucking the blood out of his little province of Germany to the last drop, like a vampire."[58] This narrative of a social gap and the prince's domination was transformed into a spectacle offered to all the subjects of the kingdom. In these stories, the underworld was constructed, inspected, and reduced in the exercise of a benevolent power that found its legitimacy there.

6

The Grand Dukes' Tour

Whether a philanthropist, a righter of wrongs, or a reporter, the "prince" ventured alone into the shadowy depths. But a competing scenario soon emerged in which there was a *collective* discovery of the underworld. Under the leadership of a guide—either a Cicero figure or a detective—a troupe of revelers would roam the lower depths of the city when night fell, seeking some of its "attractions." This tourism of the underworld, which was born in London as "fashionable slumming," quickly spread to all the capitals of the Western world and became one of the principal forms of exploring the underworld. Tourists could find everything that made bad places attractive: exoticism and culture shock, to satisfy a strange desire for repulsion, to experience the shiver of danger—and the thrill of eroticism. Moreover, there was the comforting certainty of knowing they belonged to another world! This kind of tourism achieved its most accomplished form in Paris, where it was nicknamed the "Grand Dukes' Tour," for reasons that will soon become clear. The Parisian experience serves as our guide for following the nocturnal journeys of those who sought adventure in the spectacle of poverty and vice.[1]

TOURING THE SLUMS

Roaming bad places in search of strong emotions had certainly been an activity long practiced by social elites. But it was not until the nineteenth century that it was codified in the form of a narrative and diffused as a model. This phenomenon, like many others, was born in England when Pierce Egan, a fashionable journalist who specialized in London's sporting life, published *Life in London* (1821), an amiable and lively account of the nocturnal peregrinations of two gentlemen—the Londoner Tom and his provincial cousin Jerry Hawthorn—around the lower quarters of the East End.[2] From gin palaces to coffee shops, the two companions encountered poor people, beggars, prostitutes, drunkards, pimps, and children in rags. They took part in masquerades, watched dog and cock fights, and ultimately got mixed up in a brawl where their "natural superiority" easily gave them the upper hand (Egan was also the author of a famous book on boxing).[3] This rather realistic tale precisely described both places and people, and it copiously annotated the use of slang. But the underworld, kingdom of vice and drunkenness, was just the backdrop—it was the two young aristocrats, their joys and pleasures, that occupied the foreground.

The tale of Tom and Jerry, illustrated by the Cruikshank brothers, enjoyed immense success. It was rapidly copied, plagiarized, and adapted for the theater. It inspired many similar tales, including *Doings in London* (1828) by Georges Smeeton and *The Dens of London* (1835) by John Duncombe, both based on the same scenario: the guided visit by gentlemen avid for strong sensations to the sordid entrails of the city.[4] Egan himself made sequels: *Real Life in London*, and then in 1828, *The Finish to the Adventures of Tom and Jerry*. Thereafter the vogue for "fashionable slumming" developed rather quickly. Charles Dickens, who had made *Life in London* his bedside reading,[5] recounted in 1851 his nighttime jaunts with his friend, Inspector Field, in the London dives and workhouses. In the 1860s, Donald Shaw remembers that

one of the most popular pastimes ... was going the rounds of the dens of infamy in the East End and the rookeries that then abutted the Gray's Inn Road. [. . .] To escape with one's life or one's shirt was as much as the most sanguine could expect. These dens of infamy were beyond the power of description—sing-song caves and dancing-booths, wine bars and opium dens where all day and all night Chinamen might be seen in every degree of insensibility from the noxious fumes.[6]

Shaw did not disdain losing himself (while in the company of Lord Hasting) in the hovels, soup kitchens, and *penny gaffs* of notorious quarters.

Thus it was London, that other capital of the nineteenth century, where the French sought a model for touring the underworld. Every renowned voyager tried to follow in the footsteps of Pierce Egan or Charles Dickens. The historian and critic Hippolyte Taine visited Manchester in the 1860s and was led by two detectives through the city's "bad quarters." From ten o'clock to midnight he visited shacks, brothels, and thieves' dens, which made a very strong impression: "that of a nightmare or a novel by Edgar Poe."[7] In his apocryphal memoirs, the Paris police superintendent M. Claude took a guided tour of Whitechapel and of Newgate Prison, the "opaque and mysterious world" of London crime.[8] In 1884, the chronicler Albert Wolff, from the newspaper *Le Figaro*, accompanied by a London detective, visited the shady bars to see the beggars of Whitechapel and the thieves of Spitalfields.[9] After the death of Victor Hugo, a similar tour around London was conducted by a Scotland Yard inspector for Léon Daudet, Charles Floquet, and Edouard Locroy.[10]

Then the vogue shifted to Paris, where tourism of the bas-fonds had not been completely unknown. The best-selling *Mystères de Paris* had given many a taste for the spectacle of debasement, and after the Second Empire (1852) toffs hastened to the notorious cabaret Lapin Blanc. In fact, wasn't the protagonist Rodolphe a Grand Duke, and Salvator (his alter ego from Alexandre Dumas's *Paris Mohicans*) a sort of marquis? "Almost every day," the writer and critic Charles Nisard remembered, "elegant personages arrived in carriages to breathe the emanations of Chourineur, Rodolphe, Fleur-de-Marie, of the Borgnesse, and the Schoolmaster (all of them Mystères de Paris charachters.). The old man from Bordeaux served as their Cicero, and eager tourists, holding copies of *Mystères de Paris* in their hands like a guidebook to the Versailles museum, returned from their pilgrimage quite enchanted."[11] The old "Bordelais" in question was Maurras, the proprietor of the Lapin Blanc, who did not hesitate to embellish the dramatic scene. He decorated the walls of the establishment with a portrait of author Eugène Sue and drawings illustrating the major scenes in *Mystères de Paris*, and it was rumored that he sometimes hired harlots and thugs as extras! Ultimately the cabaret became more a museum than a den of vice.[12]

But it was not until after the repercussions of Haussmann's massive urban renewal projects that the phenomenon became widespread and collective and guided tours really developed. There was a close relationship to the city's urban transformations: it seemed as if the goal of this new tourism was precisely to record the death of the old Paris and to observe the few quartiers or sordid alleys that had escaped the demolition shovels. Therefore, it was in close symbiosis with books such as *Paris disparu, Paris qui s'efface* (Disappearing), or *Paris ignoré* (Forgotten) that the first itineraries of the underworld appeared. This was notably the case with Louis Barron's *Paris étrange*, published in 1883, in which the author, persuaded by a former police agent, decided to write a guide to "the dark city that has been hidden in the somber folds of the brilliant and luxurious Paris, city of villains, beggars, and vagabonds."[13]

A dozen years later, in the mid-1890s, the formula became institutionalized and found its appellation as the "Grand Dukes' Tour," combining two phenomena. The first was the actual request, in the era of the Franco-Russian alliance, from a few grand Russian figures to visit, duly accompanied, the capital's places of ill repute. For Léon-Paul Fargue, the practice was inaugurated by some unknown "Highness" in the entourage of Tsar Alexandre III.[14] For André de Fouquières, it was invented for the Grand Duke Alexis, the tsar's younger brother, a Francophile *bon vivant*.[15] For others, such as Jean Lorrain, it was in fact Paris police chiefs Gustave Macé and, especially, Marie-François Goron who had the "ingenious idea of offering the Grand-Dukes a descent into the Parisian inferno,"[16] and this version was confirmed by Police Superintendent Morain in his memoirs published in English in 1929.[17] Moreover, Paris did not have a monopoly on the expression. In November 1871, the same Grand Duke Alexis, whom his brother had appointed ambassador to the United States to put an end to his morganatic liaison with Alexandra Zhukovskaya, disembarked in New York and asked to visit the infamous Five Points. His slumming party stopped at the music hall located in Baxter Street, which from then on became the "Grand Duke's Opera House."[18] The place remained famous under this name, which was used by Horatio Alger in 1904 in his novel *Julius the Street Boy*.

The other immediate source was the manifest taste for *encanaillement* (debasement) that affected the avant-gardes of the day. Although this was nothing new, it affected every author who wrote about the *canaille* (rogues, rascals) and became one of the salient traits of literary snobbery by the end of the century.[19] You could give yourself a roasting at Aristide Bruant's, or mingle with pimps and prostitutes, or attend in costume the *gouape* (mobster) ball in the rue Charras, or eat at the Bagne tavern where the waiters wore convict uniforms.[20]

Beginning at the end of the 1890s, the tour fed an impressive print output, which included picturesque texts describing the "very bizarre nocturnal excursion through the capital's underworld to the land of vice and poverty" offered by Paul de Chamberet in 1897,[21] but also guidebooks and almanacs such as *Paris intime et mystérieux*, which also rented out personal guides at the the Cicero guide office at 17 rue Laférière.[22] The theme of the encounter between high society and the underworld, a traditional plot of popular fiction, now gained autonomy as in the cycle *La tournée des grands-ducs*. For example, in *Mœurs parisiennes* by Dubut de Laforest, we follow a troupe of club gentlemen and pleasure seekers who roam Paris under the guidance of Harry Smith, director of the *Agence des étrangers*, "a service of guides and interpreters charged with piloting the curious through dives, poorhouses, and dens of crime."[23]

Above all, the motif prospered in avant-garde literature. In *Les Amants*, Maurice Donnay introduced young Claudine, who wanted to go to "places where one finds killers."[24] In *Les déracinés* in 1897, Maurice Barrès made Racadot and Mouchefrin the guides who facilitated excursions by the beautiful Astiné Aravian into the Paris underworld, "a taste that she shared with all the grand-dukes and the Prince of Wales." They take her into infamous Maubert cabarets and end up killing her in the middle of the night on the banks of the Seine.[25] But the champion of the tour was indisputably Jean Lorrain, a professional voyeur and aesthete of the "poisoned city." Beginning on January 14, 1899, in *Le Journal*, he recounted a Grand Dukes' Tour by Mademoiselle Odette Valéry, a star at the Folies-Bergères.[26] Two years later, he turned the tour into the main plot of his novel *La maison Philibert*, in which a band of apaches (ruffians) led by Môme l'Affreux become escorts who tout young girls to "avidly curious society people."[27] In June 1905, a Kodak in hand, Lorrain devoted another long photographic essay—to my knowledge the only one—to the subject, which was published in Pierre Lafitte's encyclopedic magazine *Je Sais Tout*.[28]

The nascent cinema followed close behind literature. In 1909, Léonce Perret shot *La Tournée des grands-ducs*, in which he showed two couples from good society who, after a restaurant meal, decide to visit a dive. There they meet an apache and a whore (played by a major star of the Polaire *café-concert*) who perform a very suggestive "apache dance" in front of them. But the unexpected arrival of a rival triggers a fight, causing the hasty departure of the respectable foursome. Shortly thereafter, Bernard Natan shot a pornographic version, also titled *La Tournée des grands-ducs*. The scenario was similar, but reduced this time to a trio (the reveler, the apache, and the streetwalker) in clearly more scabrous postures.

The tour did not disappear after World War I—far from it—but it was profoundly changed. It became banal and standardized, codified in the numerous guides that proliferated at the time to explain *Comment visiter les dessous de Paris* (How to visit the underbelly of Paris).[29] Above all, the tour's intention was transformed: it was now less a matter of visiting sordid or dangerous places and more about visiting pleasure sites such as the cabarets of Montmartre and the cafés of Montparnasse. The Grand Dukes' Tour organized by Maryse Choisy and the painter Foujita in the late 1920s was made in a Bugatti race car and consisted of visiting the fashionable brothels.[30] During the same period, according to Francis de Miomandre, the celebrated Maxim's restaurant became one of the favorite stops on the Parisian tour.[31] Most such venues relied on touristic staging for the *nouveaux riches*, for foreigners and provincials visiting the capital. There was no more poetry, complained Joseph Kessel in 1928, just "rigged dives" being exploited for commercial purposes.[32] Elie Richard added that it was now "just for *gobeurs* (suckers) and voyeurs who still believe in the myth of Montmartre."[33] The cinema took note of this decline and these shifts. In *Paris la nuit*, a film written by the Brazilian Vital Ramos and directed by Maurice Keppens in 1924, the tour is of the Montmartre nightspots and is reduced to cabaret shows. The practice was becoming a simple tourist rite, with guided commentary. "Once when a provincial or a foreigner came to the home of a family member living in Paris, he was taken to see Notre-Dame or the Eiffel Tower," wrote André Warnod in 1930, "but today he is led to the negroes of the rue Blomet or to the *apaches* of the rue de Lappe."[34] In 1930, Pierre Colombier filmed *Chiqué*, in which the audience quickly learns that the dens visited are peopled by sham ruffians.[35] The screenwriter Jacques Prévert had worked on a scenario called "Le tour des grands-ducs, ou l'*apache* mondain (The society ruffian)," but in the end it was not filmed.[36]

THE PARIS OF THE GRAND DUKES

To understand what comprised the original tour, we have to go back to the 1900s. "Alongside night-time Paris of the grands boulevards—the joyous and gallant Paris of Maxim's, Fantasio, and the cabarets of the Butte—there is another Paris, a strange Paris, sometimes dangerous, but oh-so interesting, which offers to the observer scenes and tableaux of customs worthy of the *Mysteries of Paris*."[37] This promenade was known to Parisians as the Grand Dukes' Tour. Several circuits coexisted, but they all generally converged on a few high spots, and they all featured obligatory stops. The group should not be too large (ten guests at most, a mixture of men and women) and should be guided by a "tracker" or by a policeman. The competence of this Cicero would determine the venture's success. In *La maison Philibert*, Jean Lorrain features Biscuit, "a peddler who is also a tracker" for ten to fifteen francs per evening. This individual "has piloted a real grand-duke!" and has no equal for leading swanky people to "what is most chic."[38] Henry Danjou's tracker is Maurice Arnaud, he is "the Figaro of Maubert: at once a market porter, a broker, an information man, a confidence man, an amateur clown, and a Cicero for Americans in the Paris underworld."[39]

They started the promenade around midnight, as the theaters were getting out. "Midnight sounded in the belfry of Saint-Merri when we plunged into the network of muddy alleys surrounding the old church. [. . .] At the sound of our feet on the old cobbles, the clients of a horrible bistro looked at us with distrust. A thick voice yelped: 'it's the grands ducs on a stroll.'"[40] Most of the route was within a contained perimeter: "a modern Suburra that began at Place Maubert and ended at the Porte Saint-Martin, encompassing the whole Les Halles quarter."[41] This was the heart of old Paris, which Haussmannization had eviscerated but which still maintained the vestiges of a Gothic city. It was composed of three distinct sectors. The Maubert quartier ("La Maub") was the heart of the route and contained some famous dives such as Le Père Lunette, "the most celebrated stop on the Grand Dukes' tour," explained Jean Lorrain, where "real burglars and the really miserable" gathered,[42] and the Château Rouge, called the Guillotine, rue des Anglais, which attracted the same types. But the Maubert quartier was also the place of most ostensible poverty, the "subhuman" neighborhood, wrote Elie Richard.[43] In the streets, on the embankments, under the bridges, one could see a swarm of tramps, beggars, sellers of arlequins (leftovers) and drunken women—in short, "the vermin of nameless shelters and hidden alleyways."[44] There were even amphitheaters for clandestine anatomical dissections.

Quite close but on the other side of the Seine, the Saint-Merri quartier was the second focus point. Most of its street arteries—la rue Brisemiche, la rue de Venise, la rue Pierre-au-lard—were repugnant. This was the "favorite haunt of the lowest of the Parisian criminal classes," wrote Georges Cain in 1912, the lair of the lowest forms of prostitution.[45] "Dangerous vagabonds and scoundrels out of the correctional system strode along the cobblestones in quest of evil deeds to perform, of lingering passers-by to attack."[46] Les Halles, on the other side of the boulevard Sebastopol, closed the central triangle. Like the Maub, this quartier contained notorious establishments (Chez Fradin, the Grappe d'Or, the Caveau, the Ange Gabriel) and a population of easily observable *misérables*: beggars on the rue Pierre Lescot and unfortunates sleeping on the street in rue Montorgueil and rue Baltard. "The ragged poor, the exhausted old women, the homeless who wandered shivering or dozing for a few hours seated near a lodge [. . .] dragged themselves around, a lamentable human debris at the hour of the soup kitchens."[47]

Most of the route lay within this narrow central perimeter where the vestiges of pre-Haussmann Paris were concentrated, along narrow and sinuous alleys that had escaped the massive renovation. Other places on the periphery could be included in the tour for those who wished for more shivers. These might be more dangerous establishments that were frequented by bad types, such as the Bal d'Austerlitz or the Polonceau where brawls still took place, and Mother Cassefléche's cabaret in Saint-Denis. Then there were the sinister and dangerous neighborhoods: the outskirts of the Combat metro, with its debased prostitution (on the rue Monjeol); the areas of Javel and Grenelle, the perimeters of ancient fortifications, especially to the south, toward Gentilly, the Kremlin-Bicêtre, Malakoff; and still more the embankments of the Seine between Auteuil and Billancourt, the *Point du Jour*.

Whatever the chosen circuit, any tour that wanted to offer "sensational spectacles"[48] had to combine visits to three different types of places. First you had to see a *garni* (furnished room) or a night shelter, full of the truly poor. There lay the residents of the underworld, the ragged wrecks of the great city in mean hovels where people slept *à la corde*, meaning where "they laid their heads along a rope stretched the length of each room."[49] Three such establishments were particularly famous: the Auberge Fradin at 35 rue Saint-Denis "is the *pièce de résistance* of the tour, the great sensational stop for all miseries, the supreme refuge for all kinds of degradation, the terminus of all kinds of suffering," wrote Jean Lorrain.[50] For four *sous*, you got a bowl and bit of ground. The Grappe d'Or, rue Courtalon, was its direct rival: there, you had to drink in order so sleep, periodically ordering "Aramon wine, high in alcohol, which warmed the stomach but deadened the head and softened the legs. As soon as you had imbibed, you had to lie down."[51] The refreshment gave you the right to sleep on a bench or the hard ground—the descriptions are apocalyptic. Listen to Henry Danjou:

> In a sort of crypt, sheltered from ship's cradles, and heavy pillars, 250 miserable people were sleeping, collapsed onto heavy tables. [. . .] Hunkered alongside a stove, others were lying on wine barrels; still others had collapsed against the wall. There were people lying in the wine cellar, on the steps, on the beaten ground. They had fallen there like cadavers. Almost naked torsos emerged from ragged pantaloons. Sturdy fellows lay next to rickety spines. A frightful odor emerged from the pile of bodies.[52]

The last establishment was of another kind, the night shelter called Maison Livois, the first one to open (in June 1879) at 59 rue de Tocqueville in the seventeenth *arrondissement*, which all visitors describe with admiration. Queen Nathalie of Serbia, who visited it in May 1908 in the company of her lady of honor and the Marquis de Saint-Lieux, was so charmed by the cleanliness of the place that she left a gift of two hundred francs.[53]

The spectacle of poverty was necessarily associated with a shiver of danger. So, the second stop on the tour had to include (if only furtively) a site considered to be unsafe. The simplest option was to enter one of the dissolute *bals-musette* (dance halls) frequented by pimps and whores, choosing "in the Gobelins, the Bal d'Alcazar, one of the most dangerous places in Paris,"[54] or else the Bal des Gravilliers, in the street of the same name, "almost exclusively frequented by outlaws and low-rent pimps."[55] Other places invited shudders: the *Point du Jour* in Billancourt, where women's corpses were often discovered, or certain corners of the suburbs such as the terrible Route de la Révolte in Clichy, "one of the worst places in the suburbs," an assortment of wastelands, cul-de-sacs, and miry alleys, bordered by rough-and-tumble barracks such as the Cité du Soleil and the Cité Foucault.[56]

Finally, the tour would end in a festive place, which ideally should also be a place of ill repute. Therefore, most of these excursions ended in Les Halles, which offered the advantage of staying open all night. You sat down to cheese or onion soup either at the Ange Gabriel, where you encountered prowlers, burglars, and whores (this was where the *Casque d'or* affair—the Homeric fight between two pimps for the love of a prostitute—took place in 1902), or at the Caveau, rue des Innocents, frequented by "tattered wastrels of all kinds and people who had singular trades,"[57] or else the less infamous *Chien qui fume*, at the *Grand Comptoir* or in the Baratte restaurant. Overall the excursion would take about six hours.[58]

FROM CANTON TO LIMEHOUSE

"Each city has its underworld, its secret places, its places of intrigue and vice, and its culprits," the British journalist Stanley Scott wrote in 1925.[59] And so each city also had its Grand Dukes' Tour. In 1905, the reporter for the Havas agency, Georges de la Salle, who at the time was covering the Russo-Japanese War, undertook his in Manchuria. The dramatist Eugène Brieux did his Grand Dukes' Tour in Canton: "They had me make the traditional tour of gambling houses and dives."[60] In Berlin, Joseph Kessel felt nauseous just at the idea of "making the customary Tour that every foreigner could have if he appointed an obsequious guide."[61] Nevertheless, it was thanks to two local truands, Albert and Dick, that Kessel discovered the Berlin *Unterwelt.* In 1929, Louis Bertrand remembered the "bomb," "the imbecilic and traditional tourist Tour" that he had of Algiers in the company of a few other "new arrivals" (including two future ministers) under the leadership of a "vague ruffian who answered to the name of Lagoun, a gibbous and deformed imp" who took them around the vicinity of the prefecture, then to the Kasbah.[62] Two years later, a true Grand Dukes' Tour was guided by a policeman named Slimane around the Kasbah of Algiers. This was where Gaby met Pépé le Moko, an encounter that would lead to his death.[63]

In New York, the Five Points district had long attracted visitors ranging from Tocqueville to Davy Crockett and Abraham Lincoln. In 1842, Charles Dickens was escorted by two police officers and described the slum with repulsion in his *American Notes*.[64] From the middle of the century, specific books appeared to assist in discovery of these impoverished neighborhoods. A reader of Pierce Egan, whom we met as an explorer of London, the American George Foster (reporter at the *Aurora* and then the *New York Tribune*) was the first to publish one; his *New York by Gas-Light* (1850) claimed to be a comprehensive guide to the hidden realties of the city by "lifting the veil."[65] The reader was invited to follow him in the "festivities of prostitution, the orgies of pauperism, the dens of robbery and murder, the scenes of drunkenness and bestial debauchery." No tableau was missing: the third-rate brothels, gambling dens, shady clubs, *cafés-concerts* and music halls, Five Points at midnight, the theaters, "*artistes'* exhibitions in which naked women appeared in living tableaux." In its wake, Foster published other guidebooks on harems (1855) and seraglios (1857). In 1867, the novelist Horatio Alger published *Ragged Dick, or Street Life in New York with the Bootblacks*, a series in which a street urchin begins his rise through the city's social strata. In the 1890s, veritable "slumming parties" became fashionable in society circles.[67] The jaunt was comparable to the one around Paris. One left around 9 PM from Bleecker Street station in the company of a policeman or one of the many private detectives who could be hired to show you "the darkest parts of the city at midnight." The itinerary, explained the naturalist and explorer Ernest Ingersol (who performed such a nocturnal journey in lower Manhattan at the beginning of the 1890s),[68] took in the most sordid tenements of Five Points such as Mulberry Bend, the dives and brothels of the Bowery, with stops at certain well-known places including the Harry Hill music hall, the Grand Duke's Opera House (of course), and the bars and opium dens of Chinatown, nicknamed "joints," the most famous of which were located between Pearl and Dover streets near the Brooklyn Bridge.

In London, where our history began, nobody seemed to tire of visiting the underworld. In 1888, the crimes of Jack the Ripper even boosted its popularity. One took the omnibus to Whitechapel to do the "Ripper Tour": "Each night a swarm of young men who had never been to the East End in their lives descends on houses where the murders were committed. They chat with frightened women and go to visit the overcrowded night shelters."[69] Bus tours were organized to Whitechapel and Shoreditch, and their itineraries were described in the Baedeker guidebooks.[70] Were Londoners going too far? Was a guilty feeling at work in a bourgeoisie sickened by its own voyeurism? In the following decade, many observers diagnosed a death of fashionable slumming. "Is slumming played out?" asked James Adderley in 1893.[71] He thought that the scope of the actual social crisis, the fear aroused by the rediscovery of poverty in Charles Booth's investigation, and the pricks to the Victorian conscience that resulted, had all tarnished these practices. The vogue had passed:

> The fashionable slumming of eight years ago is given up as a wholesale practice. The languid ladies have disappeared who would be driven down Commercial Road to the Docks and back, 'just to see what it was like' and then at her evening reception would say: 'Ah, Mr.___ you don't know where I have been today. I have seen a stevedore!'"

In fact, Sir Edward Bradford, who led the Metropolitan Police from 1890 to 1903, decided the police should no longer collaborate in this kind of visit:

> "Furthermore, I have done away with the practice of letting the police serve as guides to slumming parties. I found when I took hold here, that the police were practically keeping certain places open in order to have something ready and handy to show to strangers."[72]

In fact, tourism of the underworld had merely taken other paths and was assuming partly imperial colors. Around Limehouse beginning in the 1860s the presence of numerous migrants from the Empire, principally Indians and Malaysians, showed a shifting underworld phenomenon. Despite the very low number of authentic Chinese who lived there (slightly more than 700 in 1921) and the narrowness of the site (only two streets), people started to speak of "Chinatown;" George Sim utilized the expression in *Li Ting of London* (1905).[73] The area's reputation was obviously linked to opium, and it truly began to grow after the widely publicized visit by the Prince of Wales to an opium den in New Court in 1860.[74] The drug was in fashion and aroused curiosity among aristocrats. "The soft light of shaded lamps hanging from the ceiling disclose a spacious hall. The feet sink in the rich, heavy carpet as the visitor passes on to the next floor, where there is an excellent restaurant with weird Chinese decorations and a menu that offers a variety of seductive Chinese dishes. Its patrons sometime include Society women seeking a new sensation," noted the *South London Advertiser* on December 28, 1910, and the newspapers published many accounts of jaunts to Limehouse, mostly centering on opium, its pleasures and its dangers.[75] In *East London* (1901), Walter Besant evoked opium dens as pleasant places: opium is an ambivalent product, either a poetic artifact or an instrument of the devil.[76] There, too, in the gloom of opium smoke, was where Oscar Wilde's Dorian Grey tried to find oblivion. In January 1890, the *East London Observer* noted the death of Mr. Johnston, called Ah Sing, a Chinaman of Limehouse who had married an Englishwoman and directed Johnston's, a famous den that Dickens had used as a model for *The Mystery of Edwin Drood*. Readers of this obituary discovered that many upper-class Londoners had frequented his establishment.

Beginning in the 1900s, however, both the literature and representations were clearly more hostile, in a context marked by the Boxer Rebellion and the "Yellow Peril". There was mention of Chinese proneness to cruelty, of secret societies, clandestine workers, and the cynical figure of Jack Chinaman, who seduced and drugged naïve young Englishwomen. Opium dens were represented as sordid and diabolical places, Chinatown as a mysterious and dangerous land where women (especially) risked being lost. The opium den, a place of debauchery, was asserted to be the absolute antithesis of home, the sacred symbol of British respectability.[77] In this racist and Sinophobe context, in 1913 Sax Rohmer created the figure of the demonic Doctor Fu-Manchu. *Limehouse Nights*, published by Thomas Burke in 1916, insisted instead on the fantastic aspect of the area, its mysterious and poetic character, and the love that sometimes occurred between Chinamen and Englishwomen. But terrible crime stories were being reported by the press. On November 28, 1918, Billie Carleton, a young and popular actress, was found dead in her suite at the Savoy Hotel. It was learned that she was a drug addict and her dealers got their supplies in Chinatown. In 1926 came the death of Freda Kempton, a dancer who had frequented Brilliant Chang's establishment. Also noted was the rarity of Chinese women in these places, giving rise to fantasies about the sexual exploitation of white women supposedly taking place in Limehouse. "Young White Women Hypnotized by Yellow Men" was the headline in *The Evening News* in October 1920.[78] The sexual cruelty of Chinese opium addicts became a recurrent motif: "I have read that the Chinese tie their women to a post and beat them with a leather strap. I would die for a man who would beat me like that. The English are so ridiculously suave with women," declared a heroine in *Dope*, a 1913 novel by Sax Rohmer.[79]

Was this the reason tourists became ever-more numerous in Limehouse? Thomas Burke's *Nights in Town* (1915) can be considered a veritable guide to slumming in Chinatown: "If you are tired of the West End and life in general, you must go East, young man, Go East! [...] Hatred, filth, love, brawls, and death—all these fundamental things are present here, unvarnished."[80] By 1913, one could buy tickets for "Limey-Housey-Causey-Way" at Ludgate Circus, and during the summer season Cook's agency offered tours of Chinatown every Tuesday, Thursday, and Saturday afternoons.[81] In 1928, the same agency organized circuits in Pullman cars of the whole East End: "Whitechapel—the Ghetto—the People Palace, Limehouse and Chinatown, Dockland, the Rotherhithe Tunnel, London Bridge and the Old Borough of Southwark." In Chinatown, travelers generally had the right to witness a few arranged scenes, especially a gang fight between Chinese bandits dressed in traditional costumes and armed with fearsome knives.[82] But fashionable slumming in Limehouse had declined by the 1930s, when a portion of the Limehouse shacks were destroyed and when other underworlds, especially the ones exported by Hollywood, had come to occupy cinema screens.

THE SPECTACLE OF DEGRADATION

"All of us have a more or less an uncontrollable taste for the horrible, the abnormal, and the monstrous," wrote Émile Gautier in his prison treatise published in 1888.[83] That idea was by no means new. The French elites of the Restoration and of the July Monarchy had rushed to Bicêtre to witness the convicts being put in irons and shipped off in chain gangs, and Parisians particularly appreciated visiting the morgue; the English had long flocked to witness the hanging of criminals, celebrated ones or not.[84] But the Grand Dukes' Tour, especially in its original Paris version, offered a few remarkable cultural and social singularities.

The tour had begun by reinventing a city that was partly real and partly fantasy. This was evident in Paris where, as we have seen, it gave rise to a sort of hollow city, an inverted city that tried to expose the spaces forgotten by Haussmann's urban renewal or to invent others, mounds that testified to a disappeared Paris. But the same was true for New York and for London, where this form of tourism paradoxically turned a few sordid and miserable sites into national patrimony. Every city required its underside—its social, moral, aesthetic, or urban opposite—which ironically was necessary to provide the city above with its sparkle and luster. In Paris, the tour, as an ordered itinerary of the worst of the lower depths, was the exact antithesis of the boulevard, so it was not by chance that it emerged precisely at the moment of triumph for Haussmann's renovated city. The new Paris needed a dark face, and so the remaining alleys or buildings that could represent the vanished city were overexploited. Or else a dark side was simply invented.

Moreover, history was happening in real time, and the most popular establishments disappeared at the very moment a tour to them was organized: Père Lunette was gone by 1896 and Château Rouge in 1898. In fact, the Grand Dukes' Tour was always perceived in a nostalgic way. "The Grand Dukes' Tour is dead," wrote Georges Caïn in *Le Figaro* on October 8, 1911. This nostalgia not only related to urban criteria but also to its narrative. A story such as that of the tour had more than anecdotal scope; it arose from regret for the past, for a world that was finished, only a few vague images of it could be resuscitated. "One kind of Paris dies along with the Grand Dukes' Tour," noted Elie Richard.[85] This characteristic became strongly accentuated after World War I. Like Montmartre, like the fortifications and little bistros tucked into the barriers, the tour became one of the constituents of the Belle Époque imaginary. "It was the age of the flashy foreigners living in Paris for gambling, prostitution and other kinds of transgressions, of princes in exile, and other improbable kings," Joseph Casanova wrote in 1920. The boulevard assumed the aspect of the Suburra (ancient Rome's red-light district), and French fantasy enjoyed its low-life wallow."[86] Joseph Kessel's retrospective was explicit, making the tour one of the outstanding motifs of Paris circa 1900: "It was the era of the 'Grand Dukes' Tour,' of floozies and courtesans. . . . The era of the first automobiles. And also the era of the first fascination with boxing."[87] The time frames that resulted were complex: simultaneously observing poverty and vice in the contemporary moment yet inscribing them in a past that was over, or at least dying. This produces a derealizing effect that dissociates the tableau from its whole social dimension and projects it backward onto the horizon of spectacle.

The very strong codification of the tour accentuates this aspect. As we have seen, the circuit was limited in both its geography and its themes. But, from the beginning, it was accused of subtly theatrical effects, of offering rigged scenes and arranged encounters. The very presence of the policeman or copper, succeeded by that of "trackers" or tour guides, guaranteed both the existence and safety of the spectacle. The Père Lunette was "a *bouge au chiqué* (simulated dive), as they say in Paris. Here there is nothing to fear,"[88], remembered a guide in 1904. This was not novel either. The Lapin Blanc had been somewhat refitted after Maurras's era, and many writers were already complaining in the 1880s about the "pseudo-Middle Ages cabarets whose customers were actually daubers and reporters."[89] In Dubut de Laforest's novel, the tour has an impresario, the business agent Harry Smith, who prepared the attractions: "Tonight I must make them witness (after some excursions) a rowdy police raid on a den."[90] Such jaunts gradually assumed a more commercial nature, favoring establishments that could offer dramatically staged scenes. "At the right moments, they knew when to shout, to draw a knife from the pocket, and to calm down when offered a big bowl of *vin brûlé*. The lovely ladies fainted into the arms of the guides or went into raptures with little bird cries."[91] According to Harry Greenwall, the Paris correspondent of the *Daily Express* during the Great War, the guides offering to lead tourists into apache bars or nightclubs had become so numerous (and most of them so dishonest) that they were one of the plagues of Paris.[92] In any case, they signaled the now fully standardized dimension of this form of tourism. The perils of the tour—being robbed, fleeced, or kidnapped, even murdered—were now no more than pretexts for ideological or crudely moralizing novels.[93] "It smelled of theatrics. The [real] *apaches* were elsewhere."[94] Moreover, establishments were being created all over the place to exploit this stratagem. Between the wars a false dive of this type existed in Algiers that was called (naturally) *Les Bas-Fonds*. "This is the abusive name given to an old barn camouflaged as a café where they dislodged the rats in order to poison the people," explained Lucienne Favre.

> The ostentatious taste of the *Chat Noir*, the Bruant, and of parts of Montmartre devoted to foreign customers, all endure in a somewhat anachronistic manner. [. . .] On the walls slathered with whitewash, the chops of Mistinguett, the face of Damia [the "realistic" singer whose songs were of hooligans and prostitutes], and the mask of Charlie [Chaplin] face each other. Fragments of a skeleton arranged in a panoply and desiccated manly attributes conserved in soup tureens are the principal attractions of these places.[95]

Some gradually isolated motifs came to symbolize this Parisian underworld. This was the case with the "apache dance," a particularly brutal waltz or java, combined with slaps and punches that were supposed to simulate the relationship between pimp and prostitute. Its spectacular dimension made it a strong cinematographic trope from the beginning. It was the key scene in Yves Mirande's scenario for *La tournée des grand-ducs* (1910). Then Feuillade made it into a much-anthologized scene in the first episode of the *Vampires* serial in 1915. The apache dance gradually shifted into a music hall number meant to characterize the Paris of pleasure and of crime, and the American cinema became particularly fond of it. Chaplin used it in a memorable scene in *City Lights* in 1931. Lewis Seiler pushed it to an extreme in *Charlie Chan in Paris* (1935): the dancer is killed at the end of the number. Other films, such as William Clemens's *Sweater Girl* (1942) and William Castle's *Crime Doctor's Gamble* (1947), made it the symbol of the agitated life in Paris, which in turn was parodied in Carlo Bragaglia's *Toto le Moko* (1949). In fact, the world of the lower depths was now being exhibited as cabaret scenes. In Paris in the 1950s, "there still existed on the Rue des Anglais a *bal musette* with anachronistic décor of tables and benches screwed into the floor, *apaches* and female gigolos at the bar, costumed attractions, and 'tough java' dances for the last of the night-owl Romantics."[96]

But even this ersatz version did not prevent the tour from arousing a whole palette of strong sensations and passions that would evolve over time. Foppish Tom and Jerry's underworld in the 1820s had been dominated by gin and vice, but it was also a world full of jovial figures, a carnivalesque universe where the poorest took good-natured part in a general pantomime. Logic says to Tom, "I am quite satisfied in my mind that it is the lower order of society who really enjoy themselves. They eat with a good appetite. [...] They drink with a zest [...] and among all the scenes that we have witnessed together where the lower orders have been taking their pleasure, I confess they have appeared all happiness. I am sorry I cannot say as much for the higher ranks of society."[97] The atmosphere was comparable in Smeeton's *Doings in London*, which described a joyous free-for-all among various kinds of marginals who gave no thought to tomorrow and became inebriated with good humor. "Black-legs, Gamblers, Dandies, Fortune-hunters, fraudulent Bankrupts, Lawyers, Pigeons, Greeks, Quacks, Chimney-sweeps, Pimps, Bawds, Prostitutes, Bullies and Panders, Clergymen, Soldiers, Sailors, Thieves, Sprigs of Nobility, [and] upstart Gentry"[98] arranged the chaos of their joy and insouciance together. But the tone changed in the second half of the nineteenth century when more repulsive realities were being depicted. Again, we have to distinguish the spectacle of crime from that of degradation, which the French expression *les bas-fonds* strongly connotes. Visiting infamous neighborhoods and encountering sinister glances from pimps and fallen girls delivered a "delicious shiver" to those who were bored with ordinary pleasures. "One entered the Assassins [club] with a delicious contraction of one's innards," remembers Elie Richard.[99] The troubling but spicy sensation of this promiscuity, like that of a kinky relationship, was both existential and aesthetic and had linked the poets' world to that of the bandits since the times of François Villon (the truand poet of the Middle Ages). But now the forbidden, the exotic, the erotic, the desire for shadows and transgression, was topped off with the anxiety provoked by a menacing glance or a fierce gesture. That savoring of the picturesque belonged to a well-known register and was augmented by the pleasure of being able to boast (after the fact) about the aureole of some evil perilously confronted. As a gentleman told a lady: "This dance-hall is a very dangerous place, exclusively frequented by hookers and procurers. Do you know that, mademoiselle?"—"Perfectly. In fact, that special audience is what attracts us here."[100]

But the spectacle of extreme poverty after descending into the abyss was quite different. There, whether exotic or spicy, the spectacle became "nauseating and sinister,"[101] a plunge into the unnamable and abject. Seeing vague forms lying on benches or on the ground, piles of human flesh and rags accompanied by snoring and groaning, wheezing and screaming, drove the desire for social voyeurism to its limits. In flophouse rooms or night shelters, the senses were subjected to another kind of ordeal, which was almost unbearable. Seeing how low degradation could go was one thing, but hearing and, especially, smelling it was quite another. The Grappe d'Or "smelled of wine, muck, and moldy clothing." The dirt and the residues of vomit and excrement became unbearable. "An odor of wild animals, horribly acrid, gripped us by the throat so that it was difficult to stay more than a few minutes," noted Paul de Chamberet. "We could hold on no longer, we were suffocating, we needed to breathe," added Jean Lorrain. "Air, some air!" Even the philanthropic alibi is swallowed up in this type of encounter. Rare were the visitors who, like Charlie Chaplin, managed to perceive the "beauty in the slums [. . .] despite the dirt and sordidness. There are people reacting toward another there—there is LIFE, and that's the whole thing."[102]

The Tour gradually deserted these sordid places where one met "the face without make-up, the soul without pantomime, belonging to the atrocious extras of the lower depths."[103] Instead it stuck to a few pleasure establishments that were increasingly normalized as the sources of the new meaning of the term. Although the expression had grown roots—and made fortunes—it was at the cost of a radical inversion of meaning. Even in modern times, doing the Grand Dukes' Tour means undertaking a nighttime razzle with friends to chic restaurants, select bars, or trendy nightclubs. And the expression is all the more commonly employed because the eponymous and successful film by André Pellenc (1953)—with the comic actor Louis de Funès—is often shown on French TV as if to recall the existence of the tour. Accomplished in barely half a century, this astonishing semantic reversal testifies to both the gradual democratization of leisure and to its takeover by the cultural industries, which try to neutralize those aspects judged to be inconvenient or unproductive while exploiting their references and traditions. Viewing the poor is still possible on an organized trip, such as that depicted by novelist Lydie Salvayre in *Les belles âmes*,[104] but this is no longer possible as part of a respectable *soirée*.

The Grand Dukes' Tour (or its equivalent) does not exhaust the multiple forms of immersion used by the "superior" classes to experience the underworld. Neither the charitable ladies who tried to bring relief to impoverished areas, nor prison visitors, nor the missionaries and Salvation Army folk, nor the Oxford and Cambridge students who at the end of the nineteenth century settled in "social colonies" of London's East End[105] would recognize themselves in this tour. It incarnates only one extreme type of interaction, almost a caricature. That it focused the attention of writers and journalists to an obsessive extent necessarily raises questions. Jean Lorrain explained: "It is a very twentieth century story in the sense that the worst of the criminal underworld is mingled with the most upper crust elements."[106] Lorrain was manifestly speaking as a connoisseur. The fortune of the underworld in the order of representations was born of its confrontation with its perfect antithesis, the universe of high society and the social elites—perhaps because they exist truly only by confronting each other and in an unveiling that can only come from above. This major dialectic is constantly dramatized in literature and the press. A major impetus behind "popular" fiction is to bring high society and the underworld to gaze at each other, and to insist on the secret correspondences that might unite them. Hence the importance these novels grant to "the underworld of the upper crust," which is actually peopled with revelers, seducers, lecherous and perverted aristocrats, with "noble outcasts" and with "pretty horse-breakers" or Skittles. In 1926, the serial writer Marcel Priollet devoted a series of fifteen installments to these *Gueux en habit noir* (Outcasts in tuxedos).[107] But the most transparent example in French is Bruant's novel, *Les bas-fonds de Paris.* One of the main characters epitomizes the synthesis of the two worlds. Comte Roger de Charmeuse, a "satanic incarnation of the most notorious vices,"[108] does not shrink from any disgrace in order to gratify his unwholesome passions. He buries himself in the deepest of Parisian hells, "and we know the law of acceleration of falling bodies!"[109] After having murdered an accomplice near the city wall, he assumes the identity of apache Jules Blanchon and moves in with Nini, whom he makes walk the streets, then puts her in a brothel because she earns more that way. "See the guys from up there who come into our dumps and screw our dames!"[110] Meanwhile, to compensate, the sinister predator of Paris sidewalks, Raquedalle, becomes Oscar de Püllna, the heir of a noble Bohemian family.

7

Poetic Flight

Our final scenario is quite different in nature: roaming the underworld is a poetic endeavor that combines nostalgia, populism, and a certain fascination with transgression—with the certainty (even if implicit or rudimentary) that some form of reality (otherwise inaccessible) lies at the heart of these representations. The streets and wastelands, the rubble and trash piles, the slums and slaughterhouses, the scaffolding and heavy fog that cover communal pits, all bespeak something about life that cannot be found elsewhere. Significations are entangled and do not lead in any specific direction; here the "poetic" dissimulates (behind words, images, or melodies) a refusal of any explanation, any univocal reading. Meaning seems to be exhausted in a sort of flight that is open to any interpretation. We owe to Romanticism, in its most bohemian and darkest version, the first expressions of this desperate underworld, but it became established primarily through the plaintive accents of realistic songs or guitar chords, the dead and cold angles of photography, the tragic and artificial settings of "poetic realism."

BOHEMIA AND THE UNDERWORLD

Relations between bohemia and the bas-fonds were close from the beginning.[1] The two worlds, in their modern form, emerged at the same time amid the dark decade of the 1840s, which was marked by ennui, despair, and dark Romanticism. Of course, "bohemia" had been brooding for a while in the streets of Paris. In 1830, Nodier published his *Histoire du roi de bohème et de ses sept châteaux* (History of the king of bohemia and his seven chateaux), and the following year, in *Notre-Dame de Paris*, Hugo brought together the poet Gringoire and the beautiful gypsy Esmeralda in his romantic version of the Middle Ages. So bohemia and bohemians were already in the air. In 1843, Adolphe Dennery and Eugène Grangé brought to the stage *Les bohémiens de Paris*, and shortly afterward Balzac published *Un prince de la Bohème*. But it was not until Henry Murger's *Scènes de la vie de bohème*— a set of stories and novellas published first as a serial from 1847 to 1849, then as a book, and then adapted for the stage (by the dramatist Théodore Barrière)—that the expression really acquired its full significance.

Additional structural traits also united the two worlds. Both the basfonds and bohemia were uncertain countries, spaces in the social shadows. Yet one immediately recognized their inhabitants: they belonged to the large family of the disinherited. The same urban nomadism united them, the same taste for the margins inhabited them. Neither followed a stable set of rules, and both disdained the norms of social life and rejected the bourgeois life. The existence of these inhabitants was marked by poverty, degradation, social demotion, and a solitary death in the hospital or in the street. Then there was the very term *bohemia* and its metaphoric relation to the world of gypsies and Roma, who were major actors in the imaginary of the underworld. The Romantics expressed their fascination with these haughty tribes, who seemed to incarnate adventure and absolute freedom, amorous passion, and a refusal of constraints. Their rebellious and exotic life came to intensify the figure of the artist.[2]

However, in Paris bohemia played on registers that the lower depths did not: art and literature, creation and provocation—in short, the "artist's life" was an ideal rarely shared with armed robbers, pimps, or their companions. Moreover, the latter were scarcely appreciated by Romantic poets. It was said that Murger had, for a while, hung out with miscreants, but in fact he excluded crooks' and thugs' company from *Scènes de la vie de bohème*. The world he celebrated was that of the margins and poverty, not that of vice and crime. His quest was for the unexpected, the eccentric, the provocative (which animated disdain for the settled life); bohemians also shared an enthusiasm for insurrection and revolution. But bohemian characters sometimes spilled over into the "world of *coquins* (rascals)": beggars and tramps who sold poetry, and artists who committed theft. For example, the poet-murderer Lacenaire was a romantic hero, and the medieval François Villon was celebrated everywhere. Note that these convergences with the bas fonds did not apply to those who were referred to pejoratively as "pretentious bohemians" but remained the privilege of the "muddy bohemia," the one allied with the marginals and those who had slid down in social class, as Karl Marx observed in his view of the *Lumpenproletariat*.

A whole generation of those Alfred Delvau called "divers into the Parisian ocean"[3] roamed at night around the capital's dark retreats. There was Murger, of course, but also the lithographer Traviès, who found inspiration from drinking with ragpickers, as well as the photographer Nadar, the art critic Champfleury, the journalist Vallès, and many other "irregulars"—all associated with the underworld. In the *Nuits d'octobre* (1852), the poet Gérard de Nerval descended into the "inextricable circles of the Parisian hell," describing cabarets such as Paul Niquet's with its clientele of rag-and-bone men, and the quarries of Montmartre that accommodated vagabonds.[4] One figure more than any other incarnated these nocturnal meanders around the unknown city: Privat d'Anglemont was a friend of Murger, of Theodore de Banville, and of Charles Baudelaire, an inveterate night owl, "a vagabond without home or hearth, a bohemian 'without a cross,'" who, according to Delvau, "spends half his life in exploring the underbelly of Paris."[5] These experiences, these "nights spent in roaming the great city in search of the impossible, the strange, the new,"[6] were recounted by Alexandre Privat d'Anglemont (better known as Privat) in three books (*Voyages à travers Paris* in 1846, *Paris anecdote* in 1854, and *Paris inconnu* in 1861) in which he expressed in the purest fashion this strange romantic appropriation of the lower depths.

The city he roamed in the mid-nineteenth century was indeed one of poverty and deprivation. Two spaces that especially caught his attention were "the Latin Quarter" and the twelfth *arrondissement*. Both counted among the most poverty stricken of the capital. The *Écoles* (the area around the street of that name), the Maubert area, the Contrescarpe, the northern slope of Sainte-Geneviève hill, the Salpêtrière hospital—all these places constituted "an immense Court of Miracles."[7] This was "the city of miseries": full of hovels, insalubrious alleys, slums, and shacks. Yet Privat scarcely depicted these places, nor was he interested in the hideous people that others described at length. "There will be no question here of thieves or murderers, or taverns. Everything will take place in the family, within honest and hard-working poverty, never amidst hideous deprivation."[8] What he sought in this *other* Paris were the "originals," the members of this "great family of problematic existences,"[9] those who had no equal at inventing "unknown trades." More than places, it was individuals who fascinated him, a variegated population of working-class Paris, including the fallen and those "bastard children of the place Maubert" whose creativity and initiative seemed infinite. Privat's works featured a veritable encyclopedia of thousands of impoverished trades. In the parade was "the whole vagabond bohemia of strolling musicians, street singers, sword swallowers, people who dance on eggs, tightrope walkers, tooth pullers, and fire-eaters who are sheltered in Paris."[10] The most unimaginable occupations became ordinary: vendors of leftovers, diviners of rebuses, a woman who rents leeches, not to mention breeders of snakes to be sold in the area's restaurants in the place of eels for good fish stew. In places, we may think of Henry Mayhew (Privat was his contemporary) because both compose a "gallery" of the city's fallen ones and both list their unexpected occupations. But unlike the British Mayhew, Privat never turned them into types, and still less into outcasts. He grasped them in a sort of warm embrace that tried to account for the richness of their existence. Emanating from these individuals are touching virtues and picturesque authenticity, and especially a fertile imagination that speaks to poetry. His preference was for the rag-and-bone men, the most appealing of "all the *Lazaroni* in Paris" (thus comparing them to Neapolitan figures): it is wrong to despise their activities because they are profoundly useful, and some of them are actually artists. The "artist-ragman, the bohemian of the genre, the philosopher, the man who was once Somebody, all of whom (sometimes due to misfortune and always because of bad behavior) have tumbled down one chute after another into the lowest depths of society."[11] Privat loved these *chiffonniers*, followed them around and offered blazing representations of their "encampments."

"Quite far down there, at the bottom of an impossible faubourg, farther away than Japan, more unknown than the interior of Africa, in a quartier where nobody has ever gone, there exists something unbelievable, incomparable, curious, frightful, charming, dreadful, admirable."[12] It is the Cité Dorée, one of the "villas" of the *chiffonniers* of Paris, which starts on the boulevard de la Gare, two steps from the Orléans railway. Of course, the place was sordid, the streets were foul and damp, but Privat's benevolent empathy gradually transformed this landscape of misery into a territory of poetry. "It is the country of happiness, dreams, and tolerance that is located by chance at the heart of a despotic empire."[13]

Privat d'Anglemont was not the only one to celebrate this unsettled poetry of the street that was incarnated in the figure of the ragpicker, this inverse of the respectable bourgeois, this living symbol of social marginality. The *chiffonnier* was both a distraction to the *flâneur* and a pleasure for those who loved the picturesque, wrote Edmond Texier in *Paris Gagne-Petit* (1855).[14] Intent on describing *Ce qu'on voit dans les rues de Paris* (What you see in the Paris streets), Victor Fournel also insisted in 1858 on the ambulant world of *chiffonniers*, acrobats, street-sweepers, itinerant musicians, street kids, and all those who did odd (and often bizarre) jobs to get by.[15] Champfleury and Vallès were sensitive, too, to the poetic eccentricity that surged up from this underworld.[16] No doubt the places were dirty and sometimes sordid, but also free from the thieves, prostitutes, and hideous beggars who were whisked away in this kind of writing; they incarnated a sort of social margin that was inventive, virtuous, and picturesque, that laughed at the bourgeoisie and social norms. And this sufficed to give them a poetic force. Are these people more plausible than those depicted by moralists or reformers? That is not their function. The poetic valence that they conferred on the margins had a liberating vocation. By escaping the tyranny of the bourgeois, they symbolically opened the gates to another social world. The popular uprising in the 1871 Commune marked the end of this first bohemia. A good portion of its troops were inhabitants of the "Latin land"—defiant irregulars and other "Mohicans" of Paris—who engaged in the radical events and paid a price for it. This would give strength to the argument that the 1871 Commune was solely an emanation from the lower depths.

LA BUTTE MONTMARTRE

Nevertheless, bohemia did not disappear, and a second generation emerged a few years later, after partial displacement from the Latin Quarter to Montmartre. This time bohemia was linked to the Symbolists (the new pictorial avant-garde) and sometimes also to anarchist circles. The marginals were all the more interested in the Montmartre hill because a common destiny seemed to link penniless artists, the poor, and the disinherited, reinforcing their alliance. The older romantic bohemia had tended to exclude crooks and prostitutes, but here in Montmartre they were fully reintegrated into underworld society. Bad company even seemed to constitute the salt of life in Montmartre, over whom the tutelary figure of François Villon floated. The tragic fate of crooks and streetwalkers seemed to push to the limit, outside any moral path, a refusal of norms and conventions. In the cabarets of the Butte, such as the Zut and the Lapin Agile, "scallywags fraternized with beautiful spirits," Dorgelès remembered.[17] The former "thieves rendezvous" and then a "murderers' rendezvous," the Lapin Agile (or simply à Gill) was for a good twenty years the haunt of artists (such as composers Eric Satie and Francis Carco, and novelists Roland Dorgelès and Pierre Mac Orlan), but it also welcomed certain down-and-out and bad characters. But the latter were only glimpsed as part of an atmosphere that tried to seem heavy with mystery and anguish, though many clients did not share the artists' fascination with *mauvais garçons* (bad guys). The painters and poets of the Bateau-Lavoir were less sensitive, or else they preferred the fictional apaches who peopled the *Fantômas* series. Moreover, things did not always go well. The proprietor of the Lapin Agile, Frédéric Gérard, had no taste for the company of apaches and tried several times to throw them out. One brawl in 1910 ended with the murder of his son, killed behind the counter, which finished off the adventure.[18] But the Lapin, in which Mac Orlan situated the action of *Quai des brumes*, marked a whole generation.

People also prized the vagabond, although this figure was much decried by society at the end of the century as the principal agent of "disorder." But a whole literary tradition continued to consider the vagabond as a sort of solitary hero, a resister who symbolized the refusal of norms and the bourgeois order.[19] Baudelaire, as a solitary, had even celebrated bohemians as "the prophetic tribe with an ardent gaze" and thought they incarnated voyage and mystery and passion. In 1876, the *Chanson des gueux* gave Jean Richepin immediate celebrity—as well as a month in prison for outrage to good manners. For writers such as Vallès, Mirbeau, Bloy, Rictus, and Couté, the vagabond remained a sort of icon, a fragile and sympathetic person who had been buffeted by life, but also a poetic and dissident figure. His wandering was due to his demand for freedom; he was also a poor devil, a victim who was condemned without being heard, who was left to die in silence as in "Le gueux" (The beggar), a story that Maupassant published in *Le Gaulois* in March 1884. The occult organization to which vagabonds supposedly belonged did not necessarily signify deception and duplicity but could connote the solidarity and sentimentality that united people of the underworld. "A sort of fraternity in misfortune, of ignoble tenderness, of defiance of institutions, but with a zest for living," wrote Francis Carco later.[20]

From the Butte Montmartre also emanated a vogue for "gangland songs" that lyricized the pathetic and troubling fates of the crook, the destitute, and the tart. Song had long been the companion of marginals and the disinherited. The ballad "complaints," attested to since the sixteenth century and accompanied by broadsheets and gallows sheets, as well as convict chants, had evolved into the songs of prisons and penitentiaries. Convicts' black hymns, in which the "clinking of chains in cadence served as orchestra," had deeply marked all those who had heard them.[21] But it was only in the second half of the nineteenth century that these songs resounded with the plaints of the underworld, when conveyed by a very active network of dissemination in "small formats." This musical imaginary was borne by two successive generations. The first was linked to the world of cabarets and *cafés-concerts*, which had been on the rise since the Second Empire. In Paris at the end of the century, a veritable industry had developed around them. This was the era of the *chansonniers* (singer-songwriters) and the Chat Noir poets[22] such as Jules Jouy, Mac-Nab, Gabriel Montoya, Vincent Hyspa, Léon Xanrof, and, of course, Aristide Bruant, the uncontested champion of a song style he did much to popularize. At the Chat Noir, then at the Mirliton, Bruant composed hundreds of songs devoted to the pathetic destiny of night wanderers. "Aristide Bruant was the first to express the *pathétique* of the nightime lowlife," explained Anatole France, "he knew how to give his poetry and his personage a sustained character and an original physiognomy; he could compose from scratch the body and soul of the great rabble."[23] With the help of Oscar Méténier, writer and police bureaucrat who served as his adviser on the lower depths, Bruant brought the ballad tradition up to date. Wanting to be the spokesperson of the ragged people, he sang of back alleys and slums and the heavy fate of those permanently menaced by the shadow of prison or penal colony.

Bruant did not get good press, however. Some people saw him only as an exploiter of public misery, concerned only to fill his cabaret every night. And his nationalist and anti-Semitic involvement at the time of the Dreyfus affair obviously did not earn him friends among writers. Yet he knew how to find a form capable of revealing the tenderness that existed deep down in the slums. He knew how to capture something of the tragedy without illusions that fashioned what Johan Rictus called "the popular heart" like nobody else. A great lover and author of songs himself, the writer Mac Orlan professed great admiration for Bruant, whom he saw as "the most moving poet of this mob that reigned in the lower quarters."[24] In any case, he was the first to have nourished in song the imaginary of the underworld and to have diffused it to the mixed audience that frequented his cabaret in the boulevard Rochechouart.[25] Mac Orlan's female *alter ego* was Eugénie Buffet, and she shared his nationalist and populist involvement. The "Sidewalk Serenade" was her greatest success, but it was her appearance as the *"pierreuse,"* the prostitute of the city walls, that really made her famous. In this sense, she announced the second generation, the song "tragedians" who established the "realist" style and carried it to incandescence after World War I. They were all female singers, Fréhel and Damia the most famous ones, but they also included Lys Gauty, Yvonne George, Berthe Sylva, Nitta-jo, Andrée Turcy, Germaine Lix, and the young Edith Piaf, who ensured the transition to the following generation.[26]

Despite nuances (the style was deliberately rough and provocative among the *chansonniers*, but darker and more tragic among the *chanteuses*), all these musical artists contributed forcefully to constructing the poetry of the underworld, whose golden age in Paris was precisely from 1900 to 1930. The same inspiration animated these songs, and they are characterized by common traits. Most of them narrated short biographical destinies. In what Cocteau called "pocket tragedies," they encompassed a whole life's trajectory, or evoked it in shorthand through a crime story or a dramatic episode. Often told in the first person, they aroused emotion and solicited identification. They made each song into an individual drama that verged on the universal. These were the lives of the poor, the destinies of common folk, especially the most marginal among them, the drifting existences of streetwalkers, louts and boozers, "beggars and outcasts." The setting was in keeping: sad and sinister. The street was both refuge and trap, the joyless quartier with its bridges, embankments, and ports from which nobody ever leaves, the twilight blues, the doldrums. The story told was always of failure, lost love, a tragic outcome. The tone was grave and pathetic, and often issuing a *complaint* that was accentuated by the postures and dramatic gestures of the songstresses. The dolorous tale and its strong theatricalizing compounded the tragic sentiment and emotionalism. This imaginary was especially governed by fatalism. It was a world of out-of-luck people, each one dragged down by a fate that cannot be controlled; the criminal and the prostitute were both victims of an existence that led them to the abyss. The last resorts were disillusionment and resignation. The main character, to whom the song had briefly given humanity and soul, takes leave of us in the blackness of failure. And this blackness, this tragic lucidity about hopelessness, gave birth to poetry.

Paris did not have a monopoly of songs about the underworld. In the working-class areas of Lisbon, in the taverns of the Bairo Alto and Alfama, the *fado* (born in the nineteenth century) recounted nothing else.[27] Sad and nostalgic, it spoke of the suffering of sailors, the *saudade* (longing) of prostitutes, and the complex mixture of sensuality and fatalism that characterized the social margins. In Portuguese, the *fadista* (singer of *fado*) was also a term that could refer to either the pimp or the *mauvais garçon* (bad boy). Just as close in Hispanic culture was the *tanguero* imaginary, which flourished in Buenos Aires shortly afterward. Born in the brothels of the Boca, the tango expressed the sordid nature of the Argentine underworld. It was the song of the street, of prostitutes and *porteño* crooks, a long and plaintive song that accompanied the tragic wandering of *atorantes* (ne'er-do-wells).[28] Its tales juxtaposed stories of poverty and crime, blood and sex, and told of the jealousy and the savage hatred that animated the mysterious underworld, the *hampa*. Sensual and erotic tension were prominent, just as much as sadness, nostalgia, and solitude. "I dream / about the past and yearn / for times for which I weep / that never will return," sang Carlos Gardel in *Cuesta abajo* (Downward slope), an immense success in 1934. For just like the *complaints* from Paris's underworld, the tango was a song of loss—loss of love and of youth, loss of a world the very memory of which tended to dissipate over time. What emanated from tango was a populist and pathetic imaginary that celebrated the mystery of the margins, the nostalgic secrets of urban poetry.[29] Despite differences in rhythms and harmonies, there was a strikingly similar inspiration behind tango and the songs from the Butte Montmartre. A traveler named Jules Huret first noticed this when he disembarked in Buenos Aires, the "Paris of Latin America," at the beginning of the twentieth century.[30] Yet when the tango arrived in France shortly afterward, it was perceived as a luxury product, and as such the "new dance" was diffused among the Parisian elites[31] in an astonishing process of inverse cultural transfer.[32]

POETRY, REALISM, AND FANTASY

The interwar period carried this poetic mode to its paroxysm. Pierre Mac Orlan and others even tried to "theorize" it by forging the notion of *le fantastique social*, while its cinema versions gradually gave birth to "poetic realism." But this evolution affected the imaginary itself. With a few exceptions, writers and poets no longer really shared the life of the poor and the bad boys—or they did so merely in a superficial and episodic way. Their interest arose much more from a desire to be allied with *le peuple*, which expressed the contemporary take-off of "populism" more than an actual lifestyle choice on their part. Moreover, the vogue for Montmartre was slowly yielding to Montparnasse, with its "American bars" catering to a cosmopolitan clientele in an upscale atmosphere. In addition, because images tended to prevail over writing, slowly the poetic gaze shifted toward photography and the cinema.

The realist song registered its greatest successes between the wars and spawned new voices and new stars including Berthe Silva, Lys Gauty, and the young Edith Piaf, but the genre seemed to reach its limits and was not being reinvigorated. Conversely, novelists and journalists thought they had found in spectacular reportage a new hybrid form in which story, information, and poetry could be telescoped. After the war, such reporting reached its zenith. No subject was too intimidating. International conferences focused on the underworld explored mysteries ranging from Saturday night *bals-musettes* to the slave market in Ethiopia, and tried to account for all the underworld's enigmas. Moreover, the boundary between a literature given to the tyranny of the "lived experience" and a kind of reporting that thought of itself as a "genre" was blurring, even (as Henri Béraud wrote in 1927) as the "literature of tomorrow."[33] Mac Orlan, Carco, and Blaise Cendrars were also writing reportages, and sometimes little distinguished them from the novelists Kessel, Danjou, Marcel Montarron, or Maryse Choisy. People, places, and dreams crisscrossed each other in these texts, journalistic fictions that were endeavoring to fashion secrets into series. And it was undoubtedly around the theme of the lower depths and the "somber poetry of the zone"[34] that these convergences were best expressed, as were the enigmas emanating from them.

One enigma related to the attention paid to the décor of these locales. The lower-class areas of the city were endowed by these texts with an almost fantastic dimension that was fed by the mystery attached to dark streets, to shady bars, to ports resounding with the calls of sirens, of ships leaving, and of fires in the night. Kessel, who tried to explore the "folds" in the city, evoked "slippery streets that were hard and hostile and insidious, where sordid adolescents lurked."[35] An extreme sensuality emanated from bad places, along with indistinct and always disquieting sounds, and such glimmers as could break through tenacious fog. "Once again the humidity of the underground levels enveloped me. Once again, the pungency of badly aired cellars gripped me by the throat. It was cold, it was sad, it was heavy. A special sonority deformed every sound."[36] The night—"the brown night of *apache* songs"[37]—gave these clandestine landscapes a picturesque atmosphere of empty avenues and stairways, canals, the desolation of joyless streets. "The darkness, the silence, the solitude penetrated the passerby with a poignant melancholy," wrote Doctor Drouin in *Détective* about the rue de Venise, "one of the sewers of Paris where the prostitutes come to end their lamentable existence."[38] Wrote Francis Carco in self-defense: "Is it my fault that, on the first day, I discovered the Paris of the atmosphere of fog and desolation that ought instead to have been communicating so much charm?"[39]

The next enigma in this material and mental setting was the uncertain characters who lived there, who spoke little, but whose existential thickness (necessarily tragic) emerged by imperceptible touches. Sometimes they seemed like phantoms. "I call a phantom those human appearances you encounter in all cities, in all landscapes, which are the veritable literary creations of daily life."[40] Almost all are figures of crime, poverty, and vice, who are regarded with "astonishment mixed with fright and fascination."[41] One has scarcely any illusions about them: most are vile, cowardly, and pitiless beings. They are the "waste of social combustion," and Mac Orlan knows the "moral corruption" that governs their life.[42] But this was precisely why writers lingered over them. On the model of Bruant and the street *chanteuses*, authors lent them a complex sensibility; these bad boys had an edgy but unreflective sensibility. Behind the brutal appearances and situations was hidden an exacerbated sentimentality, which could not be admitted or expressed—only poetry could give an account of these feelings. And it was in this contrast between the intensity of this interior life and the mediocrity of the fates of reprobates, victims, and those vanquished by existence that mystery arose—and often a social fantasy too. "I saw a profound bestiality, a total amorality and, at the same time, a sort of heroism, the mystique of those who live outside the law,"[43] explained Kessel. Similarly, in 1932 Henri Danjou evoked "the hideous elegance" of kids from reformatories; they, too, were enveloped in mystery.[44] Working girls, even more than the thugs, seemed haloed with this awful humanity. They possessed, said Mac Orlan, "the sentimental knowledge of unfortunate beings" that "gives their profession a nobility that is just as moving as the one that was imposed by the sterile fanaticism of a religious order."[45] But there was more: "prostitution is often linked to poetry and to art by mysterious ties." The hovels or sidewalks these women frequented might have had a frightful aspect, but the locales were also touching in their mysterious appearance, in their "violent coloring."[46]

What writers perceived in these women—as in all the denizens of the lower depths, moreover—was the hand of destiny, the presence of a frightful fatality that governed their lives. "A dark force drew them down and kept them there," wrote Francis Carco.[47] The street laid down its laws and oriented people's destinies to the houses of correction, houses of prostitution or imprisonment and forced labor. Any love that was born on the social margins always proved tragic and desperate. *L'homme traqué* (The hunted man) by Carco (1922) presented the cursed love between a prostitute and a criminal with a troubled conscience. "The attraction of unhappiness is one of the strange laws of humanity,"[48] said Mac Orlan, and no doubt this law was most imperious in the universe of the lower depths. Inside these destinies that were doomed to crime or vice lay an existential density, a "secret life" capable of revealing feelings, real situations, and fragments of humanity that were otherwise inaccessible. One had to know how to detect the sentimental purity that was hidden in these miserable lives, in their saddening visions, in their sordid situations—and poetry emerged precisely here. One had to be attentive to words, to their emotional charge, to their power to evoke things not usually perceived, or to the incongruity of their combination. "You have to seek the truth in the dirge-like radiance that escapes from these precise words," wrote Mac Orlan, from words such as *bouge* (a hovel or a dive), prison, *trottoir* (sidewalk), *échafaud* (scaffold), *bagne* (labor colony).

> The word *bouge* is evocative, common, and somewhat fallen out of use. [. . .] One could say that this word no longer means anything specific, no longer corresponds to reality. But these places still exist, if one sticks to the images and disturbing ideas that they evoke. For in these nocturnal houses, rather well hidden so as not to seem aggressive during the day, crimes (or more exactly the origins of crime) are associated with dissolute pleasures.[49]

Although Paris dominated this imaginary, it did not saturate all represented locales. Ports were also special places: they were both the terminus where miserable destinies washed up as well as the ever-illusory promise of departing for another life elsewhere. For example, here is Nantes: "City of winos who shout and roll along the sidewalks. Lecherous old men hunting little girls, [. . .] tarts desperately descending on their prey, passersby in a hurry, imbeciles to be robbed, maladies to transmit (with due authorization), the skeleton key in the pocket. A city of ugliness, of monstrous women who combine the naive tenderness of lovers, the innocent dreams of virgins, and the petty calculations of spinsters on the marriage market."[50] But one could say as much about Le Havre, Bordeaux, or even Marseille, the southern port that allowed you to reach across the shores of the Mediterranean to that other port, Algiers. Here the French Empire opened up, though it was often reduced to Algeria, which came to occupy a growing place in this imaginary: the Algeria of the Casbah and the reserved quartiers, the doldrums, the *Légion étrangère*, and the *Bat' d'Af* (African battalion). In a book she dedicated in 1937 to Francis Carco, Lucienne Favre explored the Casbah, its "mazes of a truly Oriental purity" and the violent and sneaky poetics that emerged from them. Here "rape, homosexuality, and murder appear to be events fatally created by the ambiance, and somehow inevitable."[51] Here the tragedy of destinies seemed naked to the eye, barely complicated by a sense of the picturesque that was born of exoticism and racism. But nostalgia quickly came to an end. *Pépé le Moko*, in the novel by Ashelbé as well as in the film by Duvivier, left the Casbah and the arms of the Moorish Inès for the fatal love for Gaby and the vain hope of getting out of the city.

Pierre Mac Orlan called this imaginary the *"fantastique social."*[52] The down-and-out parts of the world—sinister alleys, brothels, agitated and dangerous wastelands—became the privileged places where poetry arose: "the phantoms that inhabit the shadows of our era," strange races that cannot be imagined, who are encountered only "in places where people have habitually gotten rid of the undesirable elements that might harm their existence,"—in short, the products of the "social *mysterium*."[53] What appeared to the pulp fiction writers or to social observers as "squalid encounters in the most impure neighborhoods"[54] were now invested (and in the same terms) with a secret and positive dimension. The force of this poetic flight was *not* that it offered an alternative vision; evading any moral judgment, it was content to "turn over" the words, to charge them with a sensual and sentimental dimension that humanized the characters. These tragic love stories born at dawn, these destinies broken by poverty or crime, these sinister and pitiable histories that plague all "the refuse of human activity"—they were always degraded pictures, "ruined images"[55] of life and the world, but now a nostalgic tenderness enveloped them. These rotten and spoiled lives were only revealed in snippets, and behind their hazardous encounters and sad passions was hidden a sentimental and poetic morality that obliterated all violence. The experience of the *fantastique social* was born of the aesthetic superimposition of exoticism upon the quotidian, with its silences, aversions, and dreams. Once again, morality was superimposed on crime, and the imaginary was the last resort.

This poetry found its fullest expression less in texts than in images. Often inspired by the German Expressionism that was dominating photographic aesthetics with its chiaroscuro use of light and stark contrasts, the pictures that accompanied most of these reportages wanted to be extensions of that spirit. Mac Orlan was particularly fond of photography and thought it was more suitable than the written text for rendering the *fantastique social*. Cendrars, too, was very impressed by its possibilities of expression and evocation. In fact, many of the images of the underworld published in the daily newspapers or in magazines—*Détective, Police Magazine, Vu, Voilà*, and so forth—were very ordinary portraits, investigative shots, or "chic" shots concocted for the occasion. Most of these standardized stills came from the agencies that proliferated at the time: Meurisse, Rol, Trampus, Keystone, Rapho, Alliance Photographic, and so on. But there were enough of the other kind to breathe a poetic dimension into the genre: for example, the pictures of Germaine Krull, whom Kessel called upon in 1928 for his reportage "Paris la nuit" in *Détective*; the dark and pessimistic photos by Elie Lotar that illustrated the "land of venal love" in the same magazine; and those of Brassaï who four years later did his own "Paris de nuit," full of "secret streets," louche bars and *mauvais garçons*. René Jacques in 1938 illustrated Francis Carco's *Envoûtement de Paris* (Enchantment of Paris) and later shot the insalubrious life of the poor for *La Zone de Clignancourt*.[56] The forceful contrasts and compositions, the white lights projected onto figures and types, contributed to aestheticizing and poeticizing the Paris underworld. Their influence was even stronger when they accompanied reporters' first-person stories, but also when similar images appeared in films. Many documentary films of the era exploited a "populist" vein. Georges Lacombe, whom Pathé-Revue had commissioned for a series on the "Rag-pickers of Paris," gathered his material into a documentary (*La zone 1928*), a simple and cruel silent film that brought him the esteem of the cinema avant-garde. In the same years, *Harmonies de Paris* by Lucie Derain (1928), *Études sur Paris* by André Sauvage (1929), and—the most famous of them all—*Nogent Eldorado du dimanche* by Marcel Carné (1929) empathetically depicted working-class Paris.

The move to the talkies in the 1930 brought cinematographic images and the underworld's imaginary even closer together. The "genre" of what was later called "poetic realism" largely sprang from this populist poetry as it inspired the screenwriters. Francis Carco himself wrote the scenarios for *Paris la nuit* directed by Henri Diamant-Berger (1930), then *Paris-béguin* by Augusto Genina (1931), and Charles Spaak adapted *La bandera* (written by Mac Orlan) and Jacques Prévert scripted *Le Quai des brumes*. At the intersection of naturalism and expressionism, the film directors could reconstruct (usually in the studio to better control the lighting) the same poverty of the working-class quartiers and the urban margins, with their dirty and desolate streets and puddles reflecting the fog. The same pariah figures were battered by fate: crooks, deserters, lost girls, "men from nowhere"—all animated by strong feelings, love or vengeance, but disillusioned and marked by cynicism and disgust, vividly conveyed in the overwrought dialogue. Crime and suicide were rediscovered, the looming fate that would close the atrocious dramas of these little people. The films of Marcel Carné (*Le Quai des brumes* and *Hôtel du Nord*, both in 1938, and *Le jour se lève* the following year) and of Julien Duvivier (*La bandera*, 1935, *Pépé le Moko*, 1937) may best incarnate the era's very rich vein, to which directors Pierre Chenal (*La Rue sans nom*, 1933) and Jean Grémillon (*Gueule d'amour*, 1937) contributed, among others. Between the world wars French cinema offered other representations of the underworld: a vein that was more picturesque and full of local color as in Maurice Tourneur's *Justin de Marseille* (1941), a more "American" style as in Raymond Bernard's *Faubourg Montmartre* (1931), and a lighter and more entertaining register, illustrated by *Fric-frac* or *Circonstances atténuantes* (1939).[57] In truth, the popular success of these later films was greater than the darker ones of Carné and Prévert. But it was poetic realism, a sort of film version of the *fantastique social*, that carried this poetry of the underworld the furthest, although this movement was also criticized for its fatalism and its populism. "Populism, you say. And so?" as Carné defended himself. "We are not afraid of the word—or of the thing itself. To describe the simple life of little people, to render the atmosphere of laborious humanity as they experience it, is that not worth more than to reconstruct the vague and overheated ambiance of dance parties, of an unreal nobility, and nightclubs from which cinema has abundantly profited up to now?"[58]

Yet this aesthetic gradually evaporated after World War II. *Les Portes de la nuit*, 1945), by the team of Carné and Prévert, pushed this style and its imaginary to an extreme. A figure of fate personified seemed to pursue the characters, heroes as well as villains, in a working-class Paris that was apparently losing its soul. The bitter failure of this film at the box office sealed the end of a model, and the exhaustion of a form.

By 1952 Jean-Paul Clébert was irritated that "the poetry and horror of the zone have been so many times described, inspected, photographed, filmed, reconstructed in the studio, and exported abroad as national patrimony (French culture and taste), utilized for literary, artistic, moralizing, and political purposes." Indignant that nobody in France had ever really undertaken an ethnology of the lower quartiers, that everybody had been content with a (re)production that he considered prefabricated,[59] he was now going to thrust the *fantastique social* "under the noses of a public that either does not know or else scorns it." Perhaps this verdict was somewhat severe. Were these "lower depths that were so fascinating to a desperate Romanticism"[60] really such a French specialty? As we have seen, Lisbon and Buenos Aires offered their own imaginaries that shared many traits with the Paris outskirts. In London, Arthur Morrison's *Tales of Mean Streets* (1894) tried to depict the desperate monotony of East End alleys, the dreary daily life, the melancholic and sometimes tragic routine of existences that never managed to escape from poverty and crime. This was also the meaning of the fate of the young Dicky Perrott, which Morrison described two years later in *A Child of the Jago*.[61] However, can one get rid of this view when depicting the unvarnished life of the underworld? Jean-Paul Clébert himself did not escape this dilemma when he roamed the Paris of tramps and beggars in 1952, and again in 1954, in the company of a photographer. Written up from penciled notes compiled over three years of vagrancy, this baroque text juxtaposed a series of itineraries in parts of the city where tourist guides did not venture, but where the experienced eye of the pedestrian knew how to recognize "poetry in its raw state [. . .]—of stones, cobbles, boundary markers, carriage doors, attic windows, tile roofs, scarce grass, rare, unexpected herbs, dead-end streets, passages, interior courtyards, storage sheds for coal or building materials, demolition shops—the poetry of work-sites, wastelands, *boules* pitches, bistros, bars, a poetry of colors but also a poetry of odors that vary at each doorstep."[62] Despite Clébert's efforts to extricate himself from it, nostalgia was attached to every page as he explored parts of the city that were disappearing piece by piece, and a zone "that is fading like a grease-spot being vigorously rubbed."[63] Concerned to take into account the wealth of the lower depths, he found that "the marvelous reigns in its natural state and in the extraordinary characters that miraculously live there."[64] Clébert, like others before him, took the path of poetic flight.

PART III

Ebbing of an Imaginary

8

Slow Eclipse of the Underworld

Like any historical construction, social imaginaries are part and parcel of an era. They have a beginning and an end, which is what renders them perceptible to the historian. Of course, no dates can be as precise as those that fix economic cycles or political régimes. Rough periodization may help by setting a tempo for the grand scansions of collective sensibility and stressing the major turning points in social awareness. However, the components of the imaginary never totally disappear but persist in a latent state; they remain available and are easily mobilized for current configurations—and subsequent reconfigurations. This is true of the underworld as well. In earlier chapters, I explained how a variety of motifs—some ancient (even timeless) and others more clearly contextualized—were combined in particular "figures" to give birth to the imaginary of *roguery* at the end of the Middle Ages, and then at the beginning of the nineteenth century to that of the *lower depths*, and at its end to that of the *underworld*. In this chapter I explain how and why these configurations gradually came undone around the middle of the twentieth century. Social and political transformations, the rise of the welfare state, and mutations in criminal practices all inclined Western societies to consider their marginal peoples (and their transgressions) differently. Many of the reflex reactions to vice, crime, and poverty remained, but the system that tightly aligned these elements was no longer operative. None of the elements of the underworld disappeared, but the specific combinatory link between these elements became out of season.

DECRIMINALIZING THE POOR

At the heart of these transformations lay a gradual shift in attitudes toward poverty. Social, scientific, and political representations of the poor shifted at the turn of the century, slowly dissociating the indigent person from the criminal. A new configuration was established that affected traditional philanthropy and reform campaigns, as well as the social sciences, and marked a gradual exit from the age of the underworld. Many innovations underlay this inflexion, and at least three of them appear decisive.

The first is linked to the emergence of new frameworks for understanding (and new taxonomies of) poverty. Classification of the impoverished and the indigent slowly disengaged from the moral presuppositions that had previously governed them.[1] The Englishman Charles Booth's great study (begun in 1866), *Life and Labour of the People of London*, provides the most resonant example of this "classificatory revolution."[2] A wealthy businessman from Liverpool and the owner of a shipping company that operated between Europe and Brazil, Booth financed and organized an immense investigation into the 4.3 million inhabitants of the British capital, neighborhood by neighborhood, district by district, street by street, dividing them into various "statistical classes." This gigantic enterprise, which took almost seventeen years, was carried out by a team composed of seven regular investigators and a huge number of informants (visitors from the London School Board, educators, philanthropists, clergymen, and policemen).[3] Booth's model remained partly naturalistic, drawing up a "ground plan of classification by which, as in the drawers of a mineralogist's cabinet, details can be classified and seen in their proper place."[4] Interviews and case studies provided the data, which was then recorded on quantitative charts in an attempt to establish "numerical relations which poverty, misery, and depravity bear to regular earnings and comparative comfort." The essential thing was to debunk the logic of the "voyage" to an unknown land and the description of "types" that had dominated the stories of journalists and

missionaries. Booth decided not to utilize "subject matter of sensational history," although it nevertheless arises in his notebooks. "The sensual laugh,
the coarse joke, the brutal fight, or the mean and petty cheating of the street
bargain are the outward sights yielded by society to soothe the inward condition of overstrain or hunger."[5] Avoiding the picturesque (which takes the
part for the whole or the effect for the cause, which merely produces confusion and anxiety), he tried to objectivize poverty by giving each element a
"quantitative value." Booth constructed a complex grid of stratifications as
a function of statistical criteria founded on a scale of income, a structure of
employment, the nature of the habitat, and so forth, that divided individuals
into eight "classes," running from A to H. The method revolutionized traditional social investigation and resulted in a series of statistical tables, which
were synthesized in the form of poverty maps established section by section.

The results concerning the East End and its nine hundred thousand
inhabitants drew the most attention. Booth demonstrated that almost a
third of the population of its neighborhoods lived below the poverty line
(defined as a little more than one pound per week for the average family).
For the city as a whole, poverty affected 1.3 million people, or more than
30 percent of residents. This revelation produced a veritable shock among
the Victorian elites. But more than this fact, it was Booth's explanations
that proved innovative. First, he showed that alcoholism, laziness, and
transgressions were much more symptoms than causes of poverty, which
resided principally in the irregular structure of employment. Above all, he
tried to distinguish the subject of the residue of outcasts from the subject
of poverty. "The hordes of barbarians of whom we have heard, who, issuing
from their slums, will one day overwhelm modern civilization, do not exist.
There are barbarians, but they are a handful, a small and decreasing percent-
age: a disgrace but not a danger."[6]

These barbarians, these parasites, this world of crime and transgression, were classified by Booth as belonging to class A: those who refuse to
work. Of course, this world existed, but it constituted only a very narrow
fringe—1.2 percent of the East End population—a world apart that lived
in a sort of extraterritoriality: "This savage semi-criminal class of people
had its golden age in the days when whole districts of London were in their
undisputed possession. They mainly desire to be alone, to be allowed to

make an Alsatia of their own."[7] The principal danger, according to Booth, lay in the risk of contagion spreading to class B: the "very poor." Those were the people with only occasional earnings who often proved incapable of regular work. To dry up the reproduction of class A (in large part hereditary, he thought), it was necessary to reduce that class by separating parents and children. Here we find again the notion of *residuum*, much in vogue at the end of the nineteenth century, but which Booth partially disengaged from moralistic premises, identifying the "residue" with precisely quantified groups. The elimination of these "unfit," too, could take place through a true urban policy. Booth's poverty map showed very precise locations for those portions of the city inhabited by class A. Isolating these streets inside a line of quarantine and then systematically abolishing them would get rid of this fringe, and then he could turn to class B, which he thought lay at the heart of the social question.

Charles Booth's investigation did not break with every moral diagnosis; degeneration remained one of the principal factors of the reproduction of "savage" and criminal populations. But in freeing itself from traditional typologies and from classifications derived from the natural sciences, and turning instead to sociological and quantified grids, it challenged the habitual representations of the underworld. Radically dissociating the narrow fringe of social outcasts from the impoverished and indigents, it invalidated the very principle on which the whole imaginary of the lower depths had been constructed. Of course, it took more than one inquiry to modify such deeply rooted social representations, but the work of Booth marked an essential stage. It helped to inflect all the classificatory methods applied after the 1890s and inspired other investigators, such as Seebohm Rowntree and his study of London poverty in 1902.[8] Above all, Booth's methods acquired quasi-official status when his former collaborator, Hubert Llewellyn Smith, became Chief Commissioner for Labour and adopted Booth's classification for use by the Board of Trade.

A second innovation was linked to the new conceptions of the working and nonworking.[9] Unemployment, as an old and structural reality of working life, was gradually reinvested with new understandings and new significations. The constant rise of new sectors—public administration, banking, the railroads, and department stores—led to the emergence of stable salaried workers who demonstrated their social, professional, and political virtues. In addition to these structural transformations, experts and reforming elites tried to stabilize the working modes of the popular classes, to promote normalized salary earnings. By stigmatizing the traditional mobility of labor, experts hoped to assign to workers a new relation with jobs and salaries. A lot of international reflection at the beginning of the twentieth century placed these new meanings of unemployment at the center of debates on social reform. Around 1900, in England, the term *unemployable* began to be substituted for the classic appellations of *pauper, homeless,* and *destitute.*[10] Use of this category tended to eliminate the traditional dichotomies on which philanthropic arrangements were based (for example, good versus bad poor, true versus false indigents), and along with them any work-related "moral epistemology." On the model of (and in close symbiosis with) Charles Booth's classifications, the new "unemployable" category enabled a gradual departure from naturalist taxonomies and the universe of the moral sciences. Work remained the cardinal value of society, but it became a more complex and more plastic reality. In this sense, the objectivization of unemployment as an economic and social fact was a profound overthrow of the previous perspective. Statistically informed, the new category implied that the jobless situation no longer necessarily derived from laziness and vice but from a disadvantaged position in the relations of production.

Yet this shift was neither total nor absolute. The idea persisted that certain work-shy individuals were perturbing the system, although they were merely a "residuum" (a term fashionable in Great Britain at the time) or "parasites" and "social detritus" (as they were called in France). Note that the exacerbation of the discourse on vagabonds and their strong stigmatization coincided with the invention of unemployment. But this fringe of the "abnormal" was now quantitatively reduced (less than 2 percent in France) and thought of as being bound to disappear.[11] Other representations also emerged that rejected the traditional sentimentalizing and insisted on the virtues, courage, or energy of the "lower classes." In Milan, young "positivist" intellectuals tried to view the subproletariat that peopled the city's underworld as the yeast that would raise another world. In New York, certain journalists (and novelists such as Stephen Crane) reassessed the value of life in the slums, from which they thought a new social vision and an alternative ethic could arise.[12]

All these shifts led to a profound renewal of forms of welfare assistance, marked by the gradual marginalization of good works and traditional philanthropy in favor of social insurance and the gradual construction of the regulatory state. Little by little, the practice of "holy violence" and of prying visits to domiciles disappeared. Naturally, most of the traditional structures subsisted, and some of them even tended to be further developed on the model of the Salvation Army (founded in England in 1865), which became established on the continent at the beginning of the twentieth century. The traditional care model was not exhausted, but the notions on which it had been founded were evolving. In France in the early twentieth century, for example, the place of the poor was modified in the theological and philosophical discourse of Catholicism:[13] there was a gradual transfer of the figure of the poor person from belonging to a "natural" anthropological (thus legitimate) perspective to someone "excluded," a victim of a process of social disqualification. At the heart of these shifts lay reflection on the concept of the "human person" that was taking place in Christian philosophy in the interwar period. Many influences—that of philosophers Maurice Blondel and Gabriel Marcel, the neo-Thomism of Jacques Maritain, the personalism incarnated by the journal *Esprit*, or the "Economy and Humanism" group—converged in the emergence of a new ethics of the person. The attitude to the poor became detached from the working world alone and now related to humanistic categories. This was especially the case in colonized countries and in national pockets isolated from industrial society, which in turn contributed to a redeployment of programs toward refugees, immigrants, prostitutes, lepers, those badly housed, and others. By associating the concept of the "human person" with the notion of social exclusion, Catholic thought eventually resulted in a veritable change of paradigm. The traditional figure of "God's poor" disappeared almost completely in favor of much less fatalistic representations that made the indigent person a casualty or a social misfit.

Consequently, the forms of philanthropic engagement also shifted. Principally in the Protestant world, new types of missions tried to combine charitable activism, education, and the social sciences. This was notable with the social settlements that developed in England and the United States at the end of the nineteenth century. The principle was inaugurated in 1884 by Reverend Samuel Barnett in Whitechapel, who replaced the traditional philanthropic visits with the settlement of outsiders as permanent residents in impoverished neighborhoods where they could offer educational and social activities. Thus young graduates from Cambridge and Oxford settled in Toynbee Hall, a sort of extension of the university in the slums.[14] Such experiments profoundly modified attitudes to the Dark Continent and its "savage hordes," and the model spread even more widely in the United States. In 1889, the American reformer Jane Adams created Hull House in Chicago, and similar settlements came to New York, Boston, and Pittsburgh. These "colonies" offered courses, lectures, and leisure activities, as well as concrete remedies for the problems of daily life (health, lodging, work relations, and so forth). They were also subtly transformed into instruments of inquiry, notably in the examination of the "sweating system" by Florence Kelley and her team over seven years, which was published in *Hull House Maps and Papers* in 1895. There was an analogous movement in Boston, where Robert Wood (who saw the settlements as a social science laboratory) founded Andover House. In general, ties between the universities and city governments were strengthened. Various initiatives emanated from the social survey movement, a series of more ambitious inquiries in the decade from 1900 to 1910.[15] These experiments tried to break down the partitions between philanthropy, reform, and the social sciences; they were linked to journalists who were investigating the same burning subjects that lay at the source of the Chicago sociological school.[16] As we have seen, a different representation of poverty was emanating from Chicago.

Such practices were less developed in France, but we find the same spirit in the Social Team movement founded in 1921 by the young Catholic philosopher Robert Garric. Struggling against social segregation and strengthened by his experience of solidarity in the trenches, Garric encouraged young graduates to live in working-class districts: in Belleville, where Garric settled, but also in several other districts on the periphery of Paris. Social Teams offered courses, opened libraries, and tried to build bridges between the poor and French culture.[17] In general, the movement led to a shift from assistance offered by social and religious elites toward welfare conceived as a social right.[18] Following Chancellor Bismarck's model in Prussia, the first to adopt social laws in the 1880s, most European states at the beginning of

the twentieth century effected reforms that extended rights to social insurance for sickness, accidents, pensions, and so on. For example, in France a
1905 law organized obligatory assistance to "the old, the infirm, and the
incurable" in the form of allowances or benefits. There was a gradual shift to
structures of mutual aid that were less personal, but rationalized, and now
administered by public authorities. This emergence of a regulatory and welfare state that made assistance a right was accompanied by the disappearance of the moral or religious distinctions on which previous philanthropic
practices had been based.[19] This major deconstruction affected all Western
societies, and Keynes's model provided a theoretical and economic justification for it. The avenue was open to the Welfare State that would triumph
after World War II.

A final evolution, more material and conjunctural, concerned the partial
destruction of the most insalubrious and degraded areas of the major cities, precisely those that had contributed to polarizing and fixing the imaginary of the underworld. Accompanying a general rise in the standards of
living in Western nations, policies of either rehabilitating or liquidating the
slums were put into effect almost everywhere. The overhaul of Paris under
Baron Haussmann had set the tone, even if it had the effect of displacing
the location of "bad places" to the peripheries of Paris. But the heart of
the city, its shop window, was now free of the lower depths, which were
merely figured symbolically, as a spectacle. The destruction of old Paris (or
of the degraded heart of London—St. Giles, Holborn, Drury Lane) was
echoed a half-century later in New York's slum clearance policies from 1895
to 1930. Launched in the wake of Jacob Riis's denunciatory photojournal-
ism, it resulted in the destruction of the worst of the Five Points tenements,
notably those of Mulberry Bend, which were razed in favor of a park that
was inaugurated in 1897. In the 1920s, on the initiative of the Tenement
House Commission directed by Robert De Forest, forty thousand tenements were destroyed, including the famous Gotham Court[20] built in 1850
on Cherry Street, which had become the symbol of a dirty, degraded, and
corrupt New York City.

Such phenomena were perceptible almost everywhere in Europe. From
the beginning of the twentieth century, municipalities and public authorities engaged in policies of sanitation and slum clearance. There was a

growing desire to reduce cities' actual underworlds and their insalubrious zones. Rouen, for example, razed the ten thousand houses that "still had completely permeable cesspits that were never emptied, and whose leaks necessarily contaminated any well located in a courtyard near the pit."[21] Many other cities obsessed by sanitation policies followed suit in the 1900s.[22] First they would do a sanitary inventory of buildings and then try to remedy the worst situations. In Limoges, the Viraclaud district (full of hovels, dives, and brothels) was destroyed, and on the ruins were erected a new prefecture and post office.[23] Lyon in 1906 celebrated the disappearance of the Grôlée district. Dijon eradicated the most unsanitary streets and houses, except for the upper portion of the rue Roulotte, which was also where the brothels were found.[24] In Algiers, the Marine district, a zone of sinister shacks containing the most sordid and indigent population, was razed between 1937 and 1943.[25] In Paris, the slow and incomplete liquidation of the "Zone" tells an analogous story. The lack of treatment of water, garbage, and excrement focused public attention; discharges that attracted flies, vermin, and rats raised a big debate in the 1920s.[26] Cesspools appeared as unbearably vile, and their disappearance was conceived of as the absolute symbol of the diminution of the underworld, both topographic and social. But the campaign that began around 1895 was not ultimately won until the 1950s.

We must be careful about the meaning of these changes: between 1920 and 1950, sordid and insalubrious places did not disappear, unfortunately, either from France or from any other Western country. Permanently pushed back into the recesses and interstices of housing projects, to the peripheries of cities or under the bridges and highway interchanges, were shacks and shantytowns and temporary encampments—intolerable "nonlife" spaces where the poorest were periodically forced to reconstitute a semblance of social living. This issue lies at the core of the history of contemporary urban reform and *cités* (projects). But something was indeed undertaken at the beginning of the twentieth century so that this environment was no longer the "natural" setting for the disadvantaged (that is, the working class.)

The traditional perception of the lower depths of poverty tended to be effaced during these upheavals, especially when other social realities came to the forefront: new topographies of poverty appeared in suburban tracts and extended like oil stains along avenues of communication and transportation. New understandings of delinquency arose, increasingly and insistently identifying it with foreign immigration. New attention was paid to situations of poverty in countries of the "Third World." For example, when in 1943 part of Marseilles' old quartiers was destroyed, the new poor—principally Armenians—were confined to *enclos* (enclosures) and shantytowns in the northern parts of the city. Poverty was not abolished, but new ways of designating the phenomenon testify to different appraisals of it. In French the expression *bas-fonds*, which was gradually reduced to symbolic or dramatic usages, was succeeded by other terms. The term *clochard* (tramp), first heard in 1895, did not become widespread until after World War I;[27] its origin was the bell (*cloche*) that rang at the Halles de Paris when the market closed, which was the moment to start recuperating leftover produce. Although this term's referents remained composite, in the interwar period it assumed an increasingly quaint dimension with the diffusion of the figure of the *bon clochard*, which became a symbol of a bohemian life that was partially voluntary, the deliberate choice of an ambivalent and unconstrained existence. At the end of the 1960s, a very different expression developed: the *quart monde* (Fourth World) was suggested by Joseph Wresinski, founder of the ATD-*Quart Monde* association. Wresinski was obviously inspired by the "Third World" phrase that had been forged by Alfred Sauvy in 1950, but he also remembered the revolutionary Dufourny de Villiers, author in 1789 of a *Cahier du quatrième ordre*, which was devoted to indigents and the poorest, whom he thought had been forgotten in the revolutionary debates.[28] By combining the themes of the French Revolution's Rights of Man with the inequalities born of colonialism, the expression offered a new field to representations of poverty.

At the end of the 1970s, the intensification of the economic and social crisis led to the appearance of new designations, among them the notions of *exclus* and *exclusion*, which René Lenoir's *Les exclus: Un Français sur dix* (Outsiders: One Frenchman in ten) introduced in 1974. From the beginning, these expressions were criticized by sociologists for their weak explanatory power. By associating very heterogeneous situations, by presenting society in a reductive binary mode (those included versus those excluded), and by stressing a state of affairs rather than the process that caused it, exclusion simplified a complex phenomenon. It eschewed factors that might have been responsible (social, economic, ideological, political) in favor of an abstract and anonymous situation that nothing seemed to have provoked. Some wanted to see it as a simple "prenotion" (in the Durkheimian sense of the term) that social demand had converted into a paradigm. What remained (the term "exclusion") had a dramaturgic function and an undeniable metaphoric scope.[29] In its wake, other designations appeared: *SDF* (*sans domicile fixe* [of no fixed address]) arose in the bureaucratic language of the police administration of the Belle Époque, but did not take root;[30] and *RMIst* (welfare recipient), the "new poor," and other terms began to appear. The massive and clearly identifiable evil of pauperism was succeeded by a host of situations of social disaffiliation that were not susceptible to overall interpretation and treatment.

INVENTION OF "MILIEU"

The weakening of the imaginary of the underworld also resulted from transformations that affected representations of the criminal world. Those of the Criminal (another great figure in this imaginary) changed drastically at the beginning of the twentieth century. The influence of new medical and anthropological knowledge in the second half of the nineteenth century began to influence the association between poverty and crime—but without abolishing it. Anthropological and biological interpretations of crime were produced by Benedict Morel, pioneer of the concept of degeneration in 1859, then by anthropologist Paul Broca, then by the Turin doctor Cesare Lombroso (author of *Criminal Man* in 1876). Many alienists were also interested in these questions.[31] What if the criminal—far from being an indigent person pushed to transgress by poverty or vice—was in fact a degenerate being who was structurally predisposed to do evil? These new matrices were superimposed upon previous representations but did not replace them. They also tended to revivify older figures, such as the Monster. Moreover, they did not claim to define the whole criminal universe. For Lombroso, born criminals represented less than a third of the ensemble of transgressors, which left aside a great number of wrongdoers (by profession or by opportunity), not to mention murderers (by passion or by madness). But the public favor given this new category and its rapid spread weakened ideas of a "social swamp," which had predominated in the early nineteenth century. For example, the composite figure of the "apache" that arose in France during the Belle Époque belonged to a closed world of incorrigible hoodlums who were almost naturally fated to do evil. Whether crime arose from one's nature or from a profession, it was no longer conceived to be the result of social degradation.

The invention of the notion of *milieu* following World War I accentuated these shifts. The expression—roughly equivalent to the English phrase "criminal environment"—has never been adequately elucidated. For a long time, police and magistrates had cited the "special milieu" of pimps and thugs, but milieu on its own was first used in 1920 in a play by Francis Carco and Aimé Picard, *Mon Homme*, to refer to a criminal society:[32] "Now it's all upside down. There are people who are not even from the *milieu*," exclaimed the tenant of a slum house. The southern slang equivalent, *mitan*, appeared two years later.

It is almost impossible to provide an "objective" definition of *milieu*. Dozens of books have tried, but they offer representations that are either nostalgic, idealized, or quaint, which all focus on the specific "mentality" of the milieu's mobsters, its rules, its code of honor and loyalty, or its quasi-feudal organization into clans or brotherhoods, in which "each person is assigned his place once and for all, from the pettiest enforcer to the biggest trafficker."[33] As a historian of the social imaginary, I find this "mythology" of the milieu interesting, but it does not help us understand the actual mutations that affected criminal societies at the beginning of the twentieth century. In this respect, the most useful definitions are the simplest, as in a 1967 judicial police report that defines the milieu as a "disparate assemblage of men [sic] living on the margins of society, camouflaging (more or less well) their illicit activities behind a suitable façade,"[34] or the even more imprecise formula of Jérôme Pierrat: "a community of men who recognize each other."[35]

In truth, what France calls "milieu" incorporates a series of transformations that took place in many places in the first half of the twentieth century that other languages labeled "organized crime." The root of the phenomenon lies in the general accumulation of wealth by criminal society.

From 1905 to 1910, the conjoined rise of the drug traffic (principally opium and cocaine that gradually spread in major Western cities) and still more of international prostitution (called the "white slave trade") both generated considerable profits, way beyond what professional gangs had traditionally reaped. A dozen years later in the United States, this was compounded by the extraordinary windfall caused by Prohibition. In less than three decades, there was a very clear process of social ascension: a significant fraction of delinquent society was getting substantially richer, and styles of clothing and posture, hangouts and décor, tended to break with the popular or working-class tradition. A new aesthetic required that hoodlums be "swank" and "decked out like lords." Henceforth gangsters "dressed with a false elegance, wearing silk or cashmere suits, two-toned shoes, their fingers weighed down by enormous gold signet rings."[36] Far from the old border prowlers or hoodlums in caps, the new bandits wore fine three-piece suits, American-style, with vibrant neckties and custom-made shoes; they drove fancy automobiles and used powerful firearms. Newspapers, photo magazines, and the cinema paid them constant attention, accentuating the phenomenon way beyond its real scope. But one thing was clear: part of the criminal world that had issued from the most sordid depths of society had gradually extricated itself and risen in the social hierarchy to the point of reaching, if not the upper strata, at least its own Milieu.

The new social relations achieved by the best-placed or most gifted among these aristocrats of crime was an important consequence of this "elevation." Not just with the police, their traditional "partner" since Vidocq, which had been almost structural given the determining role of informants in police work. Now patented gangsters publicly consorted with personalities from the political and business and entertainment worlds. This type of association was already familiar in the United States, where the Five Points blight had served since the middle of the nineteenth century as an auxiliary to Tammany Hall, the local tentacles of the Democratic Party: it supplied workers ranging from rally organizers and publicists to bouncers. This kind of alliance was also traditional in Italy, where the main criminal societies (the Sicilian Mafia, the Neapolitan Camorra, the Calabrese Ndrangheta) had built complex collusion with political powers, racketeering with businesses, and complicity with civil authorities.[37] Little studied until then in

France, this type of relation enjoyed a remarkable takeoff between the wars, notably in Marseille, which gradually earned its renown as the "capital of crime in France."[38]

Marseille had long been exceptional for lacking an underworld, and it remained gay and pleasant and marked by southern insouciance and luminosity. Things became complicated at the end of the nineteenth century: port activities, Italian emigration, and the development of prostitution had given rise to more disturbing figures, like those of the *nervis*, bands that competed during the Belle Époque for control of the Saint-Jean and Saint-Mauront districts. As a major port and magnet for immigration, Marseille was slowly taken over by the new illegal traffic—opium, cocaine, Mediterranean and Atlantic prostitution—and so an outright and wealthy Milieu emanated that earned headlines in the national newspapers. Two great figures incarnated this trend: Paul Carbone and François Spirito. Enriched by illicit gambling, opium, racketeering, and international prostitution, these two men were charged and arrested in April 1934 in an affair involving one of the magistrates investigating the murder of Stavisky, an embezzler who had been protected by the prime minister. But Carbone and Spirito were soon freed, benefiting from the protection and public support of Simon Sabiani, a regional legislator and first assistant to the mayor of Marseille. The Stavisky Affair cast a spotlight on the new relations between traffickers and politicians who seemed to be in bed together; it nearly brought down the Socialist government. Carbone and Spirito had been furnishing strikebreakers to Sabiani, who had just joined the right-wing party of Jacques Doriot.[39] The affair culminated in revelations of the existence of a second network, linking another criminal clan to the Marseilles Socialist Party, and then in 1938 vast corruption in the vice squad was exposed. Thus the Marseille Milieu represented a sort of criminal meritocracy within which a few individuals had managed (by trafficking, venality, and cronyism) to occupy very enviable positions.

Gradually becoming dissociated from the poor and the derelict, these new delinquents were no longer the symbolic dregs. They were still called vicious, immoral, and unscrupulous, but they were also becoming civilized and politicized. As products of social promotion, they could now socialize with legal elites. Although they continued to employ crooks, hotheads, or *crucibellis*—"*nervi*s and 'hard cases' fated to violent death because they killed, stole, and threatened until they had exhausted their luck"[40]—newspapers and magazines no longer focused on these second fiddles. They were condemned, of course, but their exploits were recounted with astonishment. Far from the images of yesterday, which offered the elites the image of criminal working-class mobs, the press now entertained the middle classes with representations of the wealthy Milieu. The novelist Blaise Cendrars, who visited the infamous quartier of Marseille in 1933, quickly acknowledged that he was on the wrong track. "I told myself that in order not to lose the object of my enquiry, I had to descend much lower or else aim much higher."[41]

The most significant change concerned the key hangouts, whose importance in the imaginary of the underworld we have witnessed. Here a double displacement is perceptible. The new kinds of trafficking—more mobile and more international—tended to deterritorialize criminal activities. Gone was the day when everything took place on home turf—and hence the nostalgia felt by some for the good old days. "You see [. . .] there are no more hide-outs in Paris, no more *underworld*, as it was called in my younger days," said an elderly crook. "Now you find the outlaws in bars that are like any other. They are dressed like everybody else."[42] And they had migrated to other places: the bad boys, far from the city taverns and the dives on the outskirts, now paraded in the fancy neighborhoods. "Everything takes place in the light of day," wrote Blaise Cendrars in his report on the new bandits published in 1934 in the *Excelsior* and reprinted the following year under the title *Panorama de la pègre*.[43] The term *panorama* is explicit. Gone are the shadows and the dark alleys, gone the basements and dirty tables; now everything is out in the open, in the sumptuous bars and circles of the Avenue des Champs-Élysées. No need for exploration, for revelation or unveiling: the underworld exhibits itself on the cinema screen, in the new Hollywood gangster movies.

The romantic imaginary that had given birth to the lower depths was gradually undone by these transformations. Cendrars made this predictable evolution the principal argument of his reportage. The places had already disappeared: the old Paris, the bistros on the outskirts, the banks of the Seine, the fortifications (as the singer Sylvie Fréhel was mourning in the same years). The main characters and how they looked were also vanishing, and along with them the shadows with secrets to be unveiled. Let us go back to Cendrars's limpid summary:

> Today this Romanticism is indeed outdated. The bands of capped bandits, the terrors of the neighborhood, the apaches armed with a shiv have all been succeeded by bands of gangsters in grey hats, henchmen in tuxedos, knights of chloroform and the syringe, the hotel rats and the most recent generation of society dancers who go about with bare heads, hair slicked down. Everybody struts in fashionable nightclubs and officially lives in grand hotels, where since the war they mingle with high society and rich foreigners. This quite modern promiscuity is the opposite of any Romanticism. [...] This is why, despite the growing favor that detective novels seem to enjoy, it has to be agreed that the poetry of the "Milieu" is dead, and that any literary Romanticism in this domain has expired.[44]

Still, some writers offered nuances, and rightly so. In 1927 Edmond Locard could still devote a whole chapter of his new book, *Le crime et le criminal*, to the figure of the *apache*, which had not disappeared so quickly. The newspapers of the 1920s show that crime reporters continued to use the term abundantly.[45] In December 1927, *Le Matin* published a serialized feature over three weeks that described the "Great Purge of Paris" conducted by the city's prefect: plague-ridden shacks, miserable lodging-rooms, players of three-card-monte, and prowlers of the barrier—the sordid and sinking underworld of Paris reigns in the great tradition of Eugène Sue.[46] Enduring types and newfound nostalgia mingled in these descriptions. Jean Galtier-Boissière published *La bonne vie* (The good life) in 1925, dealing with prewar prostitution and insouciant gangs. Such memoirs were also constructing the image of the Belle Époque. "I am not sad. But it's the Milieu that disgusts me. It's over. Before the war, there were still men—and some do remain. But the strongest are now forced to throw in the towel. What do you expect, life's like that," declared Bob in *Paname* (1927).[47]

Marcel Montarron, in a major 1936 article devoted to the new type of criminals, was more subtle. He, too, acknowledged that manners have changed, that the new wealth deriving from drugs and the sex trade had overthrown mob traditions, but he also noted that not all criminals had profited, and that the Depression had affected the Milieu because it is subject to the fluctuations in luxury and pleasure, and because an influx of foreigners had nourished the new-style bas-fonds.

> Unemployment and poverty used to recruit for the army of crime. You see an increase in thefts, night burglaries, raids in cars, pillaging via shop windows, blackmail, assaults. You see this new army of crime's offensive spread with disturbing speed; the jobless who are improvising at villainy come to join the ranks of gangsters low on resources. [. . .] Now a new mob, born of the forced idleness of the unemployed, of impoverished dreamers, surge up onto the Paris pavements and swell the jungle of its bas-fonds.[48]

In the spread of these new representations, we have to consider the force of attraction of images coming from the United States. Pulp fiction, serials, and especially the talkies promulgated the representation of "Chicago bandits" as incarnating modernity. In December 1927, Joseph von Sternberg's film *Underworld* was shown in Paris under the title *Les nuits de Chicago*, and it dramatized the story of Tommy O'Connor and the bloody clashes between the rival gangs of Chicago. The first issue of *Détective* (November 1, 1928) opened with a major report devoted to "Chicago, Capital of Crime" (authored by Allan Ross McDougall), and in early 1930 the weekly serialized an investigation into the "New York Underworld." The mystery writer Georges Simenon, who had not yet invented Inspector Maigret, also went to Chicago for his *Bandits de Chicago* in 1929. The following year, Géo London, the most reputable of the crime chroniclers of the day, published *Two Months with the Chicago Bandits*, in which he recounted his interview with Al Capone.[49] In 1931, Capone's trial triggered a continuous stream of publications, mostly cheap pamphlets and pulp fiction, and serials such as "True Report according to the diary of the private secretary to Al Capone." Fred Pasley's *Al Capone: The Biography of a Self-Made Man*" was issued in French with an introduction by Blaise Cendrars.[50] This complex fascination with American gangs grew thanks to technology, the automobile, firearms, and, of course, the modernity of U.S. cities—not to mention by photography and the cinema. But the image of organized crime as being rich and powerful and able to deal on an equal footing with the police and to negotiate with political and financial circles was an extraordinary motif in France, a country that had so long favored the miserablist romanticism of the lower depths. Alongside the Chicago gangs, wrote Géo London, French villains "are colorless characters and so we can understand why French writers have dealt almost sympathetically with the world of pimps at a time when André Salmon was moved by the exploits of his 'friendly scoundrels.'"[51]

Many new weeklies launched at the time contributed to this Americanization: *Détective* and *Police Magazine*, of course, but also more ephemeral sheets, such as *Police et Reportage* (1933), *Réalisme* (1933), and *Faits-divers* (1932), played a decisive role in the perception of an emerging criminal society and in the nostalgia for an old world that was vanishing. The basfonds became one of the modes of that prewar universe that was now being mourned as heroic or legendary. A former *apache* remembers: "People then were less ferocious and more loyal than nowadays. Disputes were settled with the knife or the razor, from which came death more frequently than glorious scars."[52] People deplored the disappearance of the "spirit and the law" transmitted by the older generation, of that "great family" composed of miscreants, convicts breaking bail, the pimps, the "irregulars."[53] But nostalgia is inherent in representations of the criminal world. Later on, in the 1970s, the veterans of the Milieu deplored in the same way the loss of the "mentality" that was said to reign between the wars. Still, in 2012, a newspaper story about the famous Lyonnais gang was headlined "Crooks are no longer what they used to be."[54]

The scenario described here, which strongly transformed the organization of criminal society in France, affected the particular rhythms and modes of most Western countries. This process was most advanced in the United States, but it set the tone for the rest. Prohibition accelerated the formation of powerful "organized crime," a "crime syndicate" capable of multiplying its ties to legal society via corruption and collusion. Founded on violence, but also on mutual services and clientelism, the resulting system often linked the police, business, and political milieux.[55]

The same process was at work everywhere. In Germany there was a disturbing fascination with the development of redoubtable criminal fraternities structured on the model of industrial corporations. Kessel described the *Unterwelt* as a state-within-the-State that enveloped the country in its "fearsome network." Cendrars, impressed by these new forms of organization, described "international associations of well-equipped villains who complement each other on the model of the great industrial *konzern* [and] have been able to pool their interests to guarantee exclusivity and the exploitation of crime in some port, station, city, region, border zone, seacoast, or country."[56] The Sicilian Mafia had a similar evolution, gradually losing its relationship with the world of the poor (the first occurrence of the term *maffia* [with two f's] appeared in 1868 in a dictionary of Sicilian dialect and referred to poverty)[57] to become a powerful criminal society, organized and structured, capable of dealing with those in power or even with nation-states.[58] Historians of contemporary Japan identified an identical phenomenon: contacts and agreements multiplied in the interwar period between the Yakuza and the Japanese state, and these complex networks became denser after World War II.[59] In Buenos Aires, gangsterism caused a furor in the 1920s. A new style emerged, influenced by photography and its emotional power, and by modes of spectacularizing propelled by the cinema. The gangster became a new star whose portrait was plastered in glossy magazines or on cinema screens.[60] He moved about in a fancy automobile and used all the resources of modern technology. He seemed to have definitively exited the darkness of the underworld, which migrated toward improbable and distant peripheries.

The imaginary of the bas-fonds diminished during the first half of the twentieth century. Discourse on the poor was reconfigured as criminals got rich and emancipated themselves; the social mystery changed in nature. The growling from those terrible low swamps that once threatened to engulf society in modern times receded or took the shape of other perils. The expression "lower depths" was increasingly used only in a figurative sense, and it lost its specifically social meaning and came to refer to any form of corruption. On the right, the *Action Française* decried the "underworld" of the police, the government, the Parliament. The shifty lawyer and dubious businessman Georges Anquetil was "the master of the Paris underworld" for writer Léon Daudet.[61] In the Anglophone world, the term *underworld* acquired its modern meaning of organized crime and gradually lost the connotations that linked it to the world of poverty and misery.

Les bas-fonds, Jean Renoir's 1936 film, offered a striking metaphor of this gradual eclipse. Adapted from Maxim Gorky's play by Charles Spaak and Renoir himself, the drama takes place in a poorhouse, a sordid establishment maintained (with police complicity) by a former receiver of stolen goods who is also a usurer and pimp, Kostylev. In this asylum live the needy and vagabonds (all of them alcoholics), a young consumptive, a mystical actor, a thief, prostitutes, and a former baron; they are pure products of social exploitation and comprise a perfect lower-depths mini-society. Of course, the worst character is Kostylev, a cynical and miserable exploiter, who is trying to buy the silence of the police by offering them the young Natasha. Encouraged by the vengeful fury of Pepel the Thief, the inmates revolt against the old man's tyranny, trap him in the courtyard, and massacre him in broad daylight. This collective murder has a liberating value. The accursed actor hangs himself, but Pepel and Natasha leave freely and take to the road without fear of the police; the little society disintegrates almost naturally.

This is in total contrast to the 1902 drama; in Gorky's play, the death of Kostylev has no redemptive effect. There is neither love (Natasha does not love Pepel) nor escape, and the bas-fonds inexorably sinks into misery and tragedy. "The gallows would have been better . . . that's where all of you should be sent," concludes Nastya, a former streetwalker left by her lover, "swept off into a hole!"[62] The optimism of Renoir's film and his social activism expressed the atmosphere and hopes of the French Popular Front (1936), with which it was contemporaneous, but it also explains—in a symbolic mode—the exhaustion of an imaginary.

9

Persistent Shadows

The combination of elements on which the imaginary of the underworld had been built was gradually dismantled during the twentieth century, but that did not mean that all of its components disappeared. Many components had existed even before 1840 and would continue to exist after World War II, and they could be reactivated periodically. The whole force of any social imaginary resides in the resilience of certain themes and certain figures, in their capacity to resurge in favorable contexts or to generate subsequent forms from the same inheritance. The imaginary that had been constructed around "bad places" or "spineless men and lazy girls"[1] does not escape this rule. Despite efforts made to conceive of the margins and transgressions in less anxious and stigmatizing ways, the obscurity of the underworld did not dissipate once and for all. In this chapter, I track some of its remnants, its adaptations, and its reconfigurations.

"MEN ERASED FROM HUMANITY"

Suggesting that the underworld had ended obviously does not mean that extreme poverty, crime, and prostitution have deserted our societies. What *was* partially destroyed was a mode of representation that associated crime and vice with all the figures of social exclusion. But cohorts of broken men and women persisted everywhere, people both stigmatized and excluded from social interactions. The political and social situations that accommodated that discrimination also lingered, and the French penal colonies were emblematic in many respects of these lasting remnants. Republican France had always vaunted its mission as the homeland of freedom and the Rights of Man, but the suppression of penal colonies came very late chronologically. It was not until June 1938 that a decree finally ended the overseas transportation of convicts who had been condemned to forced labor. This decision came about due to several factors: indictments made by many reporters (led by Albert Londres, whose *Au Bagne* strongly influenced public opinion in 1923), warnings from doctors about epidemics, lobbying by churches and especially the Salvation Army, criticism from various countries (especially in the Americas) that deplored the existence on their continent of these "gates of hell"[2] as a plague from another age, and, finally, actions by Gaston de Monnerville, deputy from Guyana to the French legislature, who said the penitentiaries discredited his island and were harming French prestige.[3] The 1938 decision was part of a general context that marked the gradual extinction of the underworld system.

Nevertheless, it would take almost thirty-five years for the French Republic to reabsorb the heritage and traces of this institutional underworld. In November 1938, six months after the decree suppressing the transportation of convicts, a last convoy of 666 of them left for Saint-Laurent in Guyana. A Genevan missionary named Charles Péan witnessed the departure: "A vision of human degradation! [. . .] their long straggly hair, their vague or anxious or half-witted gazes, were painful to see; most of them appeared demented."[4] Moreover, although the 1938 decree called for a halt to transportation, it explicitly stated that "there was no question of bringing back to France convicts who had been previously transported." Those convicts, as well as the "liberated" (convicts who were released were required to remain in Guyana), would still be prisoners of what was customarily called "the land of major punishment."[5] Ironically this immense underworld that had been created wholesale by France at the heart of the Amazonian forest was now achieving its autonomy, so it was up to its occupants to extract themselves from Guyana as best they could. Finally, the decree said nothing about the fate of the *relégués*, those recidivist small offenders that a law dating back to 1885 had declared "incorrigible" and who had been sentenced to perpetual "relegation" to Guyana. The overwhelming majority of them—the so-called collective inmates—were put into forced labor at the Saint-Jean-du-Maroni camp or its annexes. In 1942, a decree transferred their incarceration to penitentiary establishments in metropolitan France, but just when transportation was definitively suppressed, they were still being sent to Guyana. Those transported, whether *relégués* or liberated, amounted at the time to 5,612 individuals living in a penitentiary situation in the colonial territory.

These discarded and broken men—"erased from humanity," in Albert Camus's phrase[6]—whom the Republic was not even trying to salvage were considered the refuse of the penitentiary system. In 1941, the Vichy regime sent a new director to Guyana (a lieutenant-colonel ironically also named Camus) who had previously directed the Indo-Chinese penal colony at Poulo-Condore, the other underworld set up by France in the tropics.[7] At Cayenne, Camus instituted a régime of terror, using the dungeon and even punishments that a 1927 decree had abolished; he obliged the collective inmates to perform forced labor, and he expelled the Salvation Army that was trying to help them. Restrictions on food rations were used to starve the detainees: the bread ration fell from 750 to 500 grams, the rice ration from 100 to 60 grams. And these rations were only for men who were able to work; "tricksters" who were "habituated to hospitalization" were given even less food. The effects of this policy were disastrous for the health of the convicts, whose mortality rate reached 48 percent in 1942. One thinks of the similar fate of those interned in insane asylums and hospitals for the unfit, other categories of "social waste" equally decimated by neglect and famine during the Vichy period.[8] The fact that Guyana rallied to Free France in 1943 relaxed the conditions of detention, but during the war half the colonial penitentiary population would die. In 1945, only 837 of those transported remained, 290 *relégués*, and about one thousand "freed" ex-convicts.

After the Occupation ended, the restored Republic did nothing more for these men. Faced with a prison overpopulation caused by the purge of collaborators, some officials in the Justice Department even considered (in December 1944, and again in February 1946) resuming the convoys to

Guyana.[9] It fell to the Salvation Army to repatriate the convicts—another way of considering these men as the last of the excluded. Why? Since 1928, transportation camps had drawn the attention of the Army's Charles Péan, and he would devote twenty-five years of his life to helping them. Early on, Péan denounced the "moral disorder and cruelty of which the penal colony remains the last example and which is a task for our country's justice system."[10] In 1933, he founded three Salvation Army centers in the colony that were designed to offer work to the liberated, those cohorts of raggedy and scrawny ex-convicts, often stupefied by alcohol, who were forbidden to stay in Cayenne and whom the prison administration banned from a number of jobs. The idea was to help them pay for their return passage, to organize transport, and then offer them lodging once they got back to France. Thus, in 1945, the task of repatriating survivors quite naturally fell to the Salvation Army. In 1946, despite regular convoys, there were still two thousand ex-convicts abandoned to vegetate in Guyana. "Degradation. There remains a sludge of men sliding toward death," wrote Pierre Hamp.[11] Convoys of two to three hundred ex-convicts were leaving Saint-Laurent until 1953, but the leprous were not allowed to return. A handful of often tubercular men chose to stay where they were and would die destitute. "Some have blue masks tattooed on their faces. They are forever broken."[12] Many Indo-Chinese, mostly nationalist militants and those convicted for political reasons, also remained. They had been deported to the Guyana camp of Crique Anguille since 1931, and they did not leave there until 1963.

But the sad slog for these men did not stop once they were back in France. Some were still condemned to incarceration in metropolitan prisons, and all of them were banned from entering the *départements* where their crimes had been committed. The rest, as we have seen, were difficult to reintegrate, especially the very painful cases of *relégués* who were now back in France. Nobody knew what to do with them.[13] The complementary penalty of "relegation," aimed at getting rid of recidivist delinquents, still existed. Anyone with four correctional convictions of more than three months of prison each would automatically trigger this perpetual expulsion, if the judge so decided. This measure was not finally abolished until 1970, and it was replaced by parole until 1981. What could be done with those lost men who could no longer be exiled to Guyana? Penal philosophy and policy had both changed. The "new social defense" that had been progressing since the 1930s tried to practice rehabilitation by means of observation and prevention. After World War II, this approach influenced legislation: defended by Marc Ancel, its theories tried to give priority to the socialization and the redeployment of delinquents;[14] this current also informed the penitentiary reform propelled by Paul Amor, who became director of prison administration after 1945. Concerned to understand the social and psychological trajectories of individuals whose self-confidence they wanted to restore, it advocated the "observation" of those whom assistant director Pierre called "our brothers the recidivists."[15]

Thus the *relégués* essentially became the "observed" who were shifted from center to center as a function of the results of observations. In 1945, some of those repatriated were moved to experimental centers situated on Saint-Martin de Ré, the "island of the pariahs," as well as to Mauzac, in Haute-Garonne. In 1954, punishment was no longer obligatory, but there were still sixteen hundred *relégués* in France, a "residue" of the last vestiges of a shadowy world that was vanishing. They could be seen roaming on the edge of the Ile de France *département* because they did not dare go back to Paris, from which they were banned.[16] A new cycle began. Coming out of prison, the *relégués* were sent to the trial centers of Ré and Mauzac, where they stayed three years in a state of semifreedom while under observation. After this three-year "test period," their case files were supposed to contain work and lodging certificates to be submitted to the parole bureau of the prison administration. At this point, the Salvation Army was frequently asked to help *relégués* prepare to leave penitentiaries and to serve as their guarantors. The commission that examined the case files would then decide either on conditional liberation or on return to a "sorting" center for a new round of observation. This latter fate awaited most, who were redirected to centers in Lille, Rouen, Saint-Etienne, and Besançon—and ultimately many of them never left.

Thirty years after the elimination of penal colonies, a band of these men, a sort of separate race of detainees (who had "fallen into *relèg*"), still remained at the bottom of the incarceration scale, incapable of satisfying the requirements of provisional freedom. A few could be found in Normandy at the Salvation Army's job center, which was created in 1952 to receive *relégués* and also vagabonds, plus those liberated from prisons and psychiatric hospitals. This center functioned until 1972 and represented the last chance to extract the oldest of the *relégués* from the prison cycle. Most of these men, explained Jean-Claude Vimont, had been brutally treated by life. Many had followed the classic path leading from welfare to penitentiary colonies, then to the *Bat d'Af,* then to prison and relegation. Among them were poor farm workers who had lived on forest edges, ragpickers, carnies, *cloches* from the most sordid social margins, the indigent, a few former deportees, weak men shaken by the war who had turned into *collabos,* ex-convicts, and gypsies. Commission reports spoke of "bums" and "brutes" and the antisocial, almost all of them hereditary alcoholics, impulsive and mentally disturbed, men who had aged early, with deformed bodies, with advanced "degenerative stigmata." Many were described as "cretins," retarded, "instinctively perverse" men who had been institutionalized by penitentiaries and sometimes psychically scarred.

These portraits, which are presented in observation case files that have been conserved, tell of frightful situations. Here there is no attempt at dramatization or rhetorical effect; the files are just the product of a terrible institutional and social process that assembled all those defeated by existence, those overwhelmed by every circumstance. There were other examples: until 1972 the French Army maintained a disciplinary and penitentiary system that as far back as the 1830s had gathered the "residue of defectives."[17] Other nations did not necessarily do better: each conserved in prisons, asylums, and lodging centers men and women who would have been described in nineteenth-century terms as "the dregs of the great social machinery." Could any institution that combined repression, assistance, and stigmatization do anything but continually produce these new underworlds? With a few exceptions, at least they no longer exhibited them, perhaps in the hope that burying them would gradually lead to their extinction.

"SALAUDS DE PAUVRES!"

Proffered by a sickened Jean Gabin in the famous 1956 film by Claude Autant-Lara, *La Traversée de Paris* (Trip across Paris), the celebrated phrase *salauds de pauvres* (Rotten poor) bespoke the contempt falling upon the supernumeraries who were the weakest links in the underworld. Despite the many changes I have mentioned, the economic crises in the 1970s had seen the recrudescence of great poverty, which some believed had been eradicated. In fact, belief in the existence of the "false" and "bad" poor had never really been disavowed. Formerly a widely shared sentiment, it had become a more ideologically anchored position, an expression of an assertive political liberalism or else the heavy-handed security themes that were current in the last third of the twentieth century.

The poor were eternally suspect. "My study shows that the only beggars who should be given charity—the only ones who should be allowed to beg—are the infirm,"[18] a Breton reporter had noted in 1925. Ironically, the assistance and social protection measures that were advancing throughout the century merely accentuated this belief in the "responsibility" of the remaining poor for their situation. A new and singular figure developed between the world wars: the philosophical and happy tramp, a modern version of Diogenes, and especially the "millionaire" tramp. This variant—and new emanation of the "false poor"—was carried in a whole series of news items of somewhat debatable authenticity. Around 1925, Élie Richard reported that a university professor who had turned himself into a tramp was living on the banks of the Seine. "A philosopher resigned and defeated? It was said he earned a bit of money from confecting dissertations."[19] The edifying story of Marcel Jacquet, called "the king of *clochards*," also fed this idea. Founder in 1938 of a "committee of misery," a sort of indigents' mutual aid scheme offering work, Jacquet also launched a "tramp newspaper" whose financial pages were said to be written by a former adviser to Marthe Hanau, a fraudulent banker. This character had lived for a while in the sumptuous building owned by the Duke de Rothschild but was manifestly a crook who secured funds from many donors (including François Mauriac and Queen Wilhelmina) before he disappeared. He was finally arrested in August 1950 and sentenced to a correctional facility the following year.[20] But his personality stood out and people appreciated his truculence and rejoinders to the courtroom audience, and his story seemed to support the folklore around tramp figures. In 1959 Gilles Granger's film *Archimedes le clochard* featured a gentleman-tramp, aristocratic and cultivated, who did not want to spend the winter in prison and so decided to settle on the Côte d'Azur. The figure of a sympathetic and picturesque tramp, symbol of a new bohemia, spread widely in these years of growth and prosperity. However, some actual experiences of the margins would expose the baselessness of such representations. "The stories in the Sunday papers about beggars who die with two thousand pounds sewn into their trousers are of course lies," wrote Georges Orwell in *Down and Out in Paris and London*.[21] Apart from the permanence of traditional reactions to the "duplicity" of the poor, these fables indicated that the moral panic over vagabondage was fading. Sociologist Alexandre Vexliard's thesis (published in 1957) radically challenged the myth of the happy tramp (whether philosopher or millionaire) as a fiction "forged by the imagination of some vagabond in search of publicity, with the complicity of a reporter who had not bothered to check his sources."[22] Analyzing the stages of desocialization based on a series of case studies, Vexliard insisted on the profound anomie that characterized life on the street. The world of the tramp, wrote Vexliard, "has neither *structure* nor *organization*, meaning no *hierarchy* nor functional *divisions*."[23]

But the sequence of economic and social crises that began in the mid-1970s rapidly reactivated the figures of the bad poor and of those who profited from and exploited poverty, which illustrates how much the context determines apprehensions that are motivated by both fear and ideology. Over the long haul the tramp replaced the representations of the vagabond, but Alexandre Vexliard signaled in the introduction to *Clochard* the extreme difficulty of getting rid of the two poles that had long structured how the tramp phenomenon was assessed. On one hand was fear, the primacy given to the idea of individual responsibility and the desire to repress, and on the other hand was compassion, the notion of collective responsibility, and the desire to extend mutual aid and assistance.[24] In a more recent tense context, the resurgence of "bad poverty" is not surprising: these figures assume diverse forms, and sometimes earlier figures are revived such as "*assistés*" (welfare recipients) or "*chômeurs canapés*" (slackers) and others who "profit" from social services. New stereotypes may be added, such as "*punks à chiens*" (gutter punks), whose presence in France of the 1990s led to a flood of new municipal edicts against begging, which was sometimes countered by simply reviving classic edicts against the aggressive professional begging of "gypsies." But both strands clearly belong to the traditional suspicion of fake poverty.

This suspicion of the most vulnerable fractions of the social world—which we know to be constitutive of the underworld—also resurged in American and British debates in the 1980s, with the birth of a new and polarizing term (in some ways reminiscent of the nineteenth century): the *underclass*. First appearing in the 1970s in politics and journalism ("The American Underclass" was the *Time* cover story on August 29, 1977), this term enjoyed rapid media fame. It was notably used by the American journalist Ken Auletta in a series of articles for the *New Yorker* published in 1981 and gathered the following year in a book titled *The Underclass*.[25] Auletta assembled under this umbrella all the nation's nonassimilated people who were variously disqualified by unemployment or prostitution or addiction to drugs and alcohol. Use of the term spread from there, including in the social sciences. The American sociologist William Wilson, at the time a Harvard professor, used it at the end of the 1980s.[26] His perspective was principally *structural* since he classified as an "underclass" social categories definitively disqualified from (and thrown outside) the labor market. But other uses were proposed, notably spatial and behavioral, that clearly derived from the moral analyses of the previous century. In England, the debate crystallized around the positions taken by the American sociologist Charles Murray, whose first articles on the British underclass appeared in November 1989 in the *Sunday Times Magazine*.[27] "It is not a new concept. I grew up knowing what the underclass was; we just didn't call it that in those days." His definition exactly coincided with the traditional one of the bad poor, "the other kind of poor people," as he wrote in an explicit reference to Henry Mayhew and the social investigations of the nineteenth century.

Murray said three traits characterized these populations: the deliberate choice of idleness; the recourse to illegal, delinquent, or criminal activities; and the preponderance of "illegitimate" births. Laziness, crime, and immorality: here we find the traditional components of the underworld. These similarities were even more accentuated by the stress put on the last criterion, and on the stigmatization of single mothers that accompanied it. Illegitimate births were for Murray the principal indicator of the underclass, the reason "large numbers of young, healthy, low-income males choose not to take jobs."[28] One thinks of the famous study done at the end of the 1870s by the American sociologist Richard Dugdale. The study was conducted in the prisons of New York and identified a case study family, the Jukes, all indigents and criminals, who were closely followed over three generations. The study highlighted "fornication" and the consequent rate of "bastardy" as primarily responsible for this persistence. "In other terms," wrote Dugdale, *"fornication*, consanguineous or not, lies at the heart of their habits, flanked on one side by *pauperism* and on the other by *crime*."[29] The book was openly inspired by eugenics, and it recommended sterilization.

Without going as far as this, Murray's analyses relayed, almost term for term, certain conceptions of Victorian liberalism. The resulting debate was both scientifically and politically virulent. For Charles Murray as for Lawrence Mead,[30] the notion of an underclass was a powerful argument for defending neoconservative theories that "Welfare causes Poverty," meaning that welfare measures encourage laziness and lead to unemployment, to dislocation of the family, and to delinquency. The virulent critiques of the term "underclass" bore on both the improbable notion of "class" it carried and on the representations it conveyed. Not only did the adjective "under" introduce from the start the well-known semantic register of the vile, the low-down, and disruptive, but the term reactivated the whole imaginary of "dangerous classes" as it had been constructed in the nineteenth century: parasites, the bad poor, were fully responsible for their state, and ended up forming a nation apart that was a threat to the social order.[31] This view embraced clear ethnic and racial stigmatization because most of the groups placed under this label were not white in origin, being either West Indian or Hispanic, which tended to make underclass a "phenomenon of race."[32]

The intellectual clash produced (and still does) an immense bibliography and debates among sociologists that were as intense as their political and social presuppositions.[33] Most of the commentary was very critical of the term "underclass." Whether conceived from a structural perspective that stressed economic and behavioral determinants of attitudes said to be antisocial, or from an environmental perspective that stressed the poor neighborhoods as producers of marginality, the notion of an underclass was a "hybrid construction, half administrative and half journalistic," that continued to spur sensationalism. The underclass acted as a foil composed of marginal groups and social misfits, and it projected them into the heart of political and social discourse.[34] In that sense, the term was "irremediably polluted," noted Herbert Gans, another American sociologist.[35] However, the fact that such an expression could be forged at the end of the twentieth century and stimulate a debate that reactivated the issues of the "responsibility" and the "dangerousness" of the poor says a great deal about the insistent and insidious presence of the underworld imaginary—as if it were lying in ambush. "Underclass" has resurfaced in even more recent considerations of race.

UNDERBELLY OF THE ANTIWORLD

This persistence also has to do with chance, which continued to smile on stories of the underworld. Although the circulation of pulp fiction writing had considerably weakened in the second half of the twentieth century, cinema and then television took over, starting by simply adapting the printed series. The alleys of the *Cité*, the foggy side streets of Whitechapel, and images of shantytowns had never really stopped haunting our imaginations. One of the biggest successes of French "popular cinema" of the 1960s, the *Angélique* series, itself adapted from risqué novels, went back to the Court of Miracles and its affiliates, before turning to the slave markets along the Barbary coast.[36] From Vidocq to Jack the Ripper, via the great protagonists of "urban mysteries," graphic novels, serial fiction, and movies have known how to turn a profit from these topics. The interminable train of contemporary police and criminal TV series has explored more current territories of vice, but they have also made some structural innovations in dramatizing the social underside, mostly derived from Gothic motifs and representations.[37] The same is true of the immense *True Crime* production, a prolific genre in the Anglophone world that explores (generally quite crudely) the degraded social universe of the big cities.

One of the most notable and significant developments of the twentieth century was the gradual displacement of the underworld from the margins of society, where it was born and defined, toward the nether lands of other universes that maintained only a metaphorical relation with our social world. This migration conformed to a historical movement. The underworld, like roguery, appeared at a time when European societies were focused on themselves. Therefore, their underbelly was almost mechanically a reflection of the society above, even if some external elements—Egyptians, bohemians, or "savages" from distant countries—might sometimes complicate the scenario. In contrast, the twentieth century was marked by the exhaustion of sociocentric thought and shifted to conceptions of what the social world was—or could be—that were much more open and plural. The imaginary had accompanied this movement, and so we witnessed an accelerating multiplication of underworlds from elsewhere that were largely borne by the new media (Hollywood 3-D, graphic novels, video games). The more the medium seemed "modern" or "postmodern," the more the underworld tended to migrate toward other spatiotemporal dimensions.

In fact, this movement had begun in literature much earlier. H. G. Wells inaugurated it in 1895 with *The Time Machine*, whose action takes place in London at the end of the nineteenth century. Two antithetical descendants of the human race are sharing the Earth: the good Elois, refined and peaceful, who have made the planet a paradise regained, and the abominable Morlocks, deformed beings that haunt the entrails of the earth and periodically organize nighttime raids on the world above. Behind the dystopia lies a metaphoric description of England's end-of-the-century underworld, which obviously did not escape observers of the day. The journalist Thomas Holmes, whose *London Underworld* appeared in 1912, was worried about a representation of the inferno:

> Are we to have two distinct races! those below and those above? Is Wells' prophecy to come true; will the one race become uncanny, loathsome abortions with clammy touch and eyes that cannot face the light? Will the other become pretty human butterflies? I hope not, nay, I am sure that Wells is wrong!"[38]

If Wells's prophecy did not actually come true, it did give birth to an abundant production of fiction. The following year, the very serious Gabriel Tarde published a "fantasy" titled "Fragment of Future History" in the *Revue internationale de sociologie* in which civilization, confronted in the twenty-fifth century with a new Ice Age, takes refuge in the subterranean caverns, where (this time) it finds happiness and progress.[39] Whether utopias or dystopias, these fables belong to a tradition inaugurated by Plato describing Atlantis in the *Timaeus*. But the twentieth century gave the myth unprecedented scope. The acceleration of "popular literature" in fact saw a proliferation of subgenres—adventure novels, fantasies, prehistoric, futuristic, science fiction, *Weird Tales* and *Amazing Stories*—in which heroes plunge into subterranean worlds that depict (or make metaphoric versions of) the underbelly of our social worlds.[40] Some offered only a simple change of décor by developing the theme of a city of thieves or criminals lying buried underneath the above-ground city. In *La cité des tortures*,[41] René Thévenin imagined an underground city in the hands of a secret society of Chinese criminals who were trying to take down the West. But sometimes these are merely refuges populated by very ordinary bandits, as in *La cité des voleurs* by Maurice Level, or by pirates as with Leo Gestelys.[42] In most cases, these worlds under the earth, as with Wells, have engendered profound transformations that affect the nature of the underworld found there. The future author of *Phantom of the Opera*, Gaston Leroux, in his first novel, *The Double Life* (1901), imagined a society in the Paris catacombs without law or government that belonged to the very libertarian species called the Talpas, blind humanoids with pink groins. In 1935, the British novelist Joseph O'Neil conceived a utopian civilization established under all of England by the descendants of the Romans.[43] But the worlds described are often more threatening, and the subterranean ones are peopled with savages and monsters, creatures who recount their own stories of the underworld. A whole vein (illustrated by Arthur Conan Doyle, Henry Rider Haggard, and especially Edgar Rice Burroughs) used forgotten worlds peopled with races and civilizations but also with vanished monsters. Burroughs, who inaugurated the Pellucidar cycle with *At the Earth's Core* in 1914, is the most representative author of "lost race" novels. Rider Haggard, when he wrote the adventures of Allan Quartermain, may have remembered that he had been a rigorous social inquirer who had roamed rural England and was close to the Salvation Army, to which he dedicated two books.[44] But the earth's entrails contained a thousand other dangers: here, in *The Underground City*, people have been reduced to slavery; there, in *Agonie des civilisés*, the race of the uncultivated groans under the yoke of the lords above; farther down, beasts come out of the abyss (yetis, "cretins," gargoyles) to terrorize people. Closer to us, in the New York subway, lurk a sect of evil dwarves, the knights of Bernardus, but these stories also open windows onto parallel universes.[45] Whatever the danger that lurks in these depths, it usually recuperates the principal characteristics of the underworld—vice, evil, violence, moral and physical deformity—but it displaces them to worlds that are no longer metaphorically the inverse of our own society.

At almost the same time, American comics took charge of parallel worlds. In the wake of the dime novels at the end of the nineteenth century, in which solid detectives such as Nick Carter fought against fearsome bands of evildoers, and then the pulps at the beginning of the twentieth century that had added fantastic environments (the magazine *Weird Tales* was launched in 1923, its rival *Amazing Stories* in 1926), the comics of the 1930s confronted new superheroes with new underworlds. The superheroes of this kind of universe appeared in serried ranks: Detective Comics launched Superman in 1938, Batman the following year, and Wonder Woman in 1941; the rival Marvel, founded in 1939 to exploit this current, waited until after World War II to propel its own heroes, the *Fantastic Four*, then Spiderman, the Hulk, Daredevil, the X-Men, and Wonder Woman. Most of these characters worked to bring justice to the sordid underworlds of corrupt metropolises (Metropolis, Gotham City, Netherworld) that were dominated by evil and eroded by crime and corruption. Gotham, imagined in 1941 by Bob Kane and Bill Finger for the Batman series, is a rather transparent stand-in for New York City. But for the most part the urban worlds in which superheroes evolve are clearly situated outside our own time and place, transposing the traditional urban underbelly to fantasy worlds. Those who conceived Detective Comics invented the notions of *multiverses* (a set of parallel universes) and *infinite earths* in order to be able to shift plots and characters to other spatial and temporal dimensions. Yet their underworlds are just as deformed, dirty, vicious, and criminal as those back on earth, even though they prosper in fantastic realms. We should not be surprised to find the old Morlocks as communities of mutants taking refuge in the sewers of Manhattan. Adopting the creatures from *The Time Machine*, the producers of Marvel Comics turned them into victims of a vast massacre conducted by extraterrestrials.

These reworked underworlds became a staple of the cinema as special effects improved. The very prolific vein of modern zombies inaugurated by George Romero in *Night of the Living Dead* (1968) already offered a first transposition: a society of evil creatures issues from underground to transmit their deathlike contagion. But it was really John Carpenter's *Escape from New York* (1981) that made Manhattan into a prison city, and then Ridley Scott's *Blade Runner* (1982) popularized a bleak future, urban and apocalyptic, which has become a constant; it viewed the twenty-first-century city as a complete *underworld*. The action of Blade Runner takes place in Los Angeles in 2019, but it might be any urban space, New York or Hong Kong. "Part of *Blade Runner*'s plot takes place in the underworld of a megalopolis that could be a mixture of Chicago and New York if the two cities managed to fuse," declared director Ridley Scott.[46] The whole city has become an immense underworld: cold drizzle, oppressive, neon-lit, in which the "replicants" (androids outside the law) fight to survive. The film is characteristic of the vogue for cyberpunk that generated disturbing dystopias with bleak and alarmist visions of a near and post apocalyptic future in which information technology, artificial intelligence, and robotics lead to hybrid creatures that transform the planet into a vast underworld.

Since then, films, novels, comic books, and video games have constantly reactivated an imaginary that mixes science fiction, the fantastic, and the Gothic tradition. An immense success in the 2000s, the *Underworld* trilogy by Len Wiseman (the first film came out in 2003) dramatized a pitiless war that has been going on for hundreds of years between Lycans (sorts of werewolves) and vampires. The scenarios complicate this elementary plot with the relations between these two enemy species, who live partly in the underworlds of major cities, and humans, who are invested (despite themselves) in the millenarian confrontations. Much of contemporary American culture, including literature, seems hypnotized by the urban geography of underground worlds: Don DeLillo's novel *Underworld* (1997) combines the story of a former juvenile delinquent and the underground management of nuclear waste, and James Elroy's trilogy *Underworld USA* attempts a rereading of recent U.S. history from a somber and labyrinthine angle.[47]

Many video games, often marked by a mélange of violence, Gothic inspiration, and a medieval or fantastic ambience, also play with these themes. Some very successful ones, such as *True Crime* and *Grand Theft Auto* (1997), are set in contemporary underworlds (the players evolve in the criminal ghettos of New York, Chicago, or Los Angeles and are concerned with drugs, rackets, and prostitution, and settle violent scores with each other), but most of them favor the underbelly of an antiworld. The typical scenario invites players to explore subterranean worlds full of monsters or evil figures in "rogue-like games" or, in the case of "survival horror," a world of zombies, werewolves, gargoyles, or other monstrous "creatures." In *The Dark Descent*, the player is confronted with "Brutes," misshapen creatures whose left arm ends in a cutting blade; with "Grunts," disfigured human-oids whose left hand has claws; and with "Kaernks," invisible and amphibi-ous carnivores from another world. The dominant variation, though, is the heroic fantasy, which pits the hero against a band of deformed and vicious creatures that surge up from the degraded basements of our imaginations.

The steampunk movement is the fullest expression of this contempo-rary convergence between the underbelly of antiworlds and their origi-nal matrix. Also described as "retro-futurist," the steampunk imaginary is comprised of mixed time periods that implant modern—or modernized—plots into the nineteenth century, principally Victorian London.[48] Two novels launched this genre. In *Morlock Night* (1979), the American novelist K. W. Jeter reinvented the baleful tribe of *The Time Machine*, but the Mor-locks that Wells had projected into the future now recover the context of their original creation and thus invade the sewers of nineteenth-century London. The other founding text, Tim Powers's *The Anubis Gate* (1983), catapults its hero, Brendan Doyle, into a very Dickensian London. He plunges into the horror of the slums where he must confront sorcerers and bohemians, but also monsters, werewolves, cursed poets, and other wicked entities. Elements of science fiction, the fantastic, and the Gothic novel are combined in a particularly anachronic plot that makes connections between the underworlds of yesterday and today.[49] This vein has proven very prolific and has given birth to innumerable series, graphic novels, and films, many of them very successful, most notably *The League of Extraor-dinary Gentlemen*, a comic book by Alan Moire and Kevin O'Neil (1999). The plot unites four literary figures of the second half of the nineteenth century—Captain Nemo, Dr. Jekyll, Alan Quartermain, and the Invisible

Man—for a struggle against evil. A film was adapted in 2004, and the series has been pursued, constantly aggregating other characters, both heroes and evil geniuses. Older characters, including Vidocq, Sherlock Holmes, Jack the Ripper, Arsène Lupin, and Belphégor, have also been revived and confronted with mixed time-period underworlds that bizarrely combine the Gothic imaginary, industrial design, and fascination with the lower depths. The movement has even won over traditional superheroes who have gone back in time: Batman was sent to the 1880s in an antiquated *Gotham by Gaslight* where he meets Jack the Ripper.[50] The French pair of *bandes dessinées* (graphic novels) titled *Alchimie*[51] is rather emblematic of these improbable convergences that flout chronologies and superimpose imaginaries. The plot is set in Paris of 1842, where the serial writer Alexis Lerouge inquires into the subterranean plots of a secret society, the *Habits Noirs*. There he meets Vidocq, thanks to whom he manages to foil a plot whose origin lies in a secret of the Knights Templar. So the urban mysteries are mated with the esoteric and the fantastic, in amalgams that Eugène Sue could not have foreseen. The underworld pursues its chaotic itinerary, a sure sign that its potential for creative inspiration is far from exhausted.

10

Roots of Fascination

The cold, wet, shelter-less midnight streets of London; the foul and frowzy dens, where vice is closely packed and lacks the room to turn; the haunts of hunger and disease, the shabby rags that scarcely hold together;—where are the attractions of these things?[1]

This question by Charles Dickens in a preface to *Oliver Twist* could be asked regarding the whole of the lower depths and the underworld. Where indeed are the attractions of these things? How can we understand the fascination that the most sordid social realities constantly arouse; how can we apprehend the roots that underpin this imaginary? Such a question is even more difficult to answer because the underworld theme (like every social imaginary) lends itself to plural, polysemic, and evolving uses. Adventure, picturesque, utility, reform, protection—these are some of the justifications Vidocq (the former criminal who founded the state detective service) used in his *Mémoires*, and in fact this list covers many of the registers illustrated in the scenarios we have examined. Which motivation is foremost? Which can be dismissed as a simple alibi? How can we avoid value judgments, which should have no place in a history that is trying to understand how contemporaries gave meanings to their world? We must necessarily tackle these difficult questions without excluding ourselves—me the author, you the readers—from the inquiry. What are we looking for in these tales? What social, political, ideological, or moral needs do they answer? In short, how can we analyze the roots of a fascination that could be considered "unhealthy" but is also a powerful regulator of affects, sensibilities, and social aspirations?

MAKING SENSE OF SOCIAL REALITIES

Even though the underworld is certainly a "social imaginary," we cannot help wondering about its relation to the underlying realities represented therein: indigence, exclusion, prostitution, crime. As strong as the narrative or thematic codifications that govern these stories may be and the powerful effects their presence has in the media, real underworld situations remain elusive apart from the texts that convey them. Yet it would be untenable to radically dissociate the two. Something must necessarily be made transparent via these stories: hints of places, gestures, words, and fragments of social experience that cannot be neglected, inasmuch as the world of margins and transgressions might remain otherwise inaccessible. Moreover, what historian would not be interested in the tenuous, uncertain, and often unfathomable relations between the world of representations and the world of actual experiences? Undeniably, these texts transpose into literary figures some fragments of what is real just as much as they subvert them through either moral judgment, sensationalism, the picturesque, or parody—all the characteristic phenomena of "popular" culture.[2] Separating the true from the false obviously makes no sense inasmuch as the "false" comes to produce the true, here as elsewhere. These representations, even the most improbable, have had effects, have aroused reactions, and have led to social and legal measures to modify these realities. We have a historical requirement to circumscribe the range of experiences engendered by these stories.

However, the insistence with which writers have claimed to be doing "documentary" work may arouse suspicion. Observers and social investigators used "I saw. . . ." as a veritable leitmotiv, and they never stopped trying to prove their good faith, to justify their approach, to announce the protocols they had followed. Most of the novelists did the same. Eugène Sue opened the way by recalling that the goal of his book was indeed to "know those classes whom poverty crushes, hardens, and depraves."[3] Octave Féré, author of the *Mystères de Rouen* in 1845, is more explicit: nothing in his work "was done lightly or without study. Thanks to the interest of reading a novel, we were able to offer some details that would have been tiresome or foul if deprived of this assistance, or exposed nakedly."[4] *Les vrais mystères de Paris* (The true mysteries of Paris) by Vidocq proclaimed its mission in the title. "Fruit of labor, of observation, and a whole life's experience," these mysteries intend to be a "useful book" and to reestablish the authenticity of things, when others make a travesty of them. Thus the requirement to be truthful accompanied these "realistic" stories and novels, which in that era were ascribed a clear educational function.[5]

Reporters were even more insistent about veracity. Every "investigation" proclaimed its authenticity, often in a peremptory (and hence suspect) fashion: "The portrait we have sketched of this sort of white slave trade is exact. We have not invented anything, there is no embellishment or exaggeration."[6] Each reporter offered us the discovery, thanks to him or her, of the hidden reality of the miserable classes, the poor, the perverted, the felons. They assumed a "public safety" mission. From the first lists of medieval beggars to the warnings by modern reporters, the justification remained the same: by unveiling the methods of miscreants, honest folks were warned of the dangers that lie in wait for them. In effect, this was the supreme justification of stories that were accused of depicting abject situations. "By indicating to all honest people *How they rob us, how they kill us*," explained the private detective Eugène Villiod in the book that bears this title, "we want to teach them *ways to avoid being killed or robbed*."[7] All of these tales, all of these articles, all of these journalistic exposés that lingered over the lower depths of society defended themselves with similar rationales. Here is how the celebrated *Gazette des Tribunaux* (Court Gazette) justified its existence in its 1825 launch prospectus: "It will be a veritable service to all classes of society, especially businessmen, to reveal to them in a newspaper each day, not only the names of evildoers, but even the methods of fraud and swindle they are using." Some writers, including Vidocq, gave even more precise recommendations, making their books veritable vigilante manuals: "The reader who wishes to have nothing to fear from these climbing burglars: never leave your key on your door, do not hide your buffet key, for they will infallibly find it, keep it in your pocket;" and a further admonition: "Readers, beware of those individuals who when everybody is leaving the church or theater, try to push inside; hang on to your fob pocket watch, never carry a money wallet."[8] Explaining the argot is part of this endeavor because this "filthy language" is merely the criminal classes' way of dissimulating their methods and confidence tricks.

Do these stories truly reveal the lives, organization, and behavior of the "lower classes" on the margins of society? Some historians do find documentary value in these sources. Analyzing the lists of beggars and vagabonds at the end of the Middle Ages, the Polish historian Bronislaw Geremek observed a "character of ethnographic reportage"[9] and consequently defended their "historical realism." He explained that these nomenclatures use the technical language and categories of beggars themselves; therefore they "reflect" the actual organization of marginal milieux. Such sources, he said, "are not the effect of an external observer's classifying view but translates the internal organization of the criminal milieu. The observer does not describe but uncovers the realities of this milieu and decodes the language that it uses to present itself."[10] The documentary value of these texts was held to be confirmed by contemporary legal documents, especially interrogations, which adopted the same categories. Geremek modified this interpretation a few years later, specifying that in addition to the realities of marginal milieux these texts offer "a general image of 'ideological' attitudes and social behaviors toward indigence and the marginal milieux."[11] Some historians of the nineteenth century have supported similar views. In his famous *Laboring Classes and Dangerous Classes*, Louis Chevalier tried to validate by demographic and "biological" analysis the hypothesis that a population of pauperized migrants existed that was particularly vulnerable to crime and delinquency.[12] Some sources, such as Henry Mayhew's grand *London Labour and the London Poor*, have won the trust of many British historians, especially due to Mayhew's methods of elaboration and the interviews done with the humble folk of London in the 1850s. John Tobias saw this opus as a pertinent source for writing the history of the British criminal classes, and others such as Eileen Yeo, E. P. Thompson, and Donald Thomas also have confidence in Mayhew.[13] More recently, British and American specialists in the history of crime, although acknowledging the many biases in stories that may express the obsessions and the fantasies of elites, judge that some realities "from below" are nevertheless accessible through them.[14] Concerned to understand how criminal networks in nineteenth-century England were organized and functioned, historian Heather Shore endeavored to take seriously descriptions in tales that were based on real-life events and individuals.

I stand in this more nuanced position. These stories are undeniably teeming with notes, descriptions, and ephemera that can be used to reconstruct something of the actual lives of the downtrodden. Places (hovels, slums, and ragpickers' dens) have been quite precisely depicted. Institutional reports (from prisons, workhouses, and penal colonies) render tableaux that detail how they function. "Here is some indication of how food can be procured," said Clémence Royer in describing in *The Beggars of Paris* the operation of *"diners à un sou"* (penny diners), and we know by letters addressed to Eugène Sue how attentive readers were to the accuracy of his descriptions, how much they learned from reading the book, and that they sometimes even offered corrections.[15] Individual portraits, typical figures, practices, and behaviors do show through. Here we find an old woman who sells *arlequins* (leftovers), there some urchins with shaved heads who are playing in a stream, farther along a convict entirely covered with tattoos. There is indeed something about the real poor, the real criminals, to be found in these stories and photographs of the lower depths and underworld. But, in fact, not all of them are valid. It is easy to distinguish between investigators such as Parent-Duchâtelet, Henry Mayhew, and Jack London who immersed themselves deeply in their terrain of inquiry and tried to transcribe real people's speech, words, and destinies, on one hand, and sensationalists who merely recopied the same stereotypical descriptions, on the other. From the best documented of these stories we may draw evidence that enables us to understand a bit better the life of those who have left few traces. Therefore, quite a range of social history understandably relies on these texts to try to reconstruct the lives of the most disadvantaged.

But this knowledge cannot rest solely on fragmentary data or even on a meager sample of witness testimony (which is often indirect or secondhand anyway). The overall pictures composed from these sources are quickly overtaken by other intentions that derive from a desire to classify and to label. As we have seen, this was particularly the case with the nomenclatures of beggars and criminals that have flourished since the end of the Middle Ages. By foregrounding the internal "structures" of marginal milieux, by dividing individuals with heterogeneous trajectories and occupations into categories, these representations may be merely giving some order to the splintered and uncontrollable universe of the world's "useless ones." And the confirmations via legal documents invoked as "proof" by Geremek might just as easily derive from the circulation of these descriptions, whose categories were adopted by magistrates, bailiffs, and witnesses to "translate" deviant realities. There is scarcely any structure or any organization in the lives of the most deprived, explained the sociologist Alexandre Vexliard.[16] Analyzing the trial of Cartouche and his gang in 1720s Paris (in which 777 persons were implicated, with 350 arrests), Patrice Peveri has carefully decoded the hierarchy inside the world of thieves. The Cartouche gang formed less a "band" than an anomic world of small artisans of delinquency who associated on an ad hoc basis and then passed off their booty to hundreds of small fences. Parisian truancy was composed of a nebula of small "habitual thieves" who, contrary to the representations of literary roguery, had neither specialties nor exclusive techniques. They did a bit of everything; it was a question of opportunity. Of course, there was also a professional culture, but it remained a far cry from the hierarchies depicted in underworld tales.[17] These tales sprang from the frisson of apprehension and a desire for control in a changing society; people were trying to impose a grid of social stratification. Was the world of the marginals not just as differentiated, structured, and ordered as the new division of labor? Was the society of "scoundrels" really so demarcated from the rest of the social world? By insisting on the structure and specificity of this universe, these nomenclatures unified heterogeneous groups and made them into homogeneous entities, which is one of the stakes in the invention of the category of the "underworld."

Relations of an "objective" order that can be established between these texts and the real world have a totally different nature. Above all, they are contextual. Periods of crisis and insecurity (whether economic, social, or spiritual) coincide with the production of stories of the underworld. For example, the emergence of the fundamental theme of false poverty was inseparable from the famines, wars, and rising indigence that marked the end of the Middle Ages. Similarly, it was in a very troubled social and intellectual context that roguery emerged in the sixteenth and eighteenth centuries. Nor can we understand the underworld of the nineteenth century without the multiform anxiety born with the emergence of pauperism and its powerful replay in the 1880s. And, obviously, it was in the wake of the economic and social crises of the twentieth century that the debate on social exclusion and the underclass arose. A correlation has been established between actual dysfunction and elites' judgments about it. Fears, anxieties, panics—plus political contexts and ideological preoccupations—are just as much productive of the underworld as are poverty and criminal pressure. Real perils or fantasized perils? It is impossible to separate them, particularly inasmuch as the sources—reports and statistics from the police, the judiciary, scholars, and accounts from the press, the audiovisual media, and fiction—are intermingled, responding to and validating (or invalidating) each other. Thus we must think of these synchronies as both a product of social crisis and an expression of the anxiety and vulnerability felt by elites. The sources express, exacerbate, and simultaneously euphemize social worries. But these "objective" relations are also strategic, expressing the clear objective to stigmatize, to label, to moralize. They are also "performative," weighing on attitudes and behavior, arousing actions, whether charitable or repressive, emotional or rational. The imaginary never stops influencing the reality.

NORMALIZING SOCIETY

Representations of the underworld have always benefited from wide dissemination ranging from networks of print peddling to those of mass culture, and they become complicated by the functions of identifying culprits and normalizing social behavior. The stigmatization of the Other is an inherent reflex: the first lists appeared in order to signal suspect individuals, nomenclatures were organized to better recognize them. Thus the universe of the underworld defines and distinguishes all the undesirables: beggars, vagabonds, all types of migrants and drifters, the Irish, bohemians, foreigners, and so forth. By identifying the diverse figures as foils, then by amalgamating them in a community presented as structured and homogeneous, these stories consolidated the contours of the dominant group, which conferred identity and cohesion on it. Eugène Sue, who had signaled in the opening of *The Mysteries of Paris* the interest and "efficacy of contrasts," explains this normalizing unction as an inverted mirror. "It is perhaps a good idea to make certain characters, existences, and faces speak, in a work of art, in all their grimness, energy, and crudeness. Such representations of evil might serve to repulse the reader and propel him toward experiences of a completely different kind."[18] This is the reason these representations are particularly propagated in periods of social opacity or confusion, such as the first third of the nineteenth century. But the need to point the finger at figures of the Other is a constant in all societies. "The study of individual and social abnormalities undoubtedly contributes to deeper knowledge of the sources of a healthy and normal life, in both individuals and societies," noted the Dutch criminologist Gerard van Hamel in September 1901.[19] Their normalizing role is decisive: not only does knowledge of the margins delimit the circle of honest folk and solder the group by highlighting figures of disorder, but it also ensures a conformity of conduct. Bad conduct is drifting, laziness, drunkenness, sexual license—and this is the abyss of poverty, crime, and degradation to which such conduct leads. There is a constant intention to normalize, and a concern to dissuade and repress, and to impose social control.

This is how the invention of the underworld was able to play a role in the cultural order analogous to the one Michel Foucault attributed to prison in the management of illegality.[20] To identify a contrasting marginality, stabilize its contours, diffuse its images—all contributes to edifying a better normalized society. Thus Victorian "respectability" was partly the product of the thousands of pages depicting its inverse, the hordes of "occasional" workers brutalized by gin, given to cockfights and sexual debauchery. Republican democracy was not really established in France until the "rabble" of the underworld was definitively crushed after the Paris Commune. In the Mexico of "Porfiriato" (the years of authoritarian modernization corresponding to the presidency of Porfirio Diaz from 1876 to 1910), the country's elites forged and disseminated terrible images of the underworld that were partly real and partly fantasized in order to valorize a decent middle class and to consolidate a modern Mexican nation.[21] A whole series of working-class neighborhoods, principally the *colonias* where new migrants had settled—La Bolsa, La Maza, Valle Gomez, Morelos—were depicted as circles of hell that were peopled with the insane, alcoholics, brutes, degenerates, and assassins. The *pulquerias*, dives where *pulque* (a popular alcohol make from the agave cactus) flowed freely, were painted as the heart of an intolerably delinquent subculture. The Belém prison became the symbol of squalid *bajos fondos*, the lair of criminal and perverted monsters—and an immense bordello, too, because there was no clear separation of the sexes. Through thousands of petty crime notices and *notas rojas*, inquiries, brochures, and novels like the famous *Bandidos de Rio Frio* by Manuel Payno, whose phenomenal success in 1889 marked the apogee of the Mexican serial novel,[22] those in power encouraged the spreading of a grand national narrative designed to forge a policed and normative nation. An analogous scenario was at work in Germany in the course of its unification: the new elites proffered images of a terrifying underworld in order to specify and impose the norms requisite for the new state.[23]

Yet we should beware of overly univocal readings and interpretations; there was a mixture of processes in the reception and use of these texts. To identify the active fraction of the dangerous classes and to erect it into a bogeyman was, ironically, a means of decriminalizing and integrating a major portion of the working class. Apaches and hooligans would pay for the rest, and their stigmatization and banishment gave a sort of carte blanche to those redeemed. This was indeed the logic of the "residue" as it had been forged by Charles Booth and the late Victorian elites. It is hard to know how the moralizing process functioned and how far it reached. We must also acknowledge the element of eroticization underlying these texts, the desire for social and sexual transgression that they sometimes vicariously satisfied.[24] We do know that the culture of respectability and gentility of the manners of ordinary Londoners was accompanied by the consumption of spectacles of rare violence.[25] And we know of the reversibility (despised/admired) surrounding the figure of the notorious criminal and also of the distanced and amused view that some citizens had of the crooks' world. Discovering their methods also meant appropriating their world and taking vicarious part in their revenge.

CONDEMNING SOCIAL ILLS

Nor can we overlook the "empathic" and condemnatory functions of these representations. Individuals' intentions are always complex: mingled with the concern for others is an undeniable personal satisfaction from "good works." Many of these stories highlighted a social ill or condemned a situation judged to be unacceptable. This was the case for philanthropists, who tried as best they could to relieve suffering or cure evils; this was the case for social observers, almost all of whom were motivated by a reform project or a social welfare plan; this was also the case for many novelists and some journalists, whose reportages instigated significant reform measures. And we cannot forget the investment (sometimes heavy and difficult) of thousands of individuals who believed that their writings and actions would relieve suffering.

Philanthropists in their diversity were among the most active producers of underworld stories. Whether in the Victorian slums or the New York tenements, in the prisons of Restoration France or the penal colonies of the Third Republic, thousands of "slum travelers," missionaries, clergy, the Salvation Army, and the laity (both men and women) spent their time and energy to achieve what they thought to be just. Benjamin Appert, studying the penitentiary system in the era of the Royal Prison Society, was an ethnologist of the lower depths and an incarnation of romantic philanthropy who traversed the infamous neighborhoods in the 1820s, visiting slums and shacks, hospices and prisons, to the point of ruining himself in the creation of a colony for liberated convicts.[26] David Nasmith, founder of the City Mission Movement, first in Glasgow in 1825 and then in Edinburgh, London, and most of the nation's cities, died in poverty at age forty. James Adderley, who gave up his aristocratic life to found a "social colony" in Bethnal Green, became a priest and joined the General Strike of British dockers before founding a new church. In another vein, in Paris in June 1879 the Baron of Livois opened the first night refuge, the first institution in France to offer free lodging to the homeless. Its two dormitories could receive a hundred of the homeless for a maximum stay of three nights.[27] Ten years later, the organization had opened three other houses with a total of more than 950 beds, which led to the creation of similar municipal provision for the homeless. It is estimated that close to half a million women (excluding nuns) were engaged in philanthropic activities in England in the 1890s.[28] None of these people resembled the others; each was following personal beliefs, as well as moral, religious, and ideological premises that were seldom questioned. But all of them published stories that nourished

the underworld imaginary, and despite a variety of backgrounds and different projects, all of them did so to remedy situations that they considered to
be inhumane and intolerable.

Investigators and social observers, who are sometimes barely distin-
guishable from philanthropists, were also trying to "denounce" current
conditions. Their motivations, however, were more complex: almost all of
them forcefully described insalubrity, overcrowding, and the tragic living
conditions of the laboring classes, but many of them did so while point-
ing to the carelessness, immorality, and drunkenness of the poor—in short,
to their responsibility for their own situation. This kind of story seemed
to be more constrained by ideological postures and frameworks than
others. Among "economists" and "reformers," Louis Chevalier correctly
noted, understanding the system prevailed over observing its defects.[29]
And their intentions were also different: what they produced was prag-
matic knowledge, oriented to action, concerned to lead the way to reform
or to resolve conflicts. Observers were trying to place themselves "at the
tiller of the social machine," in the expression of Parent-Duchâtelet.[30] The
result was that the effects of dramatization or attenuation hung over their
descriptions. Whereas some of them constructed an apocalyptic image of
poverty—Engels in 1844 postulated the "dehumanization" of workers, and
Mary Carpenter in 1850 spoke of "classes about to perish"[31]—in order to
promote reforms, others such as Villermé tried to signal the overall benefi-
cial effects of mechanization. Each investigator endeavored to tame poverty
according to a particular ideological framework, with a consequence loss of
the denunciatory impact—except in cases such as Charles Booth's, where
the investigation resulted in conclusions that were accepted as scientifically
valid by everybody.

Therefore, it was up to the novelists and journalists, whose writings were
often confused with each other throughout the nineteenth century, to perform the heavy task of describing the world as it really was and to spotlight
its malfunctioning. Literature, and principally the novel, were invested
with almost exaggerated ambitions: to expose the social world in the "full
extent of its agitation," in Balzac's phrase, to speak truth, and to envision a
better future. "What do your salon manners mean to me in a society that
could not live one day if it lost its snitches, its jailers, its executioners, its

dens of gambling and debauchery, its cabarets and entertainment?" wrote Jules Janin in 1829. Therefore it was important to know who the "principal agents of social action" were, even when these writers produced were treatises of moral ugliness.[32] Victor Hugo, prince of the romantic movement who increasingly posed as the conscience of the century, was no doubt the writer who best incarnated this vocation. He began in 1829, when *The Last Day of a Condemned Man* raised the issue of penal punishment in all its factual horror: putting convicts in irons in the Bicêtre courtyard, the appalling world of prisons, the solitude and anguish of the detainee. In 1834, *Claude Gueux*, inspired by a true story, pushed Hugo's study of incarceration even further and explicitly linked crime and social issues. Finally, *Les misérables* (begun around 1845 and completed in 1862) was his most accomplished representation of the Parisian lower depths. Poverty, prostitution, penal colony, crime, police, street urchins, rioting, physical and moral hideousness—nothing was lacking from the tableau, or from Hugo's general condemnation of a society that not only tolerated, but actually produced, these horrors. The writer's ambition in revealing the extent of social damnation was to bring about a fictional reparation. In this sense, *Les misérables* was almost an antinovel of the lower depths because the intention was "to show the ascension of a soul, and to take the opportunity to depict in their tragic reality the lower depths from which it came, in order that human societies become aware of the hell on which they are based, and finally that they think of bringing a dawn to this tenebrism."[33]

But Hugo was not the only reformer; many novelists of the day seconded his denunciation, more or less effectively. Eugène Sue was not the least of them, and his hope for the *Mystères de Paris* was to "have awakened some noble sympathy for the upstanding and courageous and unmerited unfortunates, for sincere repentance, for simple and naïve honesty."[34] Sue passed almost unwittingly from critique to social reform, ranging from a proposed bank for the poor (mocked by Marx) to the remaking of the parliamentary system. Féval, in the preface to the *Mystères de Londres*, speaks of a "service rendered to humanity in revealing the vices, [in order to] destroy the laws that perpetuate poverty among the people, and the prejudices that arrest any social progress."[35] In England, the industrial novels burgeoning at the end of the 1830s were also texts of combat and contestation.[36]

This was, of course, true of the novels of Charles Dickens, whose *Oliver Twist*, published in 1837, established the enduring images of workhouses and the exploitation of children in the London underworld, but also of Elizabeth Gaskell (*Mary Barton* in 1848), Richard Horne (*The Dreamer and the Worker* in 1851) and Charles Kingsley, whose *Alton Locke* in 1849 told the life of a Chartist émigré who on the basis of his own past condemned the misery in which little people lived, the scandal of the sweating system, and the need for moral protest. Some authors did not conceal the militant dimension of their narratives. Himself a former Chartist, the radical George Reynolds defined his mission in the epilogue of the first volume of *Mysteries of London*: "There are but two words in the moral alphabet of this great city; for all virtues are summed up in the one, and all vices in the other: wealth/poverty. We have to establish a new moral, teaching a great lesson to each social class. For we are an enemy of the oppressor, a champion of the oppressed."[37]

These novels do not always defend the same values. Some are idealistic reactions against selfishness and utilitarianism, others express a nostalgia for a preindustrial England when the authority of the gentry and the parish harmoniously ordered society, and others are more radical or defend an ideal of sentimental interventionism, but they all blame (often in harsh terms) a social world that is degenerate, violent, vicious, and heading for its downfall. Later on, in the 1880s and 1890s, another literature of crisis took up the flame. Those who had pointed to *urban* or *new slums* now fixated on another abscess—the East End's world of poverty and prostitution, with its bands of youth spiraling into violence—but nevertheless they continued the tradition of condemnation. In fact, with the exception of the pulp novel in the vein of Aristide Bruant and Guy de Téramond, which dominated the fiction market and was content to align with pejorative and populist representations, most novelists who set their work in the underworld did so from a critical perspective.

By the turn of the century, literature was allowing other voices to be heard that abandoned the posture of accusation, which was considered overly conformist and moralizing and too close to the tear-jerking descriptions in popular fiction. Some literature started to praise the liveliness, energy, and inventiveness of the underworld. Arthur St. John Adcock in *East End Idylls*

(1897) and Walter Besant in *East London* (1901) tried to defend the noisy but positive effervescence of these neighborhoods. The young Alf, whom Clarence Rook featured in *The Hooligan Nights* (1899),[38] was indisputably a lout, but he was also a well-dressed lad and a good son who possessed virtues and skills. In *Maggie: A Girl of the Streets* (1893), the American Stephen Crane refrained from any sentimentalism in favor of an interior and brutal representation of slum life. The novel dramatized the decline and death of a young prostitute, but it avoided any miserabilism by espousing Maggie's values and refusing to draw a clear line between morality and immorality, obviously an unacceptable viewpoint according to the puritan ethic. Crane adopted the model of how romantic bohemia was represented, and so his underworld was promoted as an antidote to the stifling values of bourgeois life. Charles-Louis Philippe's *Bubu de Montparnasse* (1901) moved in the same direction: valorizing the pimp's job, the freedom of the strong man, and even the power conferred by syphilis.

By the end of the century, reporters and journalists became the most constant and most effective social critics, which testified to the evident supremacy of the press and the gradual takeover of the mass media. The inquiry by William Stead into the trade in young London virgins (see chapter 5) was ethically ambiguous, and its "sensational" and commercial dimensions were undeniable, but that verdict would be reductive. Stead was the son of a Congregational minister, and he considered journalism as the instrument of a new moral crusade. In Newcastle, he contributed to the creation of the Charity Organization Society; he was very close to Reverend Andrew Mearns, whose *Bitter Cry of Outcast London* he published in 1883, and to William Booth and Salvation Army circles. Moreover, it was in close collaboration with Catherine Booth, the general's wife, and with Josephine Butler, a figurehead of feminism and the British abolitionist movement, that *The Maiden Tribute* was undertaken.[39] Stead saw this exposé as a sort of new *Uncle Tom's Cabin*, centered this time on the slavery of prostitutes. In fact, the uproar following publication contributed to passage of the Criminal Law Amendment Act, which raised the age of sexual consent from thirteen to sixteen years old. And Stead faced his imprisonment in Holloway with courage. Tradition has it that he even proudly celebrated the anniversary of his incarceration each year by donning his prison uniform.

American "muckrakers" extended this conception of journalism that was oriented to reform and social amelioration but added a more social and political tone.[40] These reporters had often formerly covered *fait divers* and had explored the city's underbelly to chronicle crimes and misdemeanors; now they went on to investigate local corruption, principally the collusion between the police and criminals, but also economic circles and business trusts. The muckraking movement had been inaugurated by Jacob Riis's first inquiries into the New York slums in the early 1890s (see chapter 4). Riis broke with the customary grave moralizing tone that was contemptuous of vice and he adopted an alternative ethic that insisted on the energy and vitality that emanated from slum districts.[41] However, his criticism remained limited to descriptions of the scandalous living conditions in the tenements in southern Manhattan. But Riis did achieve some concrete effects, including the destruction of several slum zones. Reporters who came after him were more daring in offending the powerful. In 1902, articles published by Lincoln Steffens in *McClure's* magazine denounced the municipal corruption that corroded all American cities (in 1904 they were collected in a volume titled *The Shame of the Cities*); Ida Tarbell's articles revealed the illicit or violent activities of the great oil trusts, Rockefeller in the lead, to eliminate competitors.[42] The same year, Upton Sinclair spent seven weeks among workers in the Chicago slaughterhouses and canneries. "They told me their stories, one after one, and I made notes of everything. In the daytime, I would wander about the yards, and my friends would risk their jobs to show me what I wanted to see."[43] The resulting book, *The Jungle* (1906), skips over none of these terrible conditions, evoking the degradation, the alcoholism, and the prostitution that ravaged working-class neighborhoods in Chicago.[44] Here, too, the reporting had immediate consequences. Theodore Roosevelt's administration was very sensitive to reporters (the term "muckraker" was coined by Teddy himself),[45] and it ultimately appointed a commission to examine working conditions in the food industries, which led to creation of the Food and Drug Administration in 1930.

Beyond these practical and institutional effects, muckraking journalism just as strongly influenced the discipline of sociology that was currently developing at the University of Chicago. Robert Park, one of its principal figures, never forgot that he had started as a police reporter in Minneapolis; he later presented himself as "one of the first and most modest muckrakers."[46] The Chicago School of Sociology, as much by some of its methods (interviews and life stories) as by its subjects (crime, delinquency, gangs, vagabonds—mostly devoted to forms of social disorganization in the big city), developed in close proximity to investigative journalism.

This type of reporting was clearly less developed in France. However, at the beginning of the twentieth century, a reporter named Jacques Dhur mounted spectacular investigations—of the penal colony in New Caledonia, abusive confinements in mental asylums, the mistreatment of victims in military prisons—that were published in the columns of the *Journal*.[47] But Dhur was handicapped by his crude style, and he often used sensational rhetoric that discredited him. Albert Londres dealt with the same subjects after World War I, but he was subtler and much more effective. It was the same underworld that drew his attention—the penal colony, the disciplinary battalions in Algeria, insane asylums, the white slave trade in Argentina—but he did so while trying to banish melodramatic effects or overt pathos. Londres rarely stated a moral but instead let it emerge from collections of anecdotes or sketched encounters in dialogue. His more distanced (even ironic) tone lent more weight to his writing, which could then give momentum to legal corrective measures (as in the case of reforms to the Cayenne penal colony in 1923, and to military prisons the following year). The Londres style had a few emulators who also tried more delicately to put the "pen into the wound". In 1925, Pierre Rocher, in *Le populaire de Nantes*, delivered a long investigation into the slums and "leprosy of Nantes."[48] His itinerary through that city's underworld, more suggestive than descriptive, featured the evocative power of select scenes, brief notations, portrait sketches. "I saw and I told what I saw, so that people would know an evil that surpasses even what is expected." The series, like those of Londres, ended with a condemnatory plea addressed to the authorities. Henry Danjou, who wrote for the *Quotidien*, *Paris-Soir*, and *Détective*, also tried (especially in his 1932 investigation of juvenile correction houses, *Enfants du Malheur*) to offer short tales that were meant to be typical cases, to analyze without judging, "to penetrate each misery."[49] But the exercise was difficult, and painting the underworld was always liable to result in exoticism or sensationalism. Most journalists did not escape this more spectacular vein. Evoking Louis Roubaud, yet another writer about the penal colonies and correctional houses in the interwar period, the journalist Alexis Danan later wrote: "If this misery overwhelms him, it is as a spectacle, not as the expression of errors and injustice."[50]

But there was a fine line between the concern to do justice, to denounce intolerable situations, and their sensational or voyeuristic exploitation. In 1892, an American reformer, Miss Helen Campbell, who had already written a work on the open wounds of New York, teamed up with reporter Thomas Knox and a police superintendent at the head of the city's detective bureau to publish an even more alarmist but richly illustrated tableau of the crimes and immorality plaguing New York.[51] As the publisher stated on the title page, it contained "hundreds of thrilling anecdotes and incidents, sketches of life and characters, humorous stories, touching home scenes, and tales of tender pathos, drawn from the bright and shady sides of the Great Under World of New York."[52]

DESIRE FOR THE UNDERWORLD

As a general rule, respectable people do not like to read unpleasant things, wrote the American journalist Hutchins Hapgood in 1910. "If they pay attention at all to 'low' things, it is for charitable purposes. They do so to relieve distress or their own consciences."[53] Any other kind of attraction would be deemed perverse or immoral. No doubt he was right about those motives that were readily recognized and admitted. But do respectable people always admit all the motives that govern their lives? Perhaps we should pay attention to a few less respectable motives: "In repulsive objects we find something charming. Each day we take one more step towards Hell," wrote Charles Baudelaire in "To the Reader" that opens *Les fleurs du mal* (1861).[54] Poverty, crime, and filth have always seized attention. In each of us there is a fascination with low and abject things, and we could easily furnish a whole anthology to illustrate the "base instincts that attract us to a horrible spectacle."[55] It is much more difficult to explain a penchant that mingles complex and sometimes contradictory feelings. Moreover, the historian is probably not best equipped to venture into such a psychological and social labyrinth. Julia Kristeva maintains that any sentiment of abjection is divided into two phases, first repulsion and then fascination.[56] And horror has a counterpart in the admiration it exerts in the simultaneous process of individuation: it "isolates by making incomparable, incomparably unique," wrote Paul Ricœur in *Time and Narrative*, "horror is inverted veneration."[57]

The erotic and sexual dimension that partly governs this desire for the underworld is no doubt more easily detectable. Sometimes it responds merely to very material motivations: Isn't the underworld first of all the space of prostitution? So one could go there as to a brothel, or consider it a vast hunting ground open to all sexual possibilities. Recall from chapter 6 that the society people featured in Jean Lorrain's *La maison Philibert* were waiting for the apaches to procure them young women for sex parties. And Lorrain himself never hid the fact that his taste for the Grand Dukes' Tour sprang from the possibility of finding young boys available to complete his night. Proust, in *La recherche du temps perdu*, lent similar practices to Baron Charlus: "For it falls to my lot, now and then, like the Caliph who used to roam the streets of Baghdad in the guise of a common merchant, to condescend to follow some curious little person whose profile may have taken my fancy."[58] And such practices were even more frequent in the colonial world, site of all forbidden desires, the source of a sexual tourism that (whether inside or outside "reserved" quartiers) also made empires out of vast spaces of carnal domination.

But the underworld contains other attractions, other forms of seduction similar to those that exist in other communities, especially religious ones—a communion of sentiments has often united the men and women who descend into the slums. Fraternities, and even more sororities, were born of this shared experience, often partly connected to homosexual desires, whether effective or repressed.[59] For many women, especially, charity in the underworld was a means of acquiring independence and freedom, giving them a sense of community and gender solidarity. It was also possible that a sister soul might be found at the bottom of the worst lower depths, among the admirable women who were struggling against poverty and vice, or even among the lost girls that benevolent women were trying to save from the abyss. This is partly the meaning of *A Princess of the Gutter*

(1895), a novel by the very prolific L. T. Meade, that describes the ambiguous relationship between a young Cambridge graduate, Joan, and a young delinquent from the Old Nichol Rookery in London. But love in the slums could just as well involve the other sex: marriages were frequent in the "social colonies" that the Methodists or Congregationalists established in the London underworld at the end of the nineteenth century, which acted as a sort of matrimonial agency![60]

At worst, investment in the underworld might take the form of a renunciation, or of an alternative to sexuality. Yet eroticism did emanate from the spectacle of the slums.[61] It could be very direct, such as the photos of orphaned children in rags propagated in 1870s London by Dr. Thomas Barnardo, in a report by William Stead, or in the barely veiled allusions to sodomite orgies related by James Greenwood in his homeless shelter. Or it could be symbolic, as in an obsession with dirt and filth that traversed most stories told by philanthropic women, of course, but which were also a mark of a primitive desire and a way of entering into contact with bodies, albeit the most miserable ones.

Beyond sexuality, there was the strong, brutal, and excessive sensation that could be achieved by experiencing the underworld. Fright, shivers, repulsion, disgust, retching—so many reactions whose thrilling ambivalence was worth the cost of the adventure: "I love tasting in each country what is most rare," wrote Astiné Aravian to a diplomat friend. What did it matter if his Grand Dukes' Tour led to meeting thieves, assassins, "degenerates who drink the Locust mixture in an atmosphere of the hospital or prison—it gets me out of the ordinary!"[62] For Lucienne Favre, the Casbah of Algiers, in her repugnant picture, was an "atrocious *and* magnificent place."[63] This thirst for distinction by ordeal, which is also a way of reassuring yourself in the face of the spectacle of evil or of the distress of others, combined with pride that you could experience and mingle in the world of the Other. "One day I joined a band of crooks at the Porte d'Italie," explained the photographer Brassaï, not without a certain pride in hanging around louche figures.[64] And Blaise Cendrars "wandered from bar to bar," recounted his daughter Miriam, "for dangerous rendezvous that were fixed by anonymous letters, ever since the his first article appeared."[65]

Many feelings were blended in this satisfaction: provocation, rebellion, taste for the forbidden, desire for transgression. "I disappeared into the underworld of the capital that I had just discovered and into which I plunged with juvenile despair composed of both pride and revolt, pleasure and disgust, obeying a Baudelairean need for provocation, swashbuckling, and debauchery. . . . At bottom, I was very proud of frequenting the bad boys," remembered Francis Carco of his first time in Paris.[66] Yet at other times he wondered, "Where does this taste for low-life come from? At its approach why have I never felt the repulsion that normally it ought to inspire in me?" And he is not always a dupe of the romanticism that enveloped the figure of the bad boys he was seeking:

These miserable creatures are the most discouraging, most abject there can be. [. . .] In vain do they maintain that it is bad luck that has betrayed them. Laziness, drunkenness, bestiality, and falsehood have so long been rooted in their souls that they fool us (and abuse themselves) by promising they would have been other men if destiny had wished it. This is not true. They were born monsters. Their true nature leads them to do nothing, to love only evil.[67]

Others, like Joseph Kessel, wanted to see the positive things that exist in these men: "I have seen a profound bestiality, a total amorality, and at the same time a sort of heroism, the mystique of the outlaw."[68] But the real character of these men does not matter. What is essential is not inside them but in the way they are viewed. The social removal and rejection that defines them arouses (almost naturally) a sort of symbolic exacerbation: the Other, depreciated and despised, is transformed into a determining and often eroticized figure in social fantasies and imaginaries.[69] Think of the young Colette as the *ingénue libertine* who dreams of having apaches in her bed at night.[70] The whole fascination with outcasts, the whole social exoticism, functions in that vein.

But one can project other views onto them. Charlie Chaplin wanted to see beauty in the slums: movement, activity, and life.[71] Pépé le Moko remembered that "this squalid street attracted him, fascinated him. For him it was life, action, freedom. His universe began there."[72] Certain social missionaries hoped that these amoral people, once they had quit the road to perdition, would become the leavening of a new world. Fascinated by the "rabble," the young Milanese bohemians of the 1880s who came to Socialism through reading Sue, Vallès, or Zola, also thought that from this shameful sub-proletariat, this savage society of beggars, the downgraded, pimps and prostitutes, would someday emerge the true people endowed with a real class consciousness.[73] "[For] some it is an infected and dangerous place, a site of perdition and debauchery, source of all the plagues from alcoholism to drugs. For others it is a privileged place, a place of encounters, conviviality, festivity, distraction, and even culture."[74]

And then there is the desire to lose yourself, to go to the limit of debauchery, to descend, to encounter the obscure part of yourself that you habitually try to elude; to face up to evil, the dirty, the perverse, the damned, which the gradual secularization of our societies is pulling toward a secular hell and which at the same time becomes a powerful motif, even a cultural myth.[75] The Victorians, confronted more than others by both the realities and the imaginary of the underworld, whose insidious presence disturbed any certainty about social progress, were particularly sensitive to this dimension. An exemplary incarnation of bourgeois respectability, the good Dr. Jekyll arouses from within himself his evil double, Mr. Hyde, who leads him to the point of death in the abyss of the underworld. First published in 1886, Robert Louis Stevenson's story is as revealing about the hypocrisy of the "dual morality" as it is about the irrepressible interior desire to face evil that animated Victorian society.[76] This is also what Oscar Wilde's Dorian Grey was seeking (the novella was published in July 1890 in *Lippincott's Monthly Magazine*). If Dorian Grey buries himself in the underworld, it is in search of opium and prostitutes, but even more in search of the ugliness that is his own.

> Ugliness that had once been hateful to him because it made things real, became dear to him for that very reason. Ugliness was the one reality, the coarse brawl, the loathsome den, the crude violence of disordered life, the very vileness of thief and outcast, were more vivid, in their intense actuality of impression, than all the gracious shapes of art, the dreamy shadows of song. They were what he needed for forgetfulness.

Transgression, forgetting of self, death—or their symbolic equivalents—
are what some people tried to find in body-and-soul immersion in the
underworld.

These desires, this attraction to the most sordid of social margins,
appeared all the more powerful because for more than five centuries our
cultural arrangement has constantly stimulated them. Just like its partner, violence, the underworld sells well, and its gradual insertion into the
channels of industrial and media culture has only multiplied the supply.
The commercial exploitation of miserabilism or sensationalism contained
in these stories did not create the phenomenon, but the media have
known all along how to manage it, to justify and reactivate it at will. And
done so even more effectively because this theme excels at working in various registers—information, emotion, drama, suspense, horror, eroticism,
poetry—just as it excels at migrating from one genre to another, from one
medium to another.

These undeniable qualities have enabled the underworld to prevail as a
sort of total spectacle that is simultaneously moral and transgressive, serious and entertaining, ethnographic and stereotyped. Earlier I stressed how
the New York reportages by Jacob Riis aimed to condemn intolerable urban
and social realities and even managed to achieve some significant results in
slum clearance. But this did not prevent his reports from also prevailing—
contradictorily—as a popular and titillating spectacle. For example, here
is how the editor of his second grand reportage, *The Children of the Poor*
(1892), presented it:

No page is uninstructive, but it would be misleading to suppose the
book even tinctured with didacticism. It is from beginning to end as
picturesque in treatment as it is in material. The author's acquaintance
with the latter is extremely intimate. The reader feels that he is being
guided through the dirt and crime, the tatters and rags, the byways
and alleys of nether New York by an experienced cicerone. Mr. Riis,
in a word, though a philanthropist and philosopher, is an artist as
well. He has also the advantage of being an amateur photographer
accompli, and his book is abundantly illustrated from negatives of the
odd, the out-of-the-way, and characteristic sights and scenes he has

himself caught with his camera. No work yet published—certainly not the official reports of the charity societies—shows so vividly the complexion and countenance of the "Down-town Back Alleys," "The Bend," "Chinatown," "Jewtown," "The Cheap Lodging-houses," the haunts of the negro, the Italian, the Bohemian poor, or gives such a veracious picture of the toughs, the tramps, the waifs, drunkards, paupers, gamins, and the generally gruesome populace of this center of civilization.[77]

Conclusion

"The history of mankind is reflected in the history of its sewers," wrote Victor Hugo in *Les misérables*.[1] The history of the underworld obeys that rule. Despite its hybrid nature, where worries, anguish, and fantasies are mixed with fragments of actual experience, the imaginary of the underworld speaks to us of the lives of flesh-and-blood human beings. In three respects at least, the story that it tells us is essential. First, it speaks to us of the problems that afflicted Western societies during the great upheavals leading to this new world that industry, the city, democracy, and consumer culture were beginning to fashion in the first half of the nineteenth century. Confronted with a major overthrow of the social order, anxious about the eruption of new collective actors, the elites felt a need to reconsider the contours, organization, and stratification of the social world. To that end they fabricated a specter—the underworld—that aggregated gruesome and deterrent figures and then installed that specter at the heart of a symbolic geography that signified the unacceptable. But not everything was *imagined* in these imaginary representations—far from it. The essential elements were quite real: the frightful poverty that was crushing the new proletarians, the insalubrity, the promiscuity, the absence of a horizon other than the one sketched by depression, the suffering, or revolt.

Nevertheless the general focus on vice, "demoralization" and transgression, did arise from fantasy. The intention was clear: to stigmatize the intolerable, to remove responsibility from the elites, and to reaffirm the values that underlay the dominant identity. By the end of the century, the social world was clarified and its verges stabilized, and the lower depths could be slowly dismissed as a structuring motif. Emptied of most of their denizens, the underworld mutated into a "residue," assimilated to the world of marginals and professional wrongdoers, as witnessed by the very evolution of the term "underworld."

The history of the contemporary lower depths carries another lesson. It tells us of the great difficulty that collective imaginaries have in extricating themselves from the most traditional forms of representation. When the nineteenth century was shaken by the emergence of pauperism and the results of industrialization, figures able to express these fears and anxiety were needed, and social memories from the repertoire of images bequeathed by previous crises and centuries were repurposed. The "bad poor" and the outcasts at the end of the Middle Ages surged up in serried ranks. Other references were also mobilized—barbarians, savages, redskins—but *truands* dominated the assemblage. What did it matter if their profiles only imperfectly corresponded to the new industrial poor? Truands could superimpose repurposed images, now extending to a whole social class the characteristics once attributed to a group of beggars and vagabonds. Bearing the stigmata of the past, the "vicious classes" or "dangerous classes" were laden with fears about the future because they incarnated the political risk of unrest and insurrection. Even when confronted with new stakes, societies tend to replay familiar scenarios, as we have seen.

Might this suffice to disqualify the imaginary as a historical object, to throw it back into the atemporal universe of invariants and archetypes? No, for it is from these reencounters and historical telescoping that the movement of history is born. To understand this, we must pay careful attention to social rhythms and time scales, to the interweaving of motifs, to uses of representations and their repurposing. The history of imaginaries does not consist (as its detractors sometimes insist) of "recopying" the discourse of the past but rather of deconstructing its workings to expose its layers of meaning.

Finally, an intriguing psychological factor, essential but much more complex, intersects with this history of the underworld. It relates to the dark part of ourselves, to our contradictory desires, the unconscious portion of our impulses. Today as yesterday, transgressions and the margins continue to fascinate us. The symbolic consumption of horror has not wavered; in fact, it seems to increase as our world becomes more regulated, as our societies become pacified. Taken charge of by technologies, industries, and the modern media, horror may even be enjoying its grandest era. I have tried not to exploit the public taste for crime, poverty, or vice, but inevitably that taste has accompanied us, despite ourselves, and has managed here and there to interfere in the story. It will not help to deplore this, but we should not ignore it either. We must take it into account as one of the elements of history. The imaginary of the underworld teaches us about our own lives as much as the lives of our predecessors.

These descriptions of the underworld deeply marked the Western nineteenth century. They tinted it gray, gave it the bitter taste of woe and social horror, and surrounded its boundaries with tensions and fear of crime. Is Victorian London comprehensible today without *Oliver Twist*, without the engravings of Gustave Doré, or the Jack the Ripper murders? And what would Paris mean without its *Mystères* or its *Misérables*? However, have these representations now fulfilled their purpose? Have they managed to reorder and to normalize our mutating societies? The extraordinary profusion of stories of the underworld that this century has produced, and on which this book has relied, obviously pleads in this direction. But did contemporaries have real faith in all these descriptions? Did they consider all migrants as potential criminals, and did they share the same attitude to apaches and prowlers and the miserable people who spent the night in the plaster quarries outside the Paris wall? Beliefs, sensibilities, and social positions have of influenced judgments and have diversified reactions at the extremes of the opinion spectrum. Symptomatic reading, necessarily an overview that is common in the history of imaginaries, tends to harden the representations that life (inversely) is trying to soften. Have I paid too much attention to the sordid and abject, or perhaps overly accentuated what Chateaubriand called "the reserve side of society, the pleas of humanity, and the hideous machines that move the world"?[2] Many texts and much of the testimony have cast a simpler and sometimes more tender gaze on the margins. Not all of them have indulged in horror or in a competition to shock the public. Some have described poor but worthy domestic interiors, men and women at work, with difficult but ordinary lives. Others, touched by fear, empathy, or guilt, have stressed their real distress, have depicted a universe of victims, poor buggers, frightened children: "haggard and ragged beings, who seem as if excluded from the social pact, and who in solitude, resigned or shy, inoffensive due to weakness, wait for nothing but their turn to die."[3]

The voyage offered here has not exhausted the ways of exploring and speaking about the underworld. I would wager that philanthropists, clergymen, and some social workers recognize themselves only imperfectly in these pages. Other experiences, other stories might have supplied material for alternative scenarios—a female prison visitor, or a young "missionary" freshly sharpened at Oxbridge and committed to a social colony in Whitechapel, or one of those homeless bohemians traveling around a United States in crisis and desiring to follow the path of "down-and-out" writers incarnated by London or Orwell—each would tell us quite different histories. In a different genre, the journalist and novelist Sergio González Rodríguez tried to depict the nature of the Mexican underworld. Conceived as an almost kaleidoscopic to and fro between past and present, his narrative mixed many texts, places, memories, chronicles, images, and anecdotes, which altogether "and sometimes without knowing it" translated the whole effervescence of the city's shadowy zones.[4] Similarly, the camera of Lionel Rogosin, who filmed lost men without a future by ambling the Bowery for three straight days in 1955 (in dense and despairing heat) managed to open an entirely different view of the world below.

The purpose of this book was not to embrace *all the experiences* and *all the stories* of the margins, which would be an excessive (and illusory) task. Poverty and misfortune are not representable, as Hugo felt acutely. They emerge only at a few rare intersections with the world above: charity, penalty, prison.[5] In many respects, the material and moral experience of poverty is a literary *aporia* that badly suits the frameworks of representation: in fact, poverty "figures there without being able to keep itself there."[6] I tried to bring to light a social imaginary with a panoptic view that gathered and inscribed in a tableau the essence of the materials produced by contemporaries to represent social chasms and transgression. Attentive to assemblages, I postulated that societies tell themselves significant stories that engage their present and even their future. I believe in the virtue of paroxysms:[7] in the midst of panic they may reveal, even if crudely, social anguish that has been deeply buried. Finally, I have defended the idea that history is made of stories, and that, without losing any of its ambition to speak the truth and to explain the world, it may recount some of its own stories.

Notes

INTRODUCTION

1. *An Inquiry Into Destitution, Prostitution and Crime in Edinburgh* (Edinburgh: James G. Bertram, 1851).

2. Edward Crapsey, *The Nether Side of New York, or The Vice, Crime and Poverty of the Great Metropolis* (New York: Sheldon, 1872).

3. Henry Alpy, "Les enfants dans les prisons de Paris," *Revue pénitentiaire et de droit pénal* (1896): 224.

4. Pierre Zaccone, *Les nuits du boulevard* [1876] (Paris: Fayard, 1880), 296.

5. Maurice Aubenas, "Dans le canal des trespasses," *Détective*, June 28, 1934.

6. Octave Féré, *Les mystères de Rouen* [1845] (Rouen: Haulard, 1861), 248; republished 2012.

7. "He told me in 1831 what was going to happen: assassinations, conspiracies, the reign of the Jews, the hindrance to movements in France, a dearth of intelligence in the higher sphere, and the abundance of talents in the *bas-fonds* where the most courageous will be extinguished under the ashes of a cigar." Honoré de Balzac, "Z Marcas," *Revue parisienne*, July 25, 1840, 7.

8. "The wealthy classes, among whom sudden shifts in fortune sometimes cause trouble and disorder, produce from time to time famous bandit leaders who stir up and direct every subversive and cruel passion in the *bas-fonds* of a miserable and perverted population." Constantin Pecqueur, "Des améliorations matérielles dans leurs rapports avec la liberté," in *Introduction to the Study of Social and Political Economy* (Paris: Gosselin, 1840), 80.

9. Honoré Antoine Frégier, *Des classes dangereuses de la population dans les grandes villes et des moyens de les rendre meilleures* [The Dangerous Classes of People in the Big Cities and the Means of Making Them Better] (Paris: Baillière, 1840), 347.

10. Henry Monnier, *Les bas-fonds de la société: Scènes populaires* (Paris: Jules Claye, 1862).

11. *Le grande dizionario della lingua italiana* (Turin: Unione tipografico-editrice torinese, 1988) refers to the French expression.

12. "A room where low goings-on occurred," is quoted by Harold J. Dyos, "The Slums of Victorian London" [1966], in *Exploring the Urban Past: Essays in Urban History by H. J. Dyos*, ed. David Cannadine and David Reeder (Cambridge: Cambridge University Press, 1982), 129–53. According to Ellen Ross, *Slum Travelers. Ladies and London Poverty, 1860–1920* (Berkeley: University of California Press, 2007), 301, "slum" was a slang shortening of "slumber. In 1821, in *Life in London*, Pearce Egan describes the "backstreet slums" of Holy Lane and St. Giles as "low, unfrequented parts of the town," and Dickens uses the term slum in the same sense in 1840. The *Times*, January 16, 1845, makes it a synonym for "bad-lodging" and as such it came into general use. "Slumming," on the other hand, does not appear before the 1880s; the *Oxford English Dictionary* first records it in 1884.

13. Margaret Tudeau-Clayton, *Jonson, Shakespeare and Early Modern Virgil* (Cambridge: Cambridge University Press, 2006).

14. George Ellington, *The Women of New York, or The Underworld of the Great City* (New York: New York Book, 1869).

15. Helen Campbell, *Darkness and Daylight, or Lights and Shadows of New York Life* (New York: Hartford, 1892).

16. Josiah Flynt Willard, "True Stories from the Underworld," *McClure's*, June 15, 1900.

17. "A submerged, hidden or secret region or sphere, especially one given to crime, profligacy and intrigue": quoted in Donald A. Low, *Thieves' Kitchen: The Regency Underworld* (London: Dent, 1982), viii.

18. Thomas Archer, *The Pauper, the Thief and the Convict: Sketches of Some of Their Homes, Haunts, and Habits* (London: Groombridge, 1865).

19. Thomas Holmes, *London's Underworld*, with an introduction by Iain Sinclair (1912; repr. London: Anthem Press, 2006).

20. See, for example, Irwin Godfrey, *American Tramp and Underworld Slang: Words and Phrases Used by Hoboes, Tramps, Migratory Workers and Those on the Fringes of Society, with Their Uses and Origins* (New York: Sears, 1930); or slightly later in Great Britain, Eric Partridge, *A Dictionary of the Underworld, British and American, Being the Vocabulary of Crooks, Criminals, Racketeers, Beggars and Tramps, Convicts, the Commercial Underground, the Drug Traffic, the White Slave Traffic, Spivs* (London: Routledge, 1950).

21. Louis Chevalier, *Classes laborieuses et classes dangereux à Paris dans la première moitié du XIX siècle* (Paris: Plon, 1958), translated as Louis Chevalier, *Working Classes and Dangerous Classes: In Paris in the First Half of the Nineteenth Century* (New York: Howard Fertig, 2000); John Tobias, *Crime and Industrial Society* (London: Batsford, 1967).

22. For example, see Kellow Chesney, *The Victorian Underworld* (London: Temple Smith, 1970); Gāmini Salgādo, *The Elizabethan Underworld* (London: Dent, 1977); Thomas Gilfoyle, *A Pickpocket's Tale: The Underworld of Nineteenth-Century New York* (New York: Norton, 2006); Richard J. Evans, *Tales from the German Underworld: Crime and Punishment in the Nineteenth Century* (New Haven, CT: Yale University Press, 1998).

23. Deborah A. Symond, *Notorious Murders, Black Lanterns, & Moveable Goods: The Transformation of Edinburgh's Underworld in the Early Nineteenth Century* (Akron, OH: University of Akron Press, 2006), 146n25.

24. Loïc Wacquant, "L'underclass urbaine dans l'imaginaire social et scientifique américain," in *L'Exclusion. L'état des savoirs*, ed. S. Paugam (Paris: La Découverte, 1996), 248–62. On this debate, see chapter 9.

25. Heather Shore, "Undiscover'd Country: Towards a History of the Criminal Underworld," *Crimes and Misdemeanours* 1 (2007): 41–68.

26. Francisco de Veyga, "Los Lunfardos: Estudios clínicos sobre esta clase de ladrones profesionales," cited in Lila Caimari, *La ciudad y el crimen: Delito y vida cotidiana en Buenos Aires, 1880–1940* (1903; repr. Buenos Aires: Editorial Sudamericana, 2009), 56.

27. Henry James, *The American Scene* (London: Chapman and Hall, 1907), 201.

28. Caimari, *La ciudad y el crimen*, 56.

29. For example, see Alain Corbin, *The Foul and the Fragrant: Odor and the French Social Imagination* (Cambridge, MA: Harvard University Press, 1986); Judith Walkowitz, *City of Dreadful Delight: Narratives of Sexual Danger in Late-Victorian London* (Chicago: University of Chicago Press, 1992); Seth Koven, *Slumming: Sexual and Social Politics in Victorian London* (Princeton, NJ: Princeton University Press, 2004).

30. This is the case with G. Bachelard and Gilbert Durand. See Gilbert Durand, *Les structures anthropologiques de l'imaginaire* (Paris: PUF, 1960); Gilbert Durand, *Anthropological Structures of the Imaginary* (Virginia: Boombana, 1999).

31. Bronislaw Baszko, *Les imaginaires sociaux: Mémoires et espoirs collectifs* (Paris: Payot, 1984), 35.

32. Cornélius Castoriadis, *L'institution imaginaire de la société* (Paris: Seuil, 1975); Cornélius Castoriadis, *The Imaginary Institution of Society*, trans. Kathleen Blamey (Cambridge: Polity Press, 1987).

33. Pierre Popovic, *Imaginaire social et folie littéraire: Le Second Empire de Paulin Gagne* (Montreal, Quebec: Presses de l'Université de Montréal, 2008), 24.

1. IN THE DEN OF HORROR

1. Edmond and Jules de Goncourt, *Germinie Lacerteux* (Paris: Charpentier, 1864), preface. In English, see Edmond and Jules de Goncourt, *Pages from the Goncourt Journals*, trans. Robert Baldick (New York: New York Review Books Classics, 2006).

2. Eugène Sue, *Les mystères de Paris* (1842); Eugène Sue, *The Mysteries of Paris*, trans. Carolyn Betensky and Jonathan Loesberg (New York: Penguin Classics, 2015).

3. Jules Janin, *L'Été à Paris* (Paris: Curmer, 1843), 13.

4. *Mémoires de Monsieur Claude* (Paris: J. Rouff, 1881–1885), 64–65.

5. Sue, *The Mysteries of Paris*, 5.

6. Octave Féré, *Les mystères de Rouen* (Rouen: Haulard, 1861), 21.

7. Marc-Michel, *Les gueux de Marseille: Chronique contemporaine* (Marseilles, 1810; Marseilles: Imprimerie militaire, 1836), 9; Horace Bertin, *Marseille intime* (Marseilles: Société des bibliophiles de Provence, 1876), 30, quoted by Laurence Montel, "Marseille

capitale du crime: Histoire croisée de l'imaginaire de Marseille et de la criminalité organisée (1820–1940)" (PhD diss., Université de Paris 10, 2008).

8. Quoted by Françoise Barret-Ducrocq, *Pauvreté, charité et morale à Londres au XIXe siecle: Une sainte violence* (Paris: PUF, 1991), 11.

9. Charles Knight, quoted by K. Chesney, *The Victorian Underworld*, rev. ed. (London: Penguin, 1999).

10. Georges W. Reynolds, *The Mysteries of London* (1844–1846; repr. Staffordshire, UK: Keele University Press, 1996), chaps. 1, 8.

11. Quoted by Françoise Barret-Ducrocq, in "Report of the *Mission Church*" (1867), 25.

12. Quoted by T. Thomas, "Representation of the Manchester Working-Class in Fiction, 1850–1900," in *City, Class and Culture: Studies of Social Policy and Cultural Production in Victorian Manchester*, ed. Alan J. Kidd and Kenneth W. Roberts (Manchester, UK: Manchester University Press, 1985). 193–216.

13. Christian Henriot, *Belles de Shanghai: Prostitution et sexualité en Chine aux XIXe et XXe siècles* (Paris: CNRS, 1997), 231.

14. Carton De Wiart, *Le Congo d'aujourd'hui et de demain*, 1923; quoted by Amandine Lauro, "Maintenir l'ordre dans la colonie-modèle," *Crime, Histoire, & Sociétés* 15, no. 2 (2011): 97–121.

15. Tylor Anbinder, Five Points. The Nineteenth-Century New York City Neighborhood That Invented Tap Dance, Stole Elections, and Became the World's Most Notorious Slum (New York: Free Press, 2001).

16. Paul J. Erickson, *Welcome to Sodom: The Cultural Work of City-Mysteries Fiction in Antebellum America* (PhD diss., University of Texas at Austin, 2005).

17. Caimari, *La ciudad y el crimen*.

18. Féré, *Les mystères de Rouen*, 166.

19. Damien Cailloux, "Les bas-fonds nantais, XIXe–XXe siècles" (master's thesis, Université de Paris 1, 2008).

20. Henry Jacques, *Jean-François de Nantes* (Paris: Louis Querelle, 1929), 28–29.

21. Louis-François Raban, *Les mystères du Palais-Royal*, vol. 1 (Paris: Le Clère, 1845), 6; Elie Berthet, *Les catacombes de Paris* (Paris: de Potter, 1854); Pierre Zaccone, *Drames des catacombes* (Paris: Ballay aîné, 1863).

22. Henri Danjou "Dans Paris souterrain," *Détective*, no. 51, 1929.

23. Albert Londres, *Le chemin de Buenos-Aires (la Traite des blanches)* (Paris: Albin Michel, 1927), 180.

24. Jules Huret, *De Buenos Aires au Gran Chaco* (Paris: Fasquelle, 1912), 79.

25. Joseph Kessel, *Bas-fonds de Paris* (Paris: Editions des Portiques, 1932), 101.

26. Lucienne Favre, *Tout l'inconnu de la Casbah d'Alger* (Algiers: Baconnier, 1933), 76.

27. Nicole Dyonnet, "Les bandes de voleurs et l'histoire," in *Cartouche, Mandrin et autres brigands du XVIIIe siècle*, ed. Lise Andries (Paris: Desjonquières, 2010), 216.

28. Pierre Souvestre and Marcel Allain, *La voleur d'or* (Paris: Fayard, 1913; repr. Paris: Laffont, 1988), 1124–28.

29. Georges Darien, *Le voleur* (Paris: Savine, 1898; repr. Paris: Gallimard, 1987), 338.

30. Lee Grieveson, "Gangster and Governance in the Silent Era," in *Mob Culture: Hidden Histories of the American Gangster Film*, ed. Lee Grieveson, Esther Sonnet, and Peter Stanfield (New Brunswick, NJ: Rutgers University Press, 2005), 11–36.

31. Louis-René Villermé, *Des prisons telles qu'elles sont et telles qu'elles devraient être* (Paris: Méquignon-Marvis, 1820), 3.

32. Antoine-François Eve, *Tableau historique des prisons d'état en France sous le règne de Buonaparte* (Paris: Delaunay, 1814), 20.

33. Gustave Macé, *Mes lundis en prison* (Paris: Charpentier, 1889), 74.

34. Othenin d'Haussonville, "Le combat contre le vice," *Revue des deux mondes* (1887): 803.

35. François Raspail, *Réforme pénitentiaire: Lettres sur les prisons de Paris* (Paris: Tamisey and Champion, 1839), 365; Adolphe Guillot, *Paris qui souffre: Les prisons de Paris et les prisonniers* (Paris: Dentu, 1889), 466; Pierre Zaccone, *Histoire des bagnes depuis leur création jusqu'à nos jours . . .*, vol. 1 (Clichy: Dupont, 1878), 432.

36. Sue, *Les mystères de Paris*, chap. 9.

37. Victor Hugo, *Notre-Dame de Paris*, trans. Alban Krasilsheimer (London: Oxford University Press, 2009), 539.

38. Féré, *Les mystères de Rouen*, 266.

39. Mariano Felipe Pas Soldan, *Examen de las penitenciarias de los Estados Unido . . .*, 1853. Quoted by Lissel Quiroz-Perez, "Du service du roi au service de la république: Haute magistrature et construction de l'état au Pérou (1810–1870)" (PhD thesis, Université Paris 1, 2009), 260–61.

40. David Pike, *Metropolis on the Styx: The Underworlds of Modern Urban Culture, 1800–2001* (Ithaca, NY: Cornell University Press, 2007).

41. Louise Michel and Jean Guetré (Marcelle Tynaire), *La misère* (Paris: Fayard, 1890), 302.

42. Aya Umazawa, "La prison cellulaire et la folie des prisonniers (1819–1848)" (PhD thesis, Université Paris 1, 2012), 134.

43. "Les détenus," in *Les français peints par eux-mêmes*, vol. 2 (Paris: Curmier, 1839; repr. Paris: La Découverte, 2004), 532. Moreau-Christophe takes up and develops this metaphor and adds: "What is phenomenal in this mélange is that it operates without transmutation, in the sense that the impure matters in fermentation are gathered together without being mixed up. In effect, all the vices conserve their own nature, the certificate of their origin, and the rank they occupied in the world from which they came, they still occupy in the one into which they have just been incorporated": Louis Mathurin Moreau-Christophe, *Le monde des coquins: Physiologie du monde des coquins* (Paris: Dentu, 1863), 52–53.

44. Guillot, *Paris qui souffre*, 241.

45. Hector Gavin, *Sanitary Ramblings* (London: Churchill, 1848), 19.

46. Anbinder, Five Points, 19.

47. *La Iberia*, April 26, 1860, quoted by Fernando Vicente Albarran, "Los barrios negros: El ensanche sur en la formación del moderno Madrid (1860–1931)" (PhD thesis, Universidad Complutense de Madrid, 2011), 343.

48. Théodore Child, *Les républiques hispano-américaines* (Paris: Librairie illustrée, 1891), 304.

49. Alain Pessin, *Le mythe du peuple et la société française du XIXe siècle* (Paris: PUF, 1992), 133.

50. Donald A. Low, *The Regency Underworld* (London: Dent, 1982), 48; Charles Bateson, *The Convicts Ships, 1867–1869* (Glasgow: Brown, Son & Ferguson, 1959).

51. Michel Foucault, *Histoire de la folie à l'âge classique* (Paris: Gallimard, 1972), 21–30; Alain Corbin, *The Lure of the Sea: The Discovery of the Seaside in the Western World, 1750–1840* (Paris: Aubier, 1988; repr. Berkeley: University of California Press, 1994).

52. Rachel Falconer, *Hell in Contemporary Literature: Western Descent Narratives Since 1945* (Edinburgh: Edinburgh University Press, 2005).

53. Pessin, *Le mythe du peuple*, 133.

54. Jerry White, *London in the Nineteenth Century* (London: Cape, 2007).

55. Jean-Paul Clébert, *Paris insolite, authentifié par 115 photographies de Patrice Molinard* (Paris: Denoel, 1952; repr. Paris: Attila, 2009), 116–19.

56. Honoré Antoine Frégier, *Des classes dangereuses de la population dans les grandes villes et des moyens de les rendre meilleures* [The dangerous classes of people in the big cities and the means of making them better] (Paris: Baillière, 1840), 34–35.

57. Moreau-Christophe, *Le monde des coquins*, 28.

58. Mikhaïl Bakhtine, "L'oeuvre de François Rabelais et la culture populaire au Moyen Âge et sous la Renaissance," in *Rabelais and His World*, trans. Helene Iswolsky (Indiana University Press, 1969), 369.

59. G. de la Baume, *Raoul, ou 15 jours de l'année 1228*, vol. 2 (Paris: Verdière, 1826), 96.

60. Féré, *Les mystères de Rouen*, 9.

61. Andrew Mearns, *The Bitter Cry of Outcast London: An Inquiry Into the Condition of the Abject Poor* (London: James Clarke, 1883), 7–8.

62. Géo Bonneron, *Les Prisons de Paris* (Paris: Firmin-Didot, 1898), 87.

63. René Janon, *Hommes de peine et filles de joie* (Algiers: La Palangrote, 1936), 30.

64. Ashelbé, *Pépé le Moko* (Paris: EID, 1931), 137; Pierre Loti, *Les trois drames de la Kasbah* (Paris: Calmann-Lévy, 1882), 50.

65. Féré, *Les mystères de Rouen*, 41.

66. Dubut de Laforest, *La tournée des grands ducs, mœurs parisiennes* (Paris: Flammarion, 1901), 10.

67. Michel and Guetré, *La misère*, 30.

68. André Tabet, *Rue de la Marine* (Paris: Albin Michel, 1938), 190.

69. Frégier, *Des classes dangereuses*, 140.

70. Aristide Bruant, *Le bal des puces*, vol. 3 (Paris: Fayard, 1903), 296.

71. J. H. Stallard, *The Female Casual and Her Lodging* (London: Saunders, Otley, 1866), 49.

72. Féré, *Les mystères de Rouen*, 9.

73. Louis Bertrand, *Nuits d'Alger* (Paris: Flammarion, 1904), 156.

74. Favre, *Tout l'inconnu de la Casbah d'Alger*, 41.

75. George Orwell, *Down and Out in Paris and London* (New York: Harcourt Brace, 1933; repr. New York: Houghton Mifflin Harcourt, 1961).

76. Pierre Paganel, *Rapport sur les prions, maisons d'arrêt ou de police, de répression, de détention, et sur les hospices de santé, fait au nom du comité des secours publics* (Paris: Imprimerie nationale, 1794), 3.

77. Villermé, *Des prisons telles qu'elles sont et telles qu'elles devraient être*, 21.

78. Louis-François Raban, *Le prisonnier* (Paris: Dabo jeune, 1826), 8.

79. Louis Roubaud, "Démons et dements," *Détective*, February 9, 1933; Jean Genet, *Notre-Dame-des-Fleurs* (Paris: L'Arbalète, 1948; repr. Paris: Gallimard, 2002), 84; Alexandre Daumal, *Je m'appelle reviens* (Paris: Gallimard, 1995), 34.

80. Jack London, *The People of the Abyss* (New York: Macmillan, 1903), 7.

81. Elie Richard, *Le guide des grands-ducs* (Paris: Ed. du monde moderne, 1925), 92.

82. Féré, *Les mystères de Rouen*, 12.

83. Mearns, *The Bitter Cry of Outcast London*, 9.

84. Friedrich Engels, *The Condition of the Working Class in England* (Leipzig: Otto Wigand, 1844; repr. New York, Cosimo Classics, 2008), 92.

85. Frégier, *Des classes dangereuses*, 140.

86. Mearns, *The Bitter Cry of Outcast London*, 9.

87. Francesco Mastriani, *Les vers rongeurs. Études historiques sur les classes dangereuses à Naples* (Naples: L. Gargiulo, 1885).

88. Louis Fiaux, *Un nouveau régime des mœurs* (Paris: Alcan, 1908), 290.

89. Louis Fiaux, *La police des mœurs* (Paris: Dentu, 1888), 249–50.

90. Jules Vallès, *Le tableau de Paris* (1882–1883; repr. Paris: Messidor, 1989), 154.

91. René Belbenoit, *Guillotine sèche* (Paris: Les Editions de France, 1938; repr. Paris: Manufacture des Livres, 2012), 118.

92. Constancio Bernardo de Quiros and José Maria Llanas Aguilaniedo, *La mala vida en Madrid: Estudio socio-psicológico con dibujos y fotografías del natural* (Madrid: Rodríguez Sierra, 1901), 129. Quoted by Albarran, "Los barrios negros," 344.

93. Hippolyte Raynal, *Malheur et poésie* (Paris: Perrotin, 1834), 81–82.

94. C. Fergus Linnane, *London's Underworld:. Three Centuries of Vice and Crime* (London: Robson Books, 2003), 235–36; A. D. Harvey, "Prosecutions for Sodomy in England at the Beginning of the Nineteenth Century," *The Historical Journal* 21, no. 4 (1978): 939–48.

95. Djuna Barnes and T. S. Eliot, *Nightwood* (London: Faber & Faber, 1936).

96. Frégier, *Des classes dangereuses*, 192.

97. Aristide Bruant, *Les bas-fonds de Paris*, vol. 1 (Paris: Fayard, 1902), 5–6.

98. Bruant, *Les bas-fonds de Paris*, 25.

99. Child, *Les républiques hispano-américaines*, 304.

100. Cyril-Berger, *Les têtes baissées* (Paris: Ollendorff, 1913), 3.

101. Louis Paulian, *Paris qui mendie. Les vrais et les faux pauvres. Mal et remède* (Paris: Ollendorff, 1893), 82.

102. Ferdinand Moine, *Une plaie sociale, la mendicité: Le mal, le remède* (Paris: Libraires associés, 1901), 86.

103. Bruant, *Les bas-fonds de Paris*, 379.

104. *Mémoires de Canler, ancien chef du service de la Sûreté* (Paris: Hetzel, 1862), 200.

105. Maxime Du Camp, *Paris: Ses organes, ses fonctions et sa vie dans la seconde moitié du XIXᵉ siècle*, vol. 3 (Paris: Hachette, 1875), 4.

106. London, *The People of the Abyss*, 36–37.

107. Amédée Blondeau and Maxime Halbrand, *Le Palais de Justice de Paris: Son monde et ses mœurs par la presse judiciaire parisienne* (Paris: Librairies-Imprimeries réunies, 1892), 322.

108. Jean Galtier-Boissière, "De Ménilmuche à la Villetouse," *Le Crapouillot*, special ed. (May 1939).

109. Clébert, *Paris insolite*, 79.

110. Pierre Besnard, *Ces messieurs de Buenos Aires* (Paris: Editions du siècle, 1929), 69; Ludovic Garnica de la Cruz, *Nantes la brume* (Paris: Librairie française, 1905), 167.

111. André Suarez, *Marshilo* (Paris: Trémois, 1931), 63.

112. Paul Bru, *Histoire de Bicêtre* (Paris: Lecrosnier et Babe, 1890), 14.

113. Bru, *Histoire de Bicêtre*, 30.

114. Alphonse de Lamartine, *Histoire des Girondins*, vol. 2 (Paris, Furne, 1847), 7.

115. Bru, *Histoire de Bicêtre*, 108.

116. Richard, *Le guide des grands-ducs*, 270.

117. T. Gilfoyle, *A Pickpocket's Tale: The Underworld of Nineteenth-Century New York* (New York: Norton, 2007), 95–101; Gunja Sengupta, *From Slavery to Poverty: The Racial Origins of Welfare in New York, 1840–1918* (New York: New York University Press, 2009), 69–106.

118. Gilfoyle, *A Pickpocket's Tale*, 100.

119. Charles Godfrey Leland, *The English Gypsies and Their Language* (New York: Hurd and Houghton, 1873).

120. *La vie illustrée*, December 4, 1908.

121. Émile Gautier, "Le monde des prisons: Notes d'un témoin," *Archives de l'anthropologie criminelle* (1888): 419.

122. Alexis de Tocqueville, *Memoir, Letters, and Remains of Alexis de Tocqueville*, ed. Gustave de Beaumont (Paris, 1861).

123. Moreau-Christophe, *Le monde des coquins*, 54.

124. *Mémoires de M. Claude* (Paris: J. Rouff, 1881–85), 630.

125. Henry Fielding, *An Enquiry Into the Causes of the Late Increase of Robbers* (London: Millar, 1751), 4.

126. Kessel, *Bas-fonds de Paris*, 243.

127. Camille Aymard, *La profession du crime* (Paris: Bibliothèque indépendante, 1905), 31.

128. Henriette Asseo, *Les Tsiganes: Une destinée européenne* (Paris: Gallimard, 1994), 15.

129. André Charpentier, "Les mystérieux graffitis de la pègre," *Police Magazine*, 1930.

130. "Le code des gueux," *Détective*, no. 49, 1930.

131. Charpentier, "Les mystérieux graffitis de la pègre."

132. Victor Hugo, *Les misérables*, trans. Isabel Hapgood (New York: T. Y. Crowell, 1887), part 4, book 7, chap. 1.

133. I am indebted for some of these aspects to the work of Claudine Nedelec who has published decisive work on this matter since completing her thesis: Claudine Nedelec,

"Le langage de l'argot: De la vie généreuse des mercelots, gueux et bohémiens aux mystères de Paris (1596–1842)" (PhD diss., Université Paris 3, 1992). See especially Claudine Nedelec, *Les Enfants de la truche. La vie et le langage des argotiers. Quatre textes argotiques (1596–1630)* (Toulouse: Société de littérature classique, 1998); Claudine Nedelec, "Les lexicographes des bas-fonds," *Cahiers Diderot* 11 (1999): 155–68; Claudine Nedelec, "Les mystères de l'argot," *Nord'* 46 (2005): 39–61; Claudine Nedelec, "L'argot, langue des 'gens d'une même cabale,'" in Andries, ed., *Cartouche*, 62–83.

134. Henri Estienne, *Introduction au traité de la conformité des merveilles anciennes avec les modernes* (Geneva, 1566), 138; quoted by Claudine Nedelec, *Brigands*, 62.

135. Sue, *Les mystères de Paris*, 40.

136. Charles Nodier, *Notions élémentaires de linguistique* (1837), quoted by Nedelec, "Langage de l'argot," 62.

137. P. Leclair, *Histoire des brigands, chauffeurs et assassins d'Orgères* (1799), quoted by Nedelec, "Langage de l'argot," 77.

138. Bronislaw Geremek, *Les fils de Caïn* (Paris: Flammarion, 1998).

139. Georges Fronval, *Danseuses pour Buenos Aires* (Paris: Tallandier, 1932), 29; Guy de Téramond, "Hambourg ville colossale," in *Le roman-reportage* (Paris: Ferenczi, 1932).

140. Bruant, *Les bas-fonds de Paris*, 336, 353–54.

2. COURTS OF MIRACLES

1. Louis-François Raban, *Les Mystères du Palais-Royal*, vol. 1 (Paris: Le Clère, 1845), 6.

2. Fergus Linnane, *London's Underworld: Three Centuries of Vice and Crime* (London: Robson Books, 2003).

3. John Duncombe, *The Dens of London Exposed* (London, 1835), 61.

4. H. Montgomery Hyde, *The Cleveland Street Scandal* (London: Allen, 1976); Morris Kaplan, *Sodom on the Thames: Sex, Love and Scandal* (Ithaca, NY: Cornell University Press, 2005).

5. Henri Danjou, *Enfants du malheur!* (Paris: Albin Michel, 1923; repr. Paris: La manufacture de livres, 2012), 99, 76.

6. Jean Bottero, *Babylone et la Bible: Entretien avec Hélène Monsacré* (Paris: Les Belles Lettres, 1994).

7. Lynda Nead, *Victorian Babylon: People, Streets and Images in Nineteenth-Century London* (New Haven, CT: Yale University Press, 2000).

8. Ernest Bell, ed., *War on the White Slave Trade* (Chicago, IL: Charles C. Thompson, 1909), 25.

9. Henri-Émile Chevalier and Théodore Labourieu, *Les trois babylones: Paris, Londres, New-York* (Paris: Lécrivain & Toubon, 1864).

10. Catherine Salles, *Les bas-fonds de l'antiquité* (Paris: Laffont, 1982).

11. Félix Deriège, *Les mystères de Rome* (Paris: Bureau du Siècle, 1847). See the presentation by Marie-Astrid Charlier on Médias 19, http://www.medias19.org/index.php?id=631.

12. Maurice Talmeyr, *La fin d'une société: Les maisons d'illusion* (Paris: Juven, 1906), 49.

13. Alexandre Vexliard, *Introduction à la sociologie du vagabondage* (Paris: Marcel Rivière, 1956), 13.

14. Giovanni Ricci, "Naissance du poor honteux au Moyen Age: Entre histoire des idées et histoire sociale," *Annales ESC* 38, no. 1 (1983): 158–77.

15. Michel Mollat, *Les pauvres au Moyen Age: Étude sociale* (Paris: Hachette, 1978), 274.

16. G. Le Trosne, *Mémoire sur les vagabonds et les mendiants*, 1764, quoted by Michel Foucault, *Surveiller et punir: Naissance de la prison* (Paris: Gallimard, 1975), 87; Michel Foucault, *Discipline and Punish: The Birth of the Prison*, 2nd ed., trans. Alan Sheridan (New York: Random House, 1991), 84.

17. Lambin de Saint-Félix, *Mémoire sur la mendicité*, 1775, quoted by C. Romon, "Mendiants et policiers à Paris au xviiie siècle," *Histoire, Économie, Société*, no. 2 (1982): 262.

18. Jean-Baptiste Martin, *La fin des mauvais pauvres* (Seysell: Champ Vallon, 1983), 57.

19. Henriette Asseo, *Les Tsiganes: une destinée européenne* (Paris: Gallimard, 1994), 15.

20. *Journal d'un bourgeois de Paris, 1405–1449, publiés d'après les manuscrits de Rome et de Paris par Alexandre Tuetey* (Paris: Champion, 1881), quoted in Asseo, *Les Tsiganes*, 219.

21. François Vaux de Foletier, "Les Tsiganes à Paris et en Île-de-France du XVe siècle à la Révolution," *Seine et Paris*, no. 20 (October 1961): 39–47.

22. Gāmini Salgādo, *The Elizabethan Underworld* (London: Dent & Son, 1977).

23. I borrow the examples that follow principally from the work of Bronislaw Geremek, *Truands et misérables dans l'Europe moderne (1350–1600)* (Paris: Gallimard, 1980); and Bronislaw Geremek, *La potence et la pitié: L'Europe et les pauvres du Moyen Age à nos jours* (Paris: Gallimard, 1987).

24. Robert Humphrey, *No Fixed Abode: A History of Response to the Roofless and the Rootless in Britain* (Basingstoke, UK: MacMillan, 1999).

25. Alexandre Vexliard, *Introduction à la sociologie du vagabondage* (Paris: Marcel Rivière, 1956), 63–68.

26. Michel Mollat, "La notion de pauvreté au Moyen Âge: Position de problems," *Revue d'histoire de l'Église de France*, no. 149 (1966): 19.

27. Jean-Pierre Gutton, *La société et les pauvres: L'exemple de la généralité de Lyon, 1534–1789* (Paris: Les Belles Lettres, 1971); Jean-Pierre Gutton, *La société et les pauvres en Europe, XVIe–XVIIIe siècles* (Paris: PUF, 1974).

28. Quoted by Joël Cornette, "Le nain et la 'culture des images'," in *Société, culture, vie religieuse aux XVIe et XVIIe siècles* (Paris: PUPS, 1995), 125.

29. Quoted by Joël Cornette, *L'affirmation de l'état absolu* (Paris: Hachette, 2009), 150.

30. Annick Tillier, "Indigence et décrépitude: Les hospices de Bicêtre et la Salpêtrière dans la première moitié XIXe siècle," in *Imaginaire et sensibilités au XIXe siècle*, ed. Anne-Emmanuelle Demartini and Dominique Kalifa (Paris: Créaphis, 2005), 223–34.

31. Michel Foucault, *Folie et déraison: Histoire de la folie à l'âge classique* (1777; repr. Paris: Plon, 1961), 86; Michel Foucault, *Madness and Civilization: A History of Insanity in the Age of Reason*, trans. Richard Howard (New York: Vintage, 1988), 59; Gutton, *La société et les pauvres*, 295–342.

32. Claude Quétel, *Histoire de la folie* (Paris: Tallandier, 2009).

33. Jean-Pierre Gutton, *État et la mendicité dans la première moitié du XVIIIe siècle: Auvergne, Beaujolais, Forez, Lyonnais* (Saint-Etienne: Centre d'études foréziennes, 1973).

34. André Gueslin, *Gens pauvres, pauvres gens dans la France du XIXe siècle* (Paris: Aubier, 1998), 245.

35. Louis-Sébastien Mercier, *Tableau de Paris*, vol. 11 (Paris: Virchaux, 1781), 120.

36. Alan Forrest, *The French Revolution and the Poor*, (New York: St Martin's, 1981).

37. Annick Riani, "Le grand renfermement vu à travers le refuge de Marseille," *Provence historique* 32, no. 129 (1982): 283–84.

38. Etienne Pariset, "Éloge de P. Pinel," in *Mémoires de l'Académie de médecine*, vol. 1 (Paris: Baillière, 1828), 225.

39. Pierre Zaccone, *Les mystères de Bicêtre* (Paris: Charlieu & Huillery, 1864), 7.

40. Bronislaw Geremek, *Les fils de Caïn: L'image des pauvres et des vagabonds dans la littérature européenne du XVe au XVIIIe siècle* (1988; repr. Paris: Flammarion, 1991).

41. Erik von Kraemer, *Le type du faux mendiant dans les littératures romanes depuis le Moyen Age jusqu'au 17e siècle* (Leipzig: Helsingfors, 1944).

42. Quoted by Roger Chartier, "La 'monarchie d'argot' entre le mythe et l'histoire," in Bernard Vincent, *Les marginaux et les exclus dans l'histoire, Cahiers Jussieu*, no. 5 (Paris: UGE, 1979), 293.

43. *Essays of Michel de Montaigne* [1572–1573], book 3, chap. 13.

44. Chartier, "La 'monarchie d'argot'"; Roger Chartier, "Figures de la gueuserie: Picaresque et burlesque dans la Bibliothèque bleue," in *Figures de la gueuserie*, by Roger Chartier (Paris: Montalba, 1982), 11–106.

45. Noël Du Fail, *Propos rustiques*, 1547; David Ferrand, *La Muse normande*, 1625–1655, quoted by Alexandre Vexliard, *Introduction à la sociologie du vagabondage* (Paris: Marcel Rivière, 1956), 153–54.

46. *Mémoire concernant les poors qu'on appelle enfermés*, quoted by L. Cimber and F. Danjou, *Archives curieuses de l'Histoire de France*, series 1, vol. 15 (1837), 243–70; quoted by Chartier, *Figures de la gueuserie*, 41.

47. Quoted by Chartier, *Figures de la gueuserie*, 177.

48. Henri Sauval, *Histoire et recherches des antiquités de la ville de Paris* (Paris, 1724; repr. Geneva: Minkoff Reprints, 1974).

49. Henri Sauval, *La chronique scandaleuse de Paris: Chronique des mauvais lieux*, with an introduction and notes by the bibliophile Jean (Paris: Daragon, 1910).

50. Victor Hugo, *Notre-Dame de Paris*, trans. Alban Krailsheimer (Oxford, UK: Oxford University Press, 2009).

51. "The Broken Pitcher," in Hugo, *Notre-Dame de Paris*, 93.

52. Joy Wiltenburg, "True Crime: The Origins of Modern Sensationalism," *American Historical Review* 109, no. 5 (2004): 1377–1404.

53. Françoise du Sorbier, *Récits de gueuserie et biographies criminelles de Head à Defoe* (Paris: Didier érudition, 1984).

54. Jim A. Sharpe, "Last Dying Speeches: Religion, Ideology, and Public Execution in Seventeenth-Century England," *Past & Present* 107 (1985): 144–67; Victor A. Gatrell, *The Hanging Tree: Execution and the English People, 1770–1868* (Oxford, UK: Oxford University Press, 1994).

55. Sharpe, "Last Dying Speeches"; Wiltenburg, "True Crime."

56. Patrice Peveri, "Littérature de colportage et contrôle de l'opinion," in *Cartouche, Mandrin et autres brigands du XVIII⁰ siècle*, ed. Lise Andries (Paris: Desjonquières, 2010), 269–92.

57. Eric J. Hobsbawm, *Bandits* (London: Weidenfeld and Nicolson, 1969; repr. New York: The New Press, 2002).

58. Andries, *Cartouche*, 26–27.

59. Gertrude Himmelfarb, *The Idea of Poverty: England in the Early Industrial Age* (London: Faber and Faber, 1984), 421–28.

60. Luke Pike, *A History of Crime in England* (London: Smith, Elder, 1873).

61. G. de la Baume, *Raoul, ou 15 jours de l'année 1228*, vol. 2 (Paris: Verdière, 1826), 96; Théophile Dinocourt, *Le duelliste, roman de mœurs du XVII⁰ siècle* (Paris: Tenon, 1827).

62. Théophile Dinocourt, *La Cour des miracles*, vol. 4 (Paris: Vimont, 1832), 88; Paul Lacroix, *La danse macabre: Histoire fantastique du XV⁰ siècle* (Paris: Renduel, 1832), 169–70; Charles d'Arlincourt, *Les écorcheurs, ou l'usurpation et la peste* (Paris: Renduel, 1833), 47; Marie Aycart, *Marie de Mancini*, vol. 2 (Paris: Lecointe, 1833), 87–88; Philippon de la Madeleine, *Le justicier du roi*, vol. 2 (Paris: Dumont, 1834), 101–2; Théodore Muret, *Le Chevalier de Saint-Pont* (Paris: Dupont, 1834), 159. I borrowed these references from Sébastien Bracciali, *La guerre de mille ans? L'obsédante téléologie révolutionnaire aux lumières du roman historique, 1815–1835* (PhD diss., Université Paris 1, 2010), 107–9.

63. Richard Maxwell, *The Mysteries of Paris and London* (Charlottesville: University of Virginia Press, 1992).

64. Jules Janin, *L'eté à Paris* (Paris: Curmer, 1880), 13.

65. Joseph Garnier, *Les compagnons de la Coquille* (Dijon: Duvollet-Brugno, 1842), 9.

66. *Le Bourguignon salé*, June 18, 1892, quoted by Hadrien Nouvelot, "Les mystères de Dijon" (master's thesis, Université Paris 1, 2011).

67. The French term *Trouillefou* is named after the King of Truands character in the Hugo novel.

68. *Le VII⁰ arrondissement à la Belle Époque* (Paris: Musée Rodin, 1978), 30.

69. René Belbenoit, *Guillotine sèche* (Paris: Editions de France, 1938; repr. Paris: Manufacture des Livres, 2012), 73.

70. Henri Danjou, *Enfants du malheur!* (Paris: Albin Michel, 1932; repr. Paris: Manufacture de livres, 2012), 7.

71. René Héron de Villefosse, *Les ilots insalubres et glorieux de Paris* (Paris: Laurier noir, 1932), 272.

72. Quoted by Hubert Juin, in preface to Marcel Schwob, *Le roi au masque d'or et autres contes* (Paris: 10/18, 1979), 11.

73. "Besos para Golpes," in Hugo, *Notre-Dame de Paris*, 79.

3. "DANGEROUS CLASSES"

1. Alain Corbin, "Le XIX⁰ siècle ou la nécessité de l'assemblage," in *L'Invention du XIX⁰ siècle: Le XIX⁰ siècle vu par lui-même (littérature, histoire, société)*, ed. Alain Corbin

et al. (Paris: Klincksieck et Presses de la Sorbonne nouvelle, 1999), 153–59; Pierre Rosanvallon, *Le peuple introuvable: Histoire de la représentation démocratique en France* (Paris: Gallimard, 1988).

2. This phenomenon has given rise to an immense bibliography that I have tried to cover in Dominique Kalifa, "Enquête et culture de l'enquête au XIXᵉ siècle," *Romantisme*, no. 149 (2010): 3–23. I discuss some of these works in the text.

3. Victor Hugo, *Les misérables*, vol. 5, book 1, chap. 4, trans. Lee Fahnstock and Norman MacAfee (New York: Signet Classics, 1987), 839.

4. Stuart Woolf, *The Poor in Western Europe in the 18th and 19th Century* (London: Methuen, 1986).

5. Patrick Colquhoun, *A Treatise on the Police of the Metropolis* (London: Bye and Law, 1803), 49.

6. Quoted by Gueslin, *Gens pauvres, pauvres gens dans la France du XIXe siècle*, 94.

7. Saint-Marc Girardin, *Le Journal des Débats*, December 8, 1831.

8. Pierre Michel, *Un mythe romantique: Les barbares, 1789–1848* (Lyon: Presses universitaires de Lyon, 1981).

9. Louis Chevalier, *Classes laborieuses et classes dangereux a Paris dans le première moitié du XIXᵉ siècle* (Paris: Plon, 1958).

10. Thomas Plint, *Crime in England. Its Relation, Character and Extent* (London: Charles Gilpin, 1851), 146.

11. Fernando Vicente Albarran, "Los barrios negros: El ensanche sur en la formación del moderno Madrid (1860–1931)" (PhD thesis, Université Complutense de Madrid, 2011), 344–62.

12. Gareth Stedman Jones, *Outcast London: A Study in the Relationship Between Classes in Victorian Society* (Oxford: Clarendon Press, 1971); John Welshman, *Underclass: A History of the Excluded, 1880–2000* (London: Hambledon Continuum, 2006).

13. Israel Zangwill, *Children of the Ghetto* (London, 1892; repr. London: Germinal Productions, 2011).

14. Thomas Heise, *Urban Underworld: A Geography of Twentieth-Century American Literature and Culture* (New Brunswick, NJ: Rutgers University Press, 2011).

15. Alphonse Esquiros, *Les vierges folles* (Paris: Le Gallois, 1840), 83.

16. Heinrich Heine, *De la France* (Paris: Renduel, 1833).

17. Jean-Noël Tardy, *L'age des ombres: Complots, conspirations et sociétés secrètes au XIXᵉ siècle* (Paris: Les Belles Lettres, 2015).

18. Rodolphe Appony, Vingt-cinq ans à Paris (1826–1850): Journal du comte Rodolphe Apponyi, attaché à l'ambassade d'Autriche-Hongrie à Paris, vol. 2 (Paris: Plon, 1913), 121, 462.

19. Archibald Allison, "Causes of the Increase of Crime," *Blackwood's Edinburgh Magazine*, vol. 56, July 1844, 7.

20. *Journées de juin 1848 écrites devant et derrière les barricades par des témoins occulaires (sic.)* (Paris: Garnier Frères, n.d.), 14; quoted by Jean-Claude Caron, *Frères de sang: La guerre civile en France au XIXᵉ siècle* (Seyssel: Champ Vallon, 2009), 181.

21. Quoted in Caron, *Frères de sang*, 182.

22. Pierre-Antoine Pagès-Duport, *Journées de juin, récit complet des événements des 23 24 25 26 et des jours suivants* (Paris: Pitra et fils, 1848), 27; quoted in Caron, *Frères de sang*, 182–83.

23. Letter from the Chief Prosecutor of Lyon, February 14, 1859, BB30 440; quoted by Karine Salomé, *L'Ouragan homicide: L'attentat politique en France au XIXᵉ siècle* (Seyssel: Champ Vallon, 2011), 127.

24. Quoted by Caron, *Frères de sang*, 220.

25. Gabriel Tarde, *Sur le sommeil ou plutôt sur les rêves, et autres textes inédits*, presented by Louise Salmon (Lausanne: BHMS, 2010), 197–99.

26. Stedman Jones, *Outcast London*.

27. APP, BA/1900: General synthesis of the anarchist movement intended for the Prefect of Police, July 31, 1928, and March 11, 1933; quoted by Camille Boucher, "Les vrais révolutionnaires: Anarchistes individualistes français durant l'entre-deux-guerres" (master's thesis, Université Paris 1, 2010), 40.

28. Raymond Huard, "Marx et Engels devant la marginalité: La découverte du *Lumpenproletariat*," *Romantisme*, no. 59 (1988): 7.

29. Karl Marx, *The Communist Manifesto*, trans. Samuel Moore (London: 1848).

30. Marx, *The Communist Manifesto*, 646.

31. Friedrich Engels, prefatory note to "The Peasant War in Germany," in Marx and Engels, *Selected Works* (Moscow: Progress, 1969), vol. 1, 44.

32. Karl Marx, "The Eighteenth Brumaire of Louis Napoleon," (1852), in Marx and Engels, *Selected Works*, vol. 1. 295.

33. Peter Stallybrass, "Marx and Heterogeneity: Thinking the Lumpenproletariat," *Representations*, no. 31 (1990): 69–95.

34. Hippolyte Raynal, *Malheur et poésie* (Paris: Perrotin, 1834), 171.

35. Honoré A. Frégier, *Des classes dangereuses de la population dans les grandes villes et des moyens de les rendre meilleures* [The dangerous classes of people in the big cities and the means of making them better] (Paris: Baillière, 1840), 108; George Caïn, *Promenade dans Paris* (Paris: Flammarion, 1906), 58.

36. *Le Globe*, May 24, 1827.

37. Henri Cauvain, *Maximilien Heller* (Paris: Le Coffre, 1871; repr. Paris: Garnier, 1978), 96.

38. Eugène Sue, *Les mystères de Paris* (Paris, 1842–43); Eugène Sue, *The Mysteries of Paris*, trans. Carolyn Betansky and Jonathan Loeskey (London: Oxford Penguin Classics, 2015), 3.

39. Dominique Kalifa, "Archéologie de l'apachisme: Barbares et Peaux-Rouges au XIXᵉ siècle," in Kalifa, *Crime et culture au XIXe siècle*, 44–66.

40. Martine van Woerkens, *Le voyageur étranglé: L'inde des thugs, le colonialisme et l'imaginaire* (Paris: Albin Michel, 1995).

41. Andrew Davis, "Youth Gangs, Masculinity and Violence in Late-Victorian Manchester and Salford," *Journal of Social History* 32, no. 2 (1998): 350; Upamanyu Pablo Mukherjee, *Crime and Empire: The Colony in Nineteenth-Century Fictions of Crime* (London: Oxford University Press, 2003).

42. Louis Mathurin Moreau-Christophe, *Le monde des coquins: Physiologie du monde des coquins* (Paris, Dentu 1863).

43. Maxime Du Camp, *Paris: Ses organes, ses fonctions et sa vie dans la seconde moitié du XIXe siècle*, vol. 3 (Paris: Hachette, 1875), 18.

44. Friedrich Christian Avé-Lallement, *Das deutsche Gaunerthum in einer social-politischen, litterarische und linguistichen Ausbildung zu seinem heutigen Bestande* (Leipzig: Brockhaus, 1858–1862).

45. Cesare Lombroso, *Criminal Man*, trans. Mary Gibson and Nicole Rafter (Durham, NC: Duke University Press, 2008).

46. Émile Gautier, "Le monde des prisons: Notes d'un témoin," *Archives de l'anthropologie criminelle* (1888), 419.

47. James Greenwood, *Low-Life Deeps: An Account of the Strange Fish to Be Found There* (London: Guilford, 1881).

48. George R. Sims, *How the Poor Live and Horrible London* (London, Chatto & Windus, 1889), chap. 1.

49. General Booth, *In Darkest England and the Way Out* (London: International Headquarters of the Salvation Army, 1890), 11–12.

50. Anne McClintock, *Imperial Leather: Race, Gender and Sexuality in the Colonial Contest* (New York: Routledge, 1995), 120–22.

51. Jules de Goncourt, *Journal, mémoires de la vie littéraire*, vol. 2 (Paris: Flammarion, 1959), 848.

52. Quoted by Joseph McLaughlin, *Writing the Urban Jungle: Reading Empire in London from Doyle to Eliot* (Charlottesville: University of Virginia Press, 2000), 26.

53. Deborah E. Nord, "The Social Explorer as Anthropologist: Victorian Travelers Among the Urban Poor," in *Visions of the Modern City: Essays in History, Art, and Literature*, ed. William Sharpe and Leonard Wallock (New York: Columbia University Press, 1983), 118–30.

54. Nicolas Cochard, "Les bas fonds d'une ville portuaire, l'exemple du Havre au XIXe siècle," paper at the colloquium "Presse, prostitution, bas-fonds dans l'espace médiatique francophone 1830–1930," *Médias 19*; Damien Cailloux, "Les bas-fonds nantais, XIXe–XXe siècles" (master's thesis, Université de Paris 1, 2008).

55. Thomas Knox, *Underground, or Life Below the Surface: Incidents and Accidents Beyond the Light of Day* (London: Sampson, Low, 1878).

56. Gérard Cholvy, "Du Dieu terrible au Dieu d'amour: Une évolution dans la sensibilité religieuse au XIXe siècle," in *Transmettre la foi: XIXe—XXe siècles*, vol. 1 (Paris, 1984), 141–54; Ralph Gibson, "Hellfire and Damnation in Nineteen-Century France," *Catholic Historical Review* 84, no. 3 (1988): 383–401; Thomas Kselman, *Death and the Afterlife in Modern France* (Princeton, NJ: Princeton University Press, 1993), 82–83; Guillaume Cuchet, "Une révolution théologique oubliée: Le triomphe de la thèse du grand nombre des élus dans le discours catholique du XIXe siècle," *Revue d'histoire du XIXe siècle*, no. 41 (2010): 131–48.

57. Max Milner, *Le Diable dans la littérature française de Cazotte à Baudelaire* (Paris: Corti, 1960).

58. *Le Moniteur Universel*, April 25, 1844; quoted by A. Umezawa.

59. Adolphe Rueff, *Les aliénés à l'infirmerie spéciale près le dépôt de la préfecture de police* (Paris: Victorion, 1905), 29.

60. Paul Bru, *Histoire de Bicêtre* (Paris: Lecrosnier et Babe, 1890), 9.

61. Marie-Ève Thérenty and Alain Vaillant, *1836: L'An I de l'ère médiatique. Analyse littéraire et historique de* La Presse *de Girardin* (Paris: Nouveau Monde Editions, 2001).

62. Dominique Kalifa, *La culture de masse en France, 1860–1930* (Paris: La Découverte, 2001).

63. See Peter Brooks's introduction to the English translation of the complete text of Eugène Sue, *The Mysteries of Paris*, trans. Carolyn Betensky and Jonathan Loesberg (New York: Penguin Classics, 2015).

64. A team coordinated at the University of Montpellier by Marie-Eve Thérenty did an inventory of all the urban mysteries. Compare with Helle Waahlberg, "Le projet 'Mystères urbains au XIXᵉ siècle,'" Médias 19, http://www.medias19.org/index.php?id=645.

65. Oscar Méténier. *Lui!* One-act drama (Paris: Ollendorff, 1898).

66. Dominique Kalifa, *L'encre et le sang: Récits de crimes et société à la Belle Époque* (Paris: Fayard, 1995), 47–52.

67. Lee Grieveson, Peter Stanfield, and Esther Sonnet, *Mob Culture: Hidden Histories of the American Gangster Film* (New Brunswick, NJ: Rutgers University Press, 2005).

68. I use this term in the sense given it by Marc Lits, *Du récit au récit médiatique* (Brussels: De Boeck, 2008).

69. Michel Nathan, "Le ressassement, ou ce que peut le roman populaire," in *Richesses du roman populaire*, ed. René Guise and Hans-Jörg Neuschäfer (Nancy: Centre de recherches sur le roman populaire, 1986), 235–50.

70. Jean-Claude Vareille, *Le Roman populaire français (1789–1914). Idéologies et pratiques* (Limoges: Presses Universitaires de Limoges, 1994).

71. Jean Kolb and Raymond Robert, "Une soirée chez les amateurs de cocaïne," *Police Magazine*, December 14, 1930.

72. Quoted by Myriam Boucharenc, *L'écrivain-reporter au cœur des années trente* (Lille: Presses du Septentrion, 2004), 62.

73. Eugène Buret, *De la misère des classes laborieuses en France et en Angleterre*, vol. 1 (Paris: Renouard, 1841), 69.

74. Friedrich Engels, *The Condition of the Working Class in England in 1844* (London: Oxford Basil Blackwell, 1958), 145, https://www.marxists.org/archive/marx/works/download/pdf/condition-working-class-england.pdf.

75. Felix Nadar, *Le monde où l'on patauge* [The world in which one wades] (Paris: Dentu, 1883), 30.

76. Octave Féré, *Les mystères de Rouen* (Rouen: Haulard, 1861), 23.

77. Hugo, *Les misérables*, vol. 3, book 7, chaps. 1, 2, 7.

4. EMPIRE OF LISTS

1. Franco Moretti, *Atlas of the European Novel 1800–1900* (London: Verso 1998), 143.

2. Michel Foucault, *The Order of Things: An Archeology of the Social Sciences* (1966; repr. London: Verso, 1994).

3. François de Calvi, *Divisée en trois livres, I. Contenant les cruautez & méchancetez des voleurs, II. Des ruses & subtilitez des coupeurs de bourses, III. Les finesses, tromperies, & stratagèmes des filous* (Rouen: Chez la veuve de Robert Daré, 1666).

4. Richard J. Evans, "The 'Dangerous Classes' in Germany from the Middle Ages to the Twentieth Century," in *The German Underworld. Deviants and Outcasts in German History*, ed. Richard Evans (New York: Routledge, 1988), 1–28.

5. This part of Vidocq's *Memoirs* has not been translated in the British and American editions, which have favored tales of action and adventure rather than general considerations such as classification. Eugène François Vidocq, *Mémoires de Vidocq, chef de police de sûreté jusqu'en 1827* (Paris : Tenon, 1828), chap. 30.

6. Claudine Nedelec, "Le langage de l'argot: De la vie généreuse des mercelots, gueux et bohémiens aux mystères de Paris (1596–1842)" (PhD diss., Université Paris 3, 1992).

7. I studied the French memoirs in "Les mémoires de policier: L'émergence d'un genre?", in my *Crime et culture au XIXᵉ siècle* (Paris: Perrin, 2005), 67–102. For England, see Paul Lawrence, ed., *The Making of the Modern Police: 1780–1914*, vols. 2 and 3 (London: Pickering & Chatto, 2014); and for Italy see Marco Soresina, "Le memorie dei funzionari di polizia Italiani nell'eta liberale in una prospettiva comparata," *Studi Storici* 4 (2017): 1097–1131.

8. Marcel Guillaume, *Trente-sept ans avec la pègre* (Paris: Editions de France, 1938; repr. Paris: Editions des Équateurs, 2007), 123.

9. Christian Jouhaud, Dinah Ribard, and Nicolas Schapira, eds., *Histoire, Littérature. Témoignages: Écrire les malheurs du temps* (Paris: Gallimard, 2009), 34.

10. *Mémoires de Canler, ancien chef du service de la Sûreté* (Paris: Hetzel, 1862).

11. Charles Dickens, "Three Detective Anecdotes" and "On Duty with Inspector Field," *Household Words*, June 14, 1851, in *Reprinted Pieces* (London: Chapman and Hall, 1859).

12. Adolphe Gonfrier, *Dictionnaire de la racaille: Le manuscrit secret d'un commissaire de police parisien au XIXᵉ siècle* (Paris: Horay, 2010).

13. Carmen Bernand, *Buenos Aires, 1880–1936: Un mythe des confins* (Paris: Autrement, 2001).

14. Caimari, *La ciudad y el crimen*.

15. Vincent Milliot, dir., *Les mémoires policiers, 1750–1850. Écritures et pratiques policières du Centurydes Lumières au Second Empire*, Presses universitaires de Rennes, 2006.

16. Diego Galeano, *Escritores, detectives y archivistas: La cultura policial en Buenos Aires, 1821–1910* (Buenos Aires: Teseo, 2009), 111.

17. Francis Galton, "Composite Portraits," (1879), quoted by Neil Davie, *Les visages de la criminalité: A la recherche d'une théorie scientifique du criminel type en Angleterre (1860–1914)* (Paris: Kimé, 2004), 78–79.

18. Joseph-Marie de Gérando, *Le visiteur du pauvre* (Colas, 1820). See the analysis of Michelle Perrot, "L'œil du baron ou le visiteur du pauvre" (1988), in her *Les ombres de l'histoire: Crime et châtiment au XIXᵉ siècle* (Paris: Flammarion, 2001), 101–8.

19. Françoise Barret-Ducrocq, *Pauvreté, charité et morale à Londres au XIXᵉ siècle: Une sainte violence* (Paris: PUF, 1991); Seth Koven, *Slumming: Sexual and Social Politics in Victorian London* (Princeton, NJ: Princeton University Press, 2004).

20. Gérard Leclerc, *L'observation de l'homme: Une histoire des enquêtes sociales* (Paris: Seuil, 1979).

21. Henry Mayhew, *London Labour and the London Poor*, vol. 4 (London: Griffin, Bohn, 1862), 1–4. Compare with Roland Pelurson, "Mayhew entre conformisme et dissidence," in *Écrire la pauvreté: Les enquêtes sociales britanniques aux XIXᵉ et XXᵉ siècles*, ed. Jacques Carré and Jean-Paul Révauger (Paris: L'Harmattan, 1995), 67.

22. Henry Mayhew and John Binny, *The Criminal Prisons of London and Scenes of London Life* (London: Griffith, 1862), xx.

23. Frédéric Le Play, *La description des procédés métallurgiques employés dans le pays de Galles* (1846), cited in Françoise Arnaud, *Frédéric Le Play: De la métallurgie à la science sociale* (Nancy: Presses Universitaires de Nancy, 1993), 46.

24. See chapter 8 of this volume.

25. Nels Anderson, *The Hobo: The Sociology of the Homeless Man* (Chicago: Chicago University Press, 1923); and Nels Anderson, *Men on the Move* (Chicago: Chicago University Press, 1940).

26. Louis Mathurin Moreau-Christophe, *Le monde des coquins: Physiologie du monde des coquins* (Paris: Dentu 1863).

27. Jacob Riis, *How the Other Half Lives: Studies Among the Tenements of New York* (New York: Charles Scribner's Sons, 1890); Keith Gandal, *The Virtues of the Vicious: Jacob Riis, Stephen Crane, and the Spectacle of the Slum* (New York: Oxford University Press, 1997).

28. Louis Barron, *Paris étrange* (Paris: Marpon and Flammarion, 1883); Charles Virmaître, *Paris oublié* (Paris: Dentu, 1866); Paul Strauss, *Paris ignoré* (Paris: May and Motteroz, 1892); Charles Virmaître, *Paris-escarpe* (Paris: Savine, 1887); Georges Grison, *Paris horrible et Paris original* (Paris: Dentu, 1882); Paul Bellon and Georges Price, *Paris qui passe* (Paris: Savine, 1883).

29. Edward Crapsey, *The Nether Side of New York, or the Vice, Crime, and Poverty of the Great Metropolis* (New York: Sheldon, 1872).

30. Eugène Villiod, *Les plaies sociales: Comment on nous vole, comment on nous tue* (Paris: Chez l'auteur, 1905); Louis Thinet, *Histoires de voleurs* (Paris: Fayard, 1929); Alfred Morain, *The Underworld of Paris: Secrets of the Sûreté* (New York: Blue Ribbon Books, 1929).

31. Maurice Alhoy, *Les bagnes: Histoire, types, mœurs, mystères* (Paris: Havard, 1845); Maurice Alhoy, *Les brigands et bandits célèbres* (Paris: Guiller, 1845); Maurice Alhoy and Louis Lurine, *Les Prisons de Paris: Histoire, types, mœurs, mystères* (Paris: Havard, 1846).

32. See John Merriman, *Ballad of the Anarchist Bandits: The Crime Spree That Gripped the Belle Epoque* (New York: Nation Books, 2017).

33. Eugène Dieudonné, *La vie des forçats* (Paris: Gallimard, 1930; repr. Paris: Libertalia, 2007), 136.

34. Daniel Parker, *Les trafiquants de femmes, leurs méthodes de recrutement, l'organisation de la traite* (Paris: Association pour la répression de la traite de Blanches, n.d.), quoted in Agathe Lecoeur, "Les bas-fonds a contrario: Etude du discours des bas-fonds et de ses transferts autour de la ville de Buenos Aires au début du XXᵉ siècle" (master's thesis, Université Paris 1, 2011), 95.

35. Frédéric Boutet, "Ceux qui tuent," *Détective*, no. 38, 1929.

36. Jean Chiappe, *Parole d'ordre* (Paris: Figuière, 1930), 141.

37. Joseph Kessel, *Nuits de Montmartre* (Paris: Editions de France, 1932), 75.

38. Maryse Choisy, *Un mois chez les filles* (Paris: Montaigne, 1928).

39. Henri Danjou, *Place Maubert (dans les bas-fonds de Paris)* (Paris: Albin Michel, 1928), 28.

40. Albert Londres, *Marseille, port du sud* (Paris: Albin Michel, 1927).

41. Alain Bauer and Christophe Souliez, *Une histoire criminelle de la France* (Paris: Odile Jacob, 2012).

42. Howard S. Becker, *Outsiders: Studies in the Sociology of Deviance* (New York: The Free Press, 1973).

5. THE DISGUISED PRINCE

1. David Stevenson, " 'The Gudeman of Ballangeich' : Rambles in the Afterlife of James V," *Folklores*, no. 115 (2004): 187–200.

2. Robert Irwin, *The Arabian Nights: A Companion* (London: Tauris Parke, 2003); Dwight Reynolds, "A Thousand and One Nights: A History of the Text and Its Reception," in *The Cambridge History of Arabic Literature*, vol. 6, ed. Roger Allen and D. S. Richards (Cambridge: Cambridge University Press, 2006).

3. Dominique Jullien, *Les amoureux de Schéhérazade: Variations modernes sur les Mille et une nuits* (Geneva: Droz, 2009).

4. Karl Marx and Friedrich Engels, *The Holy Family, or the Critique of Critical Reason* (Frankfurt am Main,1845), chap. 8.

5. Koven, *Slumming: Sexual and Social Politics*, 61.

6. Robert Louis Stevenson, *New Arabian Nights* (London: Chatto & Windus, 1882); Robert Louis Stevenson and Fanny Van De Grift Stevenson, *More New Arabian Nights: The Dynamiter* (London: Longmans, Green, 1885).

7. Daniel Baruch, introduction to *Paris le jour, Paris la nuit*, by Louis-Sébastien Mercier (Paris: Laffont, 1990), 591–615.

8. John F. Kasson, *Rudeness and Civility: Manners in Nineteenth-Century Urban America* (New York: Hill and Wang, 1990), 110–11. On the weak legitimacy of policemen and detectives, see Dominique Kalifa, "Criminal Investigators at the Fin-de-siècle," *Yale French Studies*, no. 108 (2005): 36–47; and Dominique Kalifa, *Histoire des détectives privés en France* (Paris: Plon, 2000; Paris: Nouveau Monde, 2007).

9. Alfred Delvau, *Les Dessous de Paris* (Paris: Poulet-Malassis et de Broise, 1860), 10.

10. Jean-Louis Bory, *Eugène Sue: Dandy mais socialiste* (Paris: Hachette Littérature, 1962), 248–49.

11. *Mémoires de Monsieur Claude* (Paris: J. Rouff, 1881–1885), 73.

12. Alexandre Dumas, *Les Mohicans de Paris*, initially published in *Le Mousquetaire* from 1854 to 1859.

13. Mark Freeman and Gillian Nelson, eds., *Vicarious Vagrants: Incognito Social Explorers and the Homeless in England, 1860–1910* (Lambertville: NJ: The True Bill Press, 2008).

14. M. A., "A Night in the Casual Ward of the Work-House, in Rhyme. Dedicated to the Million" (London: News Agents' Publishing, 1866).

15. Joshua Harrison Stallard, *The Female Casual and Her Lodging* (London: Saunders, Otley, 1866), 1–79.

16. Mary Higgs, *Three Nights in Women's Lodging-Houses* (London: Mary Higgs, 1906); Georges Z. Edward, *A Vicar as Vagrant* (London: King & Son, 1910).

17. Simone Chambon and Anne Wicke, *Jack London: Entre chien et loup* (Paris: Belin, 2001).

18. Louis Paulian, *La Hotte du chiffonnier* (Paris: Hachette, 1885); Louis Paulian, *Paris qui mendie: Les vrais et les faux pauvres* (Paris: Ollendorff, 1893); Louis Paulian, *The Beggars of Paris*, trans. Lady Herschell (London: Edward Arnold, 1897).

19. Paulian, *The Beggars of Paris*, 9–10.

20. Paulian, 11.

21. Marc Michel, *Les Gueux de Marseille: Chronique contemporaine, 1810* (Marseille: Impr. militaire, 1836), quoted by Laurence Montel, "Marseille capitale du crime: Histoire croisée de l'imaginaire de Marseille et de la criminalité organisée (1820–1940)" (PhD diss., Université de Paris 10, 2008).

22. Paulian, *Paris qui mendie*, 216.

23. James Greenwood, "A Night in a Workhouse," *Pall Mall Gazette*, January 12–15, 1866.

24. James Greenwood, *The Seven Curses of London* (London, 1869); James Greenwood, *Unsentimental Journeys, or Byways of the Modern Babylon* (London, 1867); James Greenwood, *The Wilds of London* (London, 1874); James Greenwood, Low-Life Deeps (London, 1875); James Greenwood, *Odd People in Odd Places, or the Great Residuum* (London, 1883); James Greenwood, *Toilers in London, by One of the Crowd* (London, 1883); James Greenwood, *Mysteries of Modern London, by One of the Crowd* (London, 1883); James Greenwood, *On Tramp* (London, 1883).

25. Freeman and Nelson, *Vicarious Vagrants*, xx.

26. Walter Thomas Cranfield, *A Vicarious Vagrant* (London: Hurst & Blackett, 1910).

27. The most relevant analysis of the case is by Judith Walkowitz, *City of Dreadful Delight: Narratives of Sexual Danger in Victorian London* (Chicago: University of Chicago Press, 1992), 81–134.

28. Rolf Lindner, *The Reportage of Urban Culture: Robert Park and the Chicago School* (Cambridge: Cambridge University Press, 1996).

29. Frank Luther Mott, *American Journalism: A History of Newspapers in the United States Through 250 Years, 1690 to 1940* (New York: MacMillan, 1941), 442.

30. Brooke Kroeger, Nellie Bly: *Daredevil, Reporter, Feminist* (New York: Random House, 1994).

31. Elizabeth L. Banks, *The Autobiography of a "Newspaper Girl"* (New York: Dodd, Mead, 1902).

32. Georges Grison, *Paris horrible et Paris original* (Paris: Dentu, 1882), 4.

33. Marie-Ève Thérenty, "Séparatisme de genre," in *La Civilisation du journal: Histoire culturelle et littéraire de la presse française*, ed. Dominique Kalifa et al. (Paris: Nouveau Monde, 2011), 1436.

34. Georges de Lavarenne, "Les bals musette," *Police Magazine*, no. 109, 1932.

35. And the same year as a book, in a translation for Editions Crès.

36. Maryse Choisy, *Un mois chez les filles: Reportage* (Paris: Montaigne, 1928).

37. Maryse Choisy, *Un mois chez les hommes* (Paris: Éditions de France, 1929).

38. Georges Le Fevre, *Je suis un gueux: A Londres. A Berlin. A Paris* (Paris: Baudinière, 1929).

39. Jean Dorian, *Belles de lune. Reportage dans les bas-fonds de Marseille* (Paris: Haloua, 1935); Armand-Henry Flassch, "Vos papiers," *Détective*, no. 51, October 17, 1929; Maurice Aubenas, "Au dépôt," *Détective*, May 31, 1934.

40. Let us think of the famous reporting of the American journalist Hunter S. Thompson, who in 1966 entered the Hell's Angels of California, or that of Günter Wallraff, who transformed himself into a Turkish immigrant worker in Germany of 1985 (Günter Wallraff, *Lowest of the Low* [London: Methuen, 1985]). In 1977, Wallraff had already borrowed a false identity to work at *Bild-Zeitung* and to denounce the methods of a newspaper that flouted privacy and dishonored journalism. In France, Hubert Prolongeau for four months shared the life of the homeless (Hubert Prolongeau, *Sans domicile fixe* [New York: Hachette, 1993]); in the United States Barbara Ehrenreich was hired by Wall Mart to work in a warehouse (Barbara Ehrenreich, *Nickeled and Dimed* [New York: Henry Holt, 2001]); and Arthur Frayer, journalist at *Ouest-France*, worked eight months as a guard in two French prisons (Arthur Frayer, *Dans la peau d'un maton* [Paris: Fayard, 2011]).

41. Koven, *Slumming*, 13.

42. Jack London, *People of the Abyss* (New York: Macmillan, 1903), chap. 8.

43. Quoted by Jullien, *Les amoureux de Schéhérazade*, 27.

44. Letter to Beatrice Potter, November 12, 1887, quoted by Koven, *Slumming*, 13.

45. Alexandre Vexliard, *Le clochard: Étude de psychologie sociale* (Paris: Desclée de Brouwer, 1957), 30.

46. Rolf Lindner, *The Reportage of Urban Culture: Robert Park and the Chicago School* (Cambridge, UK: Cambridge University Press, 1996).

47. Sudhir Venkatesh, *Gang Leader for a Day: A Rogue Sociologist Crosses the Line* (London: Allen Lane, 2008).

48. Georges Orwell, *Down and Out in Paris and London* (London: Victor Gollancz, 1933); Georges Orwell, René-NoëRaimbualt, Gwen Gilbert, and Panaït Istrati, *La Vache enragée* (Paris: Gallimard, 1935).

49. Georges Orwell, *The Road to Wigan Pier* (London: Gollancz, 1937), 65.

50. Orwell, *The Road to Wigan Pier*, 68.

51. Koven, *Slumming*, 36.

52. An exception is Carol Ann Parssinen, "Social Explorers and Social Scientists: The Dark Continent of Victorian Ethnography," in *A Crack in a Mirror*, ed. Jay Ruby (Philadelphia: University of Pennsylvania Press, 1982), 205–19; Anthony Wohl, "Social Exploration Among the London Poor: Theater or Laboratory," *Revue française de civilisation britannique*, no. 6 (1991): 77–97.

53. Luc Boltanski, *Distant Suffering: Morality, Media and Politics*, trans. Graham Burchell (Cambridge, UK: Cambridge University Press, 1999).

54. Koven, *Slumming*, 32.

55. Raymond Schults, Crusader in Babylon: W. T. Stead and the Pall Mall Gazette (Lincoln: University of Nebraska Press, 1972), 87.

56. Koven, *Slumming*, 27–51.

57. Here I am following the demonstration by Koven, *Slumming*.

58. Karl Marx and Friedrich Engels, "Rudolph: The Revealed Mystery of All Mysteries," in *The Holy Family*, 268.

6. THE GRAND DUKES' TOUR

1. A first version of this chapter appeared in German under the title "Das Gegenstück des Boulevard: La tournée des grands-ducs und der Elendstourismus," in *Haussmann und die Folge. Vom Boulevard zur Boulevardisierung*, ed. Walburga Hülk and Gregor Schuhen (Tübingen: Narr Verlag, 2012), 67–80.

2. Pierce Egan, *Life in London, or the Day and Night Scenes of Jerry Hawthorn, Esq., and His Elegant Friend Corinthian Tom, Accompanied by Bob Logic, the Oxonian, in Their Rambles and Sprees Through the Metropolis* (London: Chatto and Windus, 1821).

3. Pierce Egan, *Boxiana, or Sketches of Ancient Modern Pugilism* (London: Virtue, 1824).

4. George Smeeton, *Doings in London, or the Day and Night Scenes of the Frauds, Frolics, Manners and Depravities of the Metropolis* (London: Hodgson, 1828); John Duncombe, *The Dens of London* (London, 1835).

5. Judith Walkowitz, ed., *Unknown London: Early Modern Visions of the Metropolis, 1815–1845* (London: Pickering and Chatto, 2000).

6. Charles Dickens, "On Duty with Inspector Field," June 14, 1851, "Down with the Tide," February 5, 1853, *Household Words*, in *Reprinted Pieces* (London: Chapman and Hall, 1859); Donald Shaw, *London in the Sixties, with a Few Digressions* (London: Everett, 1908), 91.

7. Hyppolite Taine, *Notes sur l'Angleterre* (Paris: Hachette, 1872), 322–24.

8. *Mémoires de M. Claude* (Paris: Rouff, 1881–1885).

9. Albert Wolff, "Londres ténébreux," in *Mémoires d'un Parisien: Voyage à travers le monde*, by Albert Wolff (Paris: Victor-Havard, 1884), 1–45.

10. Léon Daudet, *Fantômes et vivants* (Paris: Nouvelle Librairie Nationale, 1914), 333–35.

11. Charles Nisard, *La muse pariétaire et la muse foraine, ou les chansons des rues depuis quinze ans* (Paris: Jules Gay, 1863), 297.

12. Jean-Louis Bory, *Eugène Sue, le roi du roman populaire* (Paris: Hachette, 1962), 271.
13. Louis Barron, *Paris étrange* (Paris, 1883; repr. London: Forgotten Books, 2017).
14. Léon-Paul Fargue, *Refuges* (Paris: Emile Paul frères, 1942), 26.
15. André de Fouquières, *Mon Paris et ses parisiens, Pigalle 1900* (Paris: Horay, 1955).
16. Jean Lorrain, "La tournée des grands-ducs," *Je Sais Tout*, July 1905, 717–23.
17. Alfred Morain, *The Underworld of Paris: Secrets of the Sûreté* (New York: Blue Ribbon Books, 1929), 39.
18. Tylor Anbinder, *Five Points. The Nineteenth-Century New York City Neighborhood That Invented Tap Dance, Stole Elections, and Became the World's Most Notorious Slum* (New York: Free Press, 2001), 190.
19. Emile Carassus, *Le snobisme et les lettres françaises de Paul Bourget à Marcel Proust, 1884–1912* (Paris: Colin, 1966).
20. "Un bal shocking," *Le Gaulois*, January 8, 1885; *Guide de poche 1900: Paris la nuit* (Paris: Schwarz, 1900), 304.
21. Paul de Chamberet, *Une nuit de Paris: Au pays du vice et de la misère* (Paris: Warnier, 1897).
22. *Paris intime et mystérieux: Guide des plaisirs mondains et des plaisirs secrets à Paris* (Paris: André Hall, 1904).
23. Dubut de Laforest, *La tournée des grands ducs, mœurs parisiennes* (Paris: Flammarion, 1901); Dubut de Laforest, *Monsieur Pithec et la Vénus des fortifs*, vol. 2 (Paris: Flammarion, 1902).
24. Maurice Donnay, *Amants* (Paris: Albin Michel, 1895), 19–21.
25. Maurice Barrès, *Les déracinés* (Paris 1897; repr. Paris: Plon, 1967), 370, 397, 451 (quotation at 451). In English *The Uprooted*, 1941, first part of the trilogy *The Novel of National Energy*.
26. Jean Lorrain, *Poussières de Paris* (Paris: Klincksieck, 2006), 85–86.
27. Jean Lorrain, *La maison Philibert* (Paris: Librairie universelle, 1904), 144.
28. Lorrain, "La tournée des grands-ducs."
29. *Comment visiter les dessous de Paris, la tournée des grands ducs, les bals-musette, etc., guides parisiens* (Paris: Impr. Henry Maillet, 1931). See also Elie Richard, *Le guide des grands-ducs* (Paris: Ed. du monde moderne, 1925); Elie Richard, "La tournée des grands ducs," *Paris-Soir*, April 15–May 2, 1930; *Guide des plaisirs à Paris. Paris le jour, Paris la nuit. Ce qu'il faut voir, ce qu'il faut savoir, comment on s'amuse, ou l'on s'amuse* (Paris: Bellenand, 1931).
30. Maryse Choisy, "La tournée des grands ducs," chap. 15 in *Un mois chez les filles: Reportage* (Paris: Montaigne, 1928), 188–222.
31. Francis de Miomandre, *Dancings* (Paris: Flammarion, 1932), 89.
32. Joseph Kessel, "Paris la nuit," *Détective*, no. 3, November 15, 1928.
33. Richard, *Le guide des grands-ducs*, 232.
34. André Warnod, *Visages de Paris* (Paris: Firmin didot, 1930), 360.
35. Jenny Lefcourt, "Aller au cinéma, aller au people," *Revue d'histoire moderne et contemporaine*, no. 51–54 (2004): 98–114.
36. Michel Rachline, *Jacques Prévert* (Paris: Olbia, 1999), 78.

37. *Comment visiter les dessous de Paris*, 45.
38. Lorrain, *La maison Philibert*, 144.
39. Henri Danjou, *Place Maubert (dans les bas-fonds de Paris)* (Paris: Albin Michel, 1928), 10.
40. Georges Cain, *Les Pierres de Paris* (Paris: Flammarion, 1910), 172, quoted by Chloé Maurel, "Images et représentations du quartier Saint-Merri dans l'entre-deux-guerres," in *Les Halles: Images d'un quartier*, ed. Jean-Louis Robert and Myriam Tsikounas (Paris: Publications de la Sorbonne, 2004), 137–58.
41. Lorrain, "La tournée des grands-ducs," 719.
42. Lorrain, 720.
43. Richard, *Le guide des grands-ducs*, 95. See also Danjou, *Place Maubert*.
44. Richard, *Le guide des grands-ducs*, 82.
45. Georges Caïn, *Le long des rues* (Paris: Flammarion, 1912), 78.
46. Joseph Hémard, *Le grand clapier de Paris* (Paris: Ed. de la Tournelle, 1946), 24.
47. *Comment visiter les dessous de Paris*, 18.
48. Chamberet, *Une nuit de Paris*, 4.
49. Chamberet, 7.
50. Lorrain, "La tournée des grands-ducs," 717.
51. *Comment visiter les dessous de Paris*, 17.
52. Danjou, *Place Maubert*, 48–49.
53. Extracts from the minutes of the meetings of the Board of Governors of the *Œuvre de l'hospitalité de nuit*, quoted by Lucia Katz, *L'avènement du sans-abri: Histoire des asiles de nuit, 1871–1914* (Paris: Libertalia, 2015).
54. Lorrain, "La tournée des grands-ducs," 719.
55. Chamberet, *Une nuit de Paris*, 4.
56. Fortuné du Boisgobey, *Le Pouce crochu* (Paris, 1885; repr. Paris: Les Belles Lettres, 2006), 78.
57. Warnod, *Visages de Paris*, 211–14.
58. Chamberet, *Une nuit de Paris*.
59. Stanley Scott, *Tales of Bohemia, Taverns, and the Underworld* (London: Hurst and Blackett, 1925), 15.
60. Georges de la Salle, *En Mandchourie* (Paris: Colin, 1905) 199–201; Eugène Brieux, *Voyage aux Indes et en Indochine* (Paris: Delagrave, 1923), 22.
61. Joseph Kessel, *Bas-fonds de Paris* (Paris: Editions des Portiques, 1932), 15.
62. Louis Bertrand, *Nuits d'Alger* (Paris: Flammarion, 1929), 23–24.
63. Ashelbé, *Pépé le Moko* (Paris: EID, 1931).
64. Anbinder, *Five Points*, 2.
65. Stuart M. Blumin, "Georg G. Foster and the Emerging Metropolis," preface to *New York by Gas-Light and Other Urban Sketches*, by George C. Foster (Berkeley: University of California Press, 1990), 1–61.
66. Foster, *New York by Gas-Light*, 69.
67. Hjalmer Hjorth Boyesen, *Social Struggle: A Novel* (New York: Scribner's, 1893), 259.
68. Ernest Ingersol, *A Week in New York* (New York: Rand, McNally, 1891), 201–17.

69. *The Ottawa Free Press*, November 21, 1888, quoted by Jérôme Triebel, "Les Slummers de l'East End" (master's thesis, Université Paris 1, 2010), which inspired the following paragraphs.

70. Karl Baedeker, *London and Its Environs* (London: Leipzig, 1900), quoted by Seth Koven, *Slumming: Sexual and Social Politics in Victorian London* (Princeton, NJ: Princeton University Press, 2004), 1.

71. *English Illustrated Magazine*, quoted in Koven, *Slumming*, 6.

72. Josiah Flynt, "Police Methods in London," *North American Review* 176, no. 556 (1903): 436–49.

73. Georges Sim, *Li Ting of London, and Other Stories* (London: Chatto and Windus, 1905).

74. Virginia Berridge, *Opium and the People: Opiate Use in 19th Century England* (London: A. Lane, 1981).

75. Anne Witchard, "A Threepenny Omnibus Ticket to Limey-House-Causey-Way: Fictional Sojourns in Chinatown," *Comparative Critique Studies*, no. 4 (2007): 225–240.

76. Walter Besant, *East London* (London: Chatto and Windus, 1901), 206–7.

77. This is the analysis of Barry Milligan, *Pleasures and Pain: Opium and the Orient in Nineteenth Century British Culture* (Charlottesville: University of Virginia Press, 1995).

78. Quoted by Michael Diamond, *Lesser Breeds: Racial Attitudes in Popular British Fiction, 1890–1949* (London: Anthem Press, 2006), 20.

79. Sax Rohmer, *Dope: A Story of Chinatown and Drug Traffic* (London: Cassell, 1919), 274.

80. Thomas Burke, *Nights in Town: A London Autobiography* (London: Allen & Urwin, 1915), 75.

81. *How to See London and Places of Historical Interest*, Thomas Cook Group Ltd., Company Archives, 1928.

82. *Stepney and Limehouse, 1914. Old Ordnance Survey Map of London* (London: The Godfrey Edition, 1990).

83. Émile Gautier, *Le monde des prisons* (Lyon: Storck, 1888), 1.

84. Sylvain Rapapport, *La chaîne des forçats, 1793–1836* (Paris: Aubier, 2006); Vanessa R. Schwartz, *Spectacular Realities: Early Mass Culture in Fin-de-Siècle Paris* (Berkeley: University of California Press, 1998); Victor A. Gatrell, *The Hanging Tree: Execution and the English People, 1770–1868* (Oxford, UK: Oxford University Press, 1994).

85. Richard, *Le guide des grands-ducs*, 3.

86. Joseph Casanova, *La tournée du grand duc* (Paris: Picard, 1920), 63.

87. Joseph Kessel, *La piste fauve* (Paris: Gallimard, 1954), 126.

88. *Paris intime et mystérieux*.

89. Boisgobey, *Le Pouce crochu*, 103.

90. Laforest, *La tournée des ducs-ducs*, 156.

91. Richard, *Le guide des grands-ducs*, 92–93.

92. Harry J. Greenwall, *The Underworld of Paris* (London: Stanley Paul, 1921), 25–36.

93. This was the case with *Déracinés* by Barrès or, in another register, of the cycle by Guy de Téramond, *Bas-fonds de Paris* (Paris: Tallandier, 1929).

94. Richard, *Le guide des grands-ducs*, 149.

95. Lucienne Favre, *Dans la Casbah* (Paris: Grasset, 1937), 68–69.

96. Jean-Paul Clébert, *Paris insolite, authentifié par 115 photographies de Patrice Molinard* (Paris: Denoel, 1952; repr. Paris: Attila, 2009), 259.

97. Egan, *Life in London*, 320.

98. Smeeton, *Doings in London*, 289.

99. Richard, *Le guide des grands-ducs*, 92–93.

100. Lorrain, *La maison Philibert*, 309.

101. Lorrain, "La tournée des grands-ducs."

102. Charlie Chaplin, *My Wonderful Visit* (London: Hurst & Blackett, 1922), 130.

103. Richard, *Le guide des grands-ducs*, 6.

104. Lydie Salvayre, *Les belles âmes* (Paris: Seuil, 2000).

105. Nigel Scotland, *Squires in the Slums. Settlements and Missions in Late-Victorian London* (New York: Taurus, 2007).

106. Lorrain, *La maison Philibert*, 283.

107. Marcel Priollet, *Les gueux en habit noir (les bas-fonds du grand monde)* (Paris: Tallandier, 1926).

108. Aristide Bruant, *Le bal des puces* (Paris: Fayard, 1903), 61.

109. Bruant, *Les bas-fonds de Paris*, 407.

110. Bruant, *Les bas-fonds de Paris*, 400.

7. POETIC FLIGHT

1. The best study of the matter is by Jerrold Seigel, Bohemian *Paris: Culture, Politics, and the Boundaries of Bourgeois Life, 1830–1930* (New York: Viking, 1986). I am also using Mary Gluck, Popular Bohemia. Modernism and Urban Culture in Nineteenth-Century Paris (Cambridge MA: Harvard University Press, 2005).

2. Marylin Brown, *Gypsies and Other Bohemians: The Myth of the Artist in Nineteen Century France* (Ann Arbor: University of Michigan Press, 1985); Sarga Moussa, ed., *Le mythe des bohémiens dans la littérature et les arts en Europe* (Paris: L'Harmattan, 2008).

3. Alfred Delvau, *Les dessous de Paris* (Paris: Poulet-Malassis et de Broise, 1860), 10.

4. Gérard de Nerval, *Nuits d'Octobre* (Paris, 1852), in *Œuvres*, by Gérard de Nerval (Paris: Gallimard, 1993), v. iii, 321. See extracts in Gérard de Nerval, *Selected Writings* trans. and ed. Richard Siebrruth (London: Penguin Classics, 2006).

5. Delvau, *Les dessous de Paris*, 32.

6. Alexandre Privat d'Anglemont, *Paris inconnu* (Paris: Delahaye, 1860), 11.

7. Anglemont, *Paris inconnu*, 54. See also chapter 2.

8. Alexandre Privat d'Anglemont, *Paris anecdote: Les industries inconnues, la Childebert, les oiseaux de nuit, la villa des chiffonniers* (Paris: P. Jannet, 1854), 218.

9. Anglemont, *Paris anecdote*, 6.

10. Anglemont, *Paris inconnu*, 40.

11. Anglemont, 157.

12. Anglemont, *Paris anecdote*, 217.

13. Anglemont, 173.

14. Quoted by Dietmar Rieger, "Ce qu'on voit dans les rues de Paris: Marginalités sociales et regards bourgeois," *Romantisme*, no. 59 (1988): 19–29.

15. Rieger, "Ce qu'on voit dans les rues de Paris."

16. Miranda Gill, *Eccentricity and the Cultural Imagination in Nineteenth-Century Paris* (Oxford: Oxford University Press, 2009).

17. Roland Dorgelès, *Le château des brouillards* (Paris: Albin Michel, 1923), 41.

18. Dorgelès, *Le château des brouillards*, 8.

19. Jean-François Wagniart, *Le vagabond à la fin du XIXᵉ siècle* (Paris: Belin, 1999).

20. Francis Carco, "Chansons de Paris," in *Le Paris de M. Francis*, ed. Gilles Freyssinet (Paris: Arcadia, 2005), 153.

21. Silvain Rappaport, *La chaine des forçats: 1793–1896* (Paris: Aubier, 2006).

22. André Velter, *Les poètes du chat noir* (Paris: Gallimard, 1996).

23. Cited in Henri Marc, Aristide Bruant, le maître de la rue (Paris: Éditions France-Empire, 1989), 54.

24. Pierre Mac Orlan, *Chansons pour accordéon*, 16.

25. Catherine Dutheil Pessin, "Chanson sociale et chanson réaliste," *Cités*, no. 19 (2004): 27–42; Catherine Dutheil Pessin, La chanson réaliste. Sociologie d'un genre: le visage et la voix (Paris: L'Harmattan, 2004); Dietmar Rieger, "Aristide Bruant et la chanson naturaliste fin de siècle," in Dynamique sociale et formes littéraires: De la société de cour à la misère des grandes villes, by Dietmar Rieger (Tübingen: Gunter Narr Verlag, 1997), 201–24.

26. Joëlle Deniot, "Elles s'appelaient Rose, Nina, Pauline ou Louise," in *Les peuples de l'art*, vol. 1, ed. Joëlle Deniot and Alain Pessin (Paris: L'Harmattan, 2006), 49.

27. Agnès Pellerin, *Le fado* (Paris: Chandeigne, 2009).

28. Christophe Appril and Elisabeth Dorier Appril, "Espaces et lieux du tango: La géographie d'une danse entre mythe et réalité," in *Le voyage inachevé . . . à Joel Bonnemaison*, ed. Dominique Guillaud, M. Seysset, and Annie Walter (Paris: Orstom-Prodig, 1998), 583–90.

29. Jorge Muñoz, *La policía, el lunfardo y el tango* (Buenos Aires: Editorial Policial, 2008); Camairi, *La ciudad y el crimen:*

30. Huret, *De Buenos Aires*, 115.

31. Béatrice Humbert, "Le tango à Paris de 1907 à 1920," in Ramon Pélinski, *Tango nomade: Études sur le tango transculturel* (Montréal: Tryptique, 1995), 109–62.

32. Agathe Lecoeur, "Les bas-fonds a contrario" (master's thesis, Université de Paris 1, 2011).

33. Myriam Boucharenc, *L'écrivain-reporter au cœur des années trente* (Lille: Presses universitaires du Septentrion, 2004), 37. See also chapter 5.

34. Henri Drouin, "Service de nuit," *Détective*, no. 6, December 1928.

35. Kessel, *Bas-fonds de Paris*, 109.

36. Kessel, *Bas-fonds de Paris*, 97.

37. Drouin "Service de nuit."

38. Henri Drouin, "Au pays de l'amour venal," *Détective*, no. 33, 1929.

39. Preface to René Jacques, *Envoutement de Paris* (Paris: Grasset, 1938), 14.

40. Pierre Mac Orlan, *Rue secrètes*, (Paris: Gallimard, 1934), 147.

41. Kessel, *Bas-fonds de Paris*, 8.

42. Mac Orlan, *Rue secrètes*, 29; Pierre Mac Orlan, preface to *Ciel de cafard*, by Marcel Montarron (Paris: Gallimard, 1932), 9.

43. Kessel, *Bas-fonds de Paris*, 8.

44. Henri Danjou, *Enfants du malheur* (Paris, 1932; Paris: La manufacture des livres, 2012), 80.

45. Pierre Mac Orlan, *Le Bataillon de la mauvaise chance: Un civil chez les "Joyeux"* (Paris: Editions de France, 1933), 160.

46. Mac Orlan, *Rues secrètes*, 6; Pierre Mac Orlan, *Nuits aux bouges* (Paris: Flammarion, 1929), 77.

47. Francis Carco, *Traduit de l'argot* (Paris: Editions de France, 1931), 262.

48. Mac Orlan, *Rue secrètes*, 29.

49. Mac Orlan, *Nuits aux bouges*, 33.

50. Ludovic Garnica de la Cruz, *Nantes la brume* (Paris: Librairie Française, 1905), 292–93.

51. Lucienne Favre, *Dans la Casbah* (Paris: Grasset, 1937), 42.

52. Bernard Baritaud, *Pierre Mac Orlan, sa vie, son temps* (Geneva: Droz, 1992).

53. Pierre Mac Orlan, *Domaine de l'ombre: Images du fantastique social* (Paris: Phébus, 2000).

54. Féré, *Les mystères de Rouen*, 326.

55. Pierre Mac Orlan, "Nocturne," *Variétés*, July 15, 1929.

56. Joseph Kessel, "Paris la nuit," *Détective*, no. 3, November 15, 1928; Drouin, "Au pays de l'amour venal"; Paul Morand, *Paris de nuit*, photographs by Brassaï (Paris: Impr.-édit. Arts et Métiers graphiques, 1933); Francis Carco, *Envoutement de Paris* (Paris: Grasset, 1938); René-Jacques, *La zone de Clignancourt*, photographs, 1948.

57. The former was made by Maurice Lehmann and Claude Autant-Lara, the latter by Jean Boyer.

58. Marcel Carné, "Quand le cinéma descendra-t-il dans la rue?", *Cinémagazine*, November 1933.

59. Jean-Paul Clébert, *Paris insolite, authentifié par 115 photographies de Patrice Molinard* (Paris: Denoel, 1952; repr. Paris: Attila, 2009), 82; Luc Sante, preface in *Paris Vagabond*, by Jean-Paul Clébert, trans. Donald Nicholson-Smith (New York: New York Review Classics, 2016).

60. Pierre Rocher, "La Lèpre de Nantes," *Le Populaire*, February 19, 1925.

61. Arthur Morrison, *Tales of Mean Streets* (London: Methuen, 1894); Arthur Morrison, *A Child of the Jago* (London: Methuen, 1896).

62. Clébert, *Paris insolite*.

63. Clébert, *Paris insolite*, 92.

64. Clébert, 30.

8. SLOW ECLIPSE OF THE UNDERWORLD

1. "Classer les assistés (1880–1914)," *Les cahiers de la recherche sur le travail social* (Caen: Université de Caen, 1991).

2. Charles Booth, ed., *Life and Labour of the People in London* (London: Macmillan, 1892–1893), 5 vols. I borrow the expression "classificatory revolution" from Christian Topalov, *Naissance du chômeur, 1880–1910* (Paris: Albin Michel, 1994) and "La ville, 'terre inconnue': L'enquête de Charles Booth et le peuple de Londres, 1886–1891," *Genèses*, no. 5 (1991): 4–34.

3. Kevin Bales, *Man in the Middle: The Life and Work of Charles Booth* (London: Routledge, 1991).

4. Charles Booth, "Life and Labour of the People in London: First Results of an Inquiry Based on the 1891 Census," *Journal of the Royal Statistical Society* 56, no. 4 (December 1893): 591.

5. Booth, *Life and Labor*, vol. 4, 29. Booth has been reprinted in English but not digitized.

6. Booth, *Life and Labor*, vol. 1, 39.

7. Booth, 174.

8. Seebowm Rowntree, *Poverty. A Study of Town Life* (London: Macmillan, 1901).

9. Topalov, *Naissance du chômeur*; Nicolas Baverez, Bénédicte Reynaud, and Robert Salais, *L'invention du chômage* (Paris: PUF, 1986).

10. Mark Freeman and Gillian Nelson, eds., *Vicarious Vagrants: Incognito Social Explorers and the Homeless in England, 1860–1910* (Lambertville: NJ: The True Bill Press, 2008), 47; Gareth Stedman Jones, *Outcast London: A Study in the Relationship Between Classes in Victorian Society* (Oxford: Clarendon Press, 1971), xxv.

11. Michelle Perrot, "La fin des vagabonds," in *Les Ombres de l'histoire: Crime et châtiment au XIXᵉ siècle*, by Michelle Perrot (Paris, 1978; Paris: Flammarion, 2001), 317–36; Jean-François Wagniart, *Le vagabond à la fin du XIXᵉ siècle* (Paris: Belin, 1999).

12. Olivier Bosc, *La foule criminelle: Politique et criminalité dans l'Europe du tournant du XIXᵉ siècle* (Paris: Fayard, 2007), 231–39; Keith Gandal, *The Virtues of the Vicious: Jacob Riis, Stephen Crane, and the Spectacle of the Slum* (New York: Oxford University Press, 1997).

13. Bruno Dumons, "L'engagement des catholiques français contre la pauvreté, 1890–1960," in *Les exclus en Europe*, Gueslin and Kalifa, 390–404.

14. Nigel Scotland, *Squires in the Slums. Settlements and Missions in Late-Victorian London* (New York: Taurus, 2007); Standish Meacham, *Toynbee Hall and Social Reform, 1880–1914* (New Haven, CT: Yale University Press, 1987).

15. Antoine Savoye, "Les *social surveys* américains: La ville comme terrain d'étude et d'action," in *Les Débuts de la sociologie empirique*, by Antoine Savoye (Paris: Meridiens Klincksieck, 1994), 85–114.

16. Jean-Michel Chapoulie, *La tradition sociologique de Chicago, 1892–1961* (Paris: Seuil, 2001).

17. Pascal Bousseyroux, "Robert Garric (1896–1967), éducateur catholique du social" (PhD thesis, Université Paris-Diderot, 2011).

18. André Gueslin, *Les gens de rien: Une histoire de la grande pauvreté dans la France du XXe siècle* (Paris: Fayard, 2004).

19. Robert Castel, *La métamorphose de la question sociale* (Paris: Fayard, 1995).

20. Anbinder, Five Points. The Nineteenth-Century New York City.

21. Dr Vallin, "Les projets d'assainissement à Rouen," *Revue d'hygiène publique* (1895), quoted by Stéphane Frioux, "Les réseaux de la modernité: Amélioration de l'environnement et diffusion de l'innovation dans la France urbaine (fin XIXe siècle-années 1950)" (PhD thesis, Université Lyon 2, 2009), 42.

22. Lion Murard and Patrick Zylberman, *L'hygiène dans la République: La santé publique en France ou l'utopie contrariée (1870–1918)* (Paris: Fayard, 1996).

23. Frioux, "Les réseaux de la modernité."

24. Hadrien Nouvelot, "Les mystères de Dijon" (master's thesis, Université Paris 1, 2011), 61–63.

25. Jean-Jacques Jordi and Jean-Louis Planche, eds., *Alger 1860–1939: Le modèle ambigu du triomphe colonial* (Paris: Autrement, 1999), 141.

26. Frioux, "Les réseaux de la modernité."

27. Patrick Gaboriau, *SDF à la Belle Époque: L'univers des mendiants vagabonds au tournant des XIXe et XXe siècles* (Paris: Desclée de Brouwer, 1998), 24.

28. Michèle Grenot, "Dufourny de Villiers et les plus pauvres (1738–1796): Vaincre l'exclusion au nom des Droits de l'Homme" (PhD thesis, Université Paris 7, 2001).

29. There is a survey of the principal discussions of the term in Gueslin and Kalifa, *Les exclus en Europe.*

30. Gaboriau, *SDF à la Belle Époque.*

31. Peter Becker and Richard Wetzell, eds., Criminals and Their Scientists: The History of Criminology in International Perspective (Cambridge: Cambridge University Press, 2006).

32. Francis Carco and André Picard, *Mon Homme* (Paris: Ferenczi, 1921).

33. James Sarrazin, *Dossier M comme Milieu* (Paris: Alain Moreau, 1977), 115.

34. AD BDR 1767W29, report of the SRPJ of Marseille to the DGSN, 1967, quoted by Laurence Montel, "Marseille capitale du crime: Histoire croisée de l'imaginaire de Marseille et de la criminalité organisée (1820–1940)" (PhD diss., Université de Paris 10, 2008), 775.

35. Jérôme Pierrat, *Une Histoire du Milieu. Grand banditisme et haute pègre en France de 1850 à nos jours*, Paris, Denoël, 2003, p. 9.

36. Marcel Petit, "Où se cachent les malfaiteurs?", *Détective*, 28 February 1929.

37. T. Anbinder, *Five Points, op. cit.*; Marie-Anne Matard-Bonucci, *Histoire de la Mafia*, (Brussells: Complexe, 1994).

38. Paul Bringuier, "L'attentat de Marseille," *Détective*, 1928; Montel, "Marseille capitale du crime," which I am following for Marseillaise matters.

39. Paul Jankowski, *Communism and Collaboration: Simon Sabiani and Politics in Marseille 1919–1944* (New Haven, CT: Yale University Press, 1989).

40. Henri Danjou, "Les bas-fonds de Marseille," *Détective*, September 18, 1930, quoted by Montel, "Marseille capitale du crime."

41. Blaise Cendrars, *Panorama de la pègre* (Paris: 1935), 37.

42. Joseph Kessel, "Nuits de Montmartre," *Détective*, October 24, 1929, 3.

43. Blaise Cendrars, "Les gangsters de la Maffia," *Excelsior*, April 19–May 14, 1934; Cendrars, *Panorama de la pègre*, 286.

44. Cendrars, *Panorama de la pègre*, 13.

45. Vanessa Zerjav, "La pègre parisienne dans les années vingt" (master's thesis, Université Paris 7, 1998).

46. Adrien Bourse, "La grande épuration de Paris," *Le Matin*, December 20, 1927–January 17, 1928.

47. Francis Carco, *Paname* (Paris: Jonquières, 1927), 14.

48. Marcel Montarron, "La guerre du crime," *Détective*, no. 389, April 9, 1936.

49. Géo London, *Deux mois avec les bandits de Chicago* (Paris: Editions des Portiques, 1930).

50. Fred D. Pasley, *Al Capone le Balafré, tsar des bandits de Chicago: Sa biographie*, introduction by Blaise Cendrars (Paris: au Sans pareil, 1931).

51. London, *Deux mois avec les bandits de Chicago*, 8.

52. Paul Bringuier, "Coup de sonde," *Détective*, April 5, 1934.

53. Francis Carco, *Traduit de l'argot* (Paris: Editions de France, 1931), 262.

54. *Le Temps*, March 20, 2012.

55. Alan Bock, *East Side, West Side: Organizing Crime in New York, 1930–1950* (New Brunswick, NJ: Transaction, 1999).

56. Kessel, *Bas-fonds de Paris*, 8; Cendrars, *Panorama de la pègre*.

57. Quoted by Marco Gasparini, *Mafia: Histoire et mythologie* (Paris: Flammarion, 2011), 28.

58. Marie-Anne Matard-Bonucci, *Histoire de la Mafia* (Brussels: Complexe, 1994); Salvatore Lupo, *Histoire de la mafia des origines à nos jours* (Paris: Flammarion, 1999).

59. Eiko Maruko Siniawer, "Befitting Bedfellows: Yakusa and the State in Modern Japan," *Journal of Social History* 45, no. 3 (2012): 623–41.

60. Caimari, *La ciudad y el crimen:*

61. Léon Daudet, Bréviaire du journalisme (Paris: Gallimard, 1936), 164.

62. Maxim Gorky, *The Lower Depths*, Act 4, trans. Jenny Covan (1902; New York: Brentano's, 1922).

9. PERSISTENT SHADOWS

1. Paul Matter, "Chez les apaches," *Revue politique et littéraire* (October 1907): 626.

2. William Alison-Booth, *Hell's Outpost: The True Story of Devil's Island by a Man Who Exiled Himself There* (New York: Minton, Balch, 1931).

3. Danielle Donet-Vincent, *La fin du bagne, 1923–1953* (Rennes: Éd. Ouest-France, 1992); Danielle Donet-Vincent, *De soleil et de silences: Histoire des bagnes de Guyane* (Paris: La Boutique de l'histoire, 2003).

4. Charles Péan, *Conquêtes en terre de bagne* (Paris: Altis, 1948), 138.

5. Michel Pierre, *La terre de la grande punition* (Paris: Ramsay, 1982).

6. Albert Camus, *Alger républicain*, December 1, 1938.

7. Daniel Hémery, "Terre de bagne en mer de Chine: Poulo-Condore (1863–1953)," 2008, http://www.europe-solidaire.org/spip.php?article8969&var_recherche=prison%20 #top.

8. Isabelle Von Bueltzingsloewen, *L'hécatombe des fous: La famine dans les hôpitaux psychiatriques français sous l'Occupation* (Paris: Aubier, 2007).

9. Donet-Vincent, *La fin du bagne*, 71.

10. Charles Péan, *Terre de bagne* (Paris: La Renaissance moderne, 1930), 248.

11. Péan, *Terre de Bagne*, 10.

12. René Girier, *Je tire ma révérence* (Paris: La Table Ronde, 1977), 318.

13. On this subject, I am relying on work by Jean-Claude Vimont, especially "L'observation des relégués (1947–1970)." *Crime, Histoire et Sociétés* 13, no. 1 (2009): 49–72; Jean-Claude Vimont, "Des corps usés et maltraités, les multirécidivistes relégués de 1938 à 1970," in *Corps saccagés: Une histoire des violences corporelles du siècle des Lumières à nos jours*, ed. Frédéric Chauvaud (Rennes: Presses universitaires de Rennes, 2009), 163–74; Jean-Claude Vimont, "Les dossiers judiciaires de personnalité et la réforme pénitentiaire (1945–1970)," in *Sous l'œil de l'expert*, ed. Ludivine Bantigny and Jean-Claude Vimont (Rouen: Presses universitaires de Rouen et du Havre, 2010); Jean-Claude Vimont, "La peur des récidivistes relégués en métropole, 1945–1970," in *L'ennemie intime. La peur: perceptions, expressions, effets*, ed. Frédéric Chauvaud (Rennes: Presses universitaires de Rennes, 2011), 143–53.

14. Marc Ancel, *La défense sociale nouvelle: Un mouvement de politique criminelle humaniste* (Paris: Cujas, 1954).

15. Pierre Cannat, *Nos frères, les récidivistes: Esquisse d'une politique criminelle fondée sur le reclassement ou l'élimination des délinquants* (Paris: Sirey, 1942).

16. Clébert, *Paris insolite*, 19.

17. Dominique Kalifa, *Biribi: Les bagnes coloniaux de l'armée française* (Paris: Perrin, 2009).

18. *L'Écho de la Loire*, May 19, 1925.

19. Richard, *Le guide*, 103.

20. François Martineau, *Fripons, gueux et loubards: Une histoire de la délinquance de 1750 à nos jours* (Paris: J.-C. Lattès, 1896), 265–66; Alexandre Vexliard, *Introduction à la sociologie du vabagondage* (Paris: Marcel Rivière, 1956), 117–19.

21. Orwell, *Down and Out*, 169.

22. Vexliard, *Le clochard*, 28. On the importance of the work of Alexandre Vexliard, see Laurent Mucchielli, "Clochards et sans-abri: Actualité de l'œuvre d'Alexandre Vexliard," *Revue française de sociologie* (1998): 105–38.

23. Vexliard, *Le clochard*, 64.

24. Vexliard, 70–71.

25. Ken Auletta, *The Underclass* (New York: Random House, 1982).

26. William J. Wilson, *The Truly Disadvantaged: The Inner City, the Underclass, and Public Policy* (Chicago: University of Chicago Press, 1987). He adopts the definitions of

the Swedish sociologist Gunnar Myrdal, *Challenge to Affluence* (New York: Random House, 1963).

27. Charles Murray, *The Emerging British Underclass* (London: Institute of Economic Affairs, 1990), 24.

28. Murray, *The Emerging British Underclass*, 38.

29. Richard L. Dugdale, *"The Jukes": A Study in Crime, Pauperism, Disease and Heredity* (New York: Putnam's Sons, 1877), 13.

30. Lawrence M. Mead, *Beyond Entitlement: The Social Obligations of Citizenship* (New York: The Free Press, 1986).

31. Christopher Jencks and Paul E. Peterson, eds., *The Urban Underclass* (Washington: The Brookings Institution, 1991); Dee Cook, *Poverty, Crime and Punishment* (London: CPAG, 1997).

32. Fred Robinson and Nicky Gregson, "The Underclass, A Class Apart?", *Critical Social Policy* 12, no. 34 (1992): 38–51; Charles Murray, *Underclass: The Crisis Deepens* (London: IEA Health and Welfare Unit, 1994).

33. In the abundant bibliography, see Bill E. Lawson, ed., *The Underclass Question* (Cambridge: Harvard University Press, 1992); Michael Katz, ed., *The "Underclass" Debate: Views from History* (Princeton, NJ: Princeton University Press, 1993); Loïc Wacquant, "L'underclass urbaine dans l'imaginaire social et scientifique américain," in *L'Exclusion. L'état des savoirs*, ed. S. Paugam (Paris: La Découverte, 1996); Loïc Wacquant, *Urban Outcasts: A Comparative Sociology of Advanced Marginality* (Malden, MA: Polity Press, 2008).

34. Dee Cook, *Poverty, Crime and Punishment* (London: CPAG, 1997).

35. Herbert Gans, *The War Against the Poor: The Underclass and Antipoverty Policy* (New York: Basic Books, 1995), quoted by Wacquant, "L'underclass urbaine dans l'imaginaire social et scientifique américain."

36. *Angélique, Marquise des Anges*, 1964; *Merveilleuse Angélique*, 1965; *Angélique et le Roy*, 1966; *Indomptable Angélique*, 1967; *Angélique et le Sultan*, 1968. All were adapted from the series written by Anne and Serge Golon, whose thirteen titles ran from 1957 to 1985. Some of these bodice rippers have been translated into English by Rita Barisse for G. K. Hall; some of the movies are available on You Tube.

37. Danielle Aubry, *Du roman-feuilleton à la série télévisuelle: Pour une rhétorique du genre et de la sérialité* (Berne: Peter Lang, 2006).

38. Holmes, *London's Underworld*, 38.

39. Gabriel Tarde, "Fragment d'histoire future," *Revue internationale de sociologie* (August–September 1896): 603–54; reprinted in Gabriel Tarde, *Fragment d'histoire future* (Lyon: Storck, 1904).

40. Guy Costes and Joseph Altairac, *Les terres creuses: Bibliographie commentée des mondes souterrains imaginaires* (Amiens: Encrage, 2006).

41. René Thévenin, "La cité des tortures," *Le Journal des Voyages*, nos. 521–526 (1906).

42. Maurice Level, "La cité des voleurs," *Lectures pour tous*, May–August 1923; Leo Gestelys, *Prisonniers des pirates* (Paris: Ferenczi, 1939).

43. Gaston Leroux, *La double vie de Théophraste Longuet* (1901); Gaston Leroux, *The Double Life* (London: Forgotten Books, 2012); Joseph O'Neil, *Land Under England* (London: Victor Gollanczs, 1935).

44. Henry Rider Haggard, *Rural England* (London: Longmans, 1902); Henry Rider Haggard, *The Poor and the Land: Being a Report on the Salvation Army Colonies in the United States and at Hadleigh, England* (London: Longmans, 1905); Henry Rider Haggard, *Regeneration: Being an Account of the Social Work of the Salvation Army in Great Britain* (London: Longmans Green, 1910).

45. Bertrand Shurtleff, "The Underground City," *Amazing Stories*, September 1939; Jean-Gaston Vandel, *Agonie des civilisés* (Paris: Fleuve noir, 1953); Régis Messac, *Valcrétin* (Paris: Jean-Claude Lattes, 1973); William Lemkin, "Isle of the Gargoyles," *Wonder Stories*, February 1936; Francis Thomas, *Night Train* (New York: Pocket Book, 1984).

46. Ridley Scott, *Blade Runner*, http://www.allocine.fr/film/fichefilm-1975/secrets -tournage/.

47. Thomas Heise, *Urban Underworld: A Geography of Twentieth-Century American Literature and Culture* (New Brunswick, NJ: Rutgers University Press, 2011).

48. Etienne Bariller, *Steampunk ! L'esthétique rétro-future* (Paris: Les Moutons électriques, 2010).

49. Kevin Wayne Jeter, *Morlock Night* (New York: DAW Books, 1979); Tim Powers, *The Anubis Gate* (London: HarperCollins, 1983).

50. *Gotham by Gaslight* (New York: DC Comics, 1989).

51. Olivier Roman and Richard Nolane, *Alchimie*, vol. 1, *L'Épreuve du feu* (Toulon: Éditions Soleil, 2010); Olivier Roman and Richard Nolane, *Alchimie*, vol. 2, *Le Dernier roi maudit* (Toulon: Éditions Soleil, 2011).

10. ROOTS OF FASCINATION

1. Charles Dickens, *Oliver Twist* (London, 1837: repr. New York: Household Edition, 1861), viii.

2. Roger Chartier, *Figures de la gueuserie* (Paris: Montalba, 1982), 101.

3. Eugène Sue, *Les mystères de Paris*, vol. 3, trans. J. D. Smith, Esq. (London: Carvalho, 1844), 145.

4. Féré, *Les mystères*, 130–31.

5. Judith Lyon-Caen, "Enquêtes, littérature et savoir sur le monde social en France dans les années 1840," *Revue d'histoire des sciences humaines*, no. 17 (2007): 99–118.

6. Jean Moris, "Traite des blanches dernières formules," *Police Magazine*, no. 375, January 20, 1938.

7. Eugène Villiod, *Les plaies sociales: Comment on nous vole, comment on nous tue* (Paris: chez l'auteur, 1905), 9–10.

8. Eugène François Vidocq, *Mémoires de Vidocq, chef de police de sûreté jusqu'en 1827*, vol. 2 (Paris, 1828), 246; Eugène François Vidocq, *Les vrais mystères de Paris*, vol. 3 (Bruxelles: C. Muquardt, n.d.), 296.

9. Bronislaw Geremek, *Les fils de Caïn: L'image des pauvres et des vagabonds dans la littérature européenne du XVᵉ au XVIIIᵉ siècle* (1988; repr. Paris: Flammarion, 1991), 357.

10. Bronislaw Geremek, *Truands et misérables dans l'Europe moderne (1350–1600)* (Paris: Gallimard, 1980), 184.

11. Geremek, *Les fils de Caïn*, 38.

12. Chevalier, *Laboring Classes*.

13. John Tobias, *Crime and Industrial Society* (London: Batsford, 1967); John Tobias, *Nineteenth Century Crime: Prevention and Punishment* (London: David and Charles, 1972); Eileen Yeo and Edward P. Thomson, eds., *The Unknown Mayhew: Selections from the Morning Chronicle, 1849–1850* (London: Merlin Press, 2010); Donald Thomas, *The Victorian Underworld* (New York: New York University Press, 1998).

14. Andy Croll, "Who's Afraid of the Victorian Underworld?", *The Historian*, no. 84 (Winter 2004): 30–35; Heather Shore, "Undiscover'd Country: Towards a History of the Criminal Underworld," *Crimes and Misdemeanours* 1 (2007): 41–68; Tylor Anbinder, Five Points. The Nineteenth-Century New York City Neighborhood That Invented Tap Dance, Stole Elections, and Became the World's Most Notorious Slum (New York: The Free Press, 2001).

15. Clémence Royer, *Les mendiants de Paris* (Paris, n.d.), 116; Judith Lyon-Caen, *La lecture et la vie: Les usages du roman au temps de Balzac* (Paris: Tallandier, 2006).

16. Alexandre Vexliard, *Introduction à la sociologie du vabagondage* (XXX), 125.

17. Patrice Peveri, "La criminalité cartouchienne: Vols, voleurs et culture criminelle dans le Paris de la Régence," in *Cartouche, Mandrin et autres brigands de XVIIIᵉ siècle*, ed. Lise Andries (Paris: Desjonquères, 2010), 156–74.

18. Eugène Sue, *The Mysteries of Paris*, trans. Carolyn Betensky and Jonathan Loesberg (London: Penguin, 2015), chap. 1.

19. Gerard Van Hamel, "Discours d'ouverture du congrès international d'anthropologie criminelle," *Archives d'anthropologie criminelle* (1901): 600–601.

20. Foucault, *Discipline and Punish*.

21. James Alex Garza, *The Imagined Underworld: Sex, Crime, and Vice in Porfirian Mexico City* (Lincoln: University of Nebraska Press, 2007).

22. The novel deals with a band of terrible villains operating throughout the country, commanded by the mysterious Colonel Juan Yauez, called El Relumbro, who is quickly seen to have ambiguous ties with Santa Anna, that is to say, the preceding régime. On this monument of popular Mexican literature, see Robert Duclas, *Les bandits de Rio Frio: Politique et littérature au Mexique à travers l'œuvre de Manuel Payno* (Paris: IFAL, 1979).

23. Richard J. Evans, *Tales from the German Underworld: Crime and Punishment in the Nineteenth Century* (New Haven, CT: Yale University Press, 1998).

24. Koven, *Slumming: Sexual and Social Politics*.

25. Rosalind Crone, *Violent Victorians: Popular Entertainment in Nineteenth-Century London* (Manchester: Manchester University Press, 2012).

26. Jacques-Guy Petit, "Le philanthrope Benjamin Appert (1797–1873) et les réseaux libéraux," *Revue d'histoire moderne et contemporaine*, nos. 41–44 (1994): 667–79.

27. Lucia Katz, *L'avènement du sans-abri: Histoire des asiles de nuit, 1871–1914* (Paris: Libertalia, 2015).

28. Ellen Ross, *Slum Travelers. Ladies and London Poverty, 1860–1920* (Berkeley: University of California Press, 2007), 1.

29. Chevalier, *Classes laborieuses*, 76.

30. Alexandre Parent-Duchâtelet, *De la prostitution dans la ville de Paris, considérée sous le rapport de l'hygiène publique, de la morale et de l'administration* (Paris: Baillière, 1837), 527. Reprinted by Nabu Press, 2011 and 2013.

31. Jacques Carré, "Pauvreté et idéologie dans les enquêtes sociales," in *Écrire la pauvreté: Les enquêtes sociales britanniques aux XIXe et XXe siècles,* ed. Jacques Carré and Jean-Paul Révauger (Paris: L'Harmattan, 1995), 201–22.

32. Jules Janin, *L'âne mort et la femme guillotinée* (Brussels: Dumont et Cie, 1829), 76–77.

33. Hugo's statement appears in an 1858 preface, which was not printed on the 1862 novel. Translation by Susan Emanuel.

34. Sue, *Les mystères de Paris,* vol. 5 (Paris: Gosselin, 1844), 101.

35. Paul Féval, *Les Mystères de Londres* (Paris : Comptoir des imprimeurs unis, 1844), preface.

36. Peter J. Keating, *The Working Classes in Victorian Fiction* (London: Routledge and Kegan Paul, 1971); Himmelfarb, *The Idea of Poverty.*

37. Georges W. Reynolds, *The Mysteries of London* (1844–1846; repr. Staffordshire, UK: Keele University Press, 1996).

38. Clarence Rook, *The Hooligan Nights* (London, 1899; repr. Oxford: Oxford University Press, 1979).

39. Raymond Schults, *Crusader in Babylon: W. T. Stead and the Pall Mall Gazette* (Lincoln: University of Nebraska Press, 1972).

40. The classic book is by Louis Filler, *The Muckrakers* (1976; repr. Stanford, CA: Stanford University Press, 1993), which is complemented by Arthur and Lila Weinberg, *The Muckrakers* (Urbana: University of Illinois Press, 2001); and especially by Aileen Gallagher, *The Muckrakers: American Journalism During the Age of Reform* (New York: Rosen Publishing Group, 2006).

41. Keith Gandal, *The Virtues of the Vicious: Jacob Riis, Stephen Crane, and the Spectacle of the Slum* (New York: Oxford University Press, 1997); Robert M. Dowling, *Slumming in New York: From the Waterfront to Mythic Harlem* (Urbana: University of Illinois Press, 2007).

42. Lincoln Steffens, *The Shame of the Cities* (New York: Smith, 1904); Ida Tarbell, *The History of the Standard Oil Company* (New York: McClure, Phillips, 1904).

43. Upton Sinclair, *The Autobiography of Upton Sinclair* (New York: Harcourt, Brace and World, 1962), 109.

44. Upton Sinclair, *The Jungle* (New York: Grosset and Dunlop, 1906).

45. Gallagher, *The Muckrakers,* 5.

46. Rolf Lindner, *The Reportage of Urban Culture: Robert Park and the Chicago School* (Cambridge: Cambridge University Press, 1996), 87.

47. Kalifa, *Biribi,* 34–38.

48. Series by Pierre Rocher, in *Le populaire de Nantes,* February 19, 21, 26; March 4, 6, 14, 21, 27; April 3 10, 1925. Compare with Damien Cailloux, "Les bas-fonds nantais, XIXe–XXe siècles" (master's thesis, Université de Paris 1, 2008).

49. Henri Danjou, *Enfants du malheur* (Paris, 1932; Paris: La manufacture des livres, 2012).

50. Alexis Danan, *L'épée du scandale* (Paris: Flammarion, 1961), 172. Louis Roubaud wrote *Les enfants de Caïn* (Paris: Grasset, 1925); *36, quai des Orfèvres* (Paris: Editions de France, 1927); and *Démons et déments* (Paris: Gallimard, 1933).

51. Helen Campbell, *Darkness and Daylight, or Light and Shadow of New York Life in the Underworld of the Great Metropolis* (New York: Hartford, 1889); Helen Campbell, Thomas Knox, and Thomas Byrnes, *Darkness and Daylight, or Lights and Shadows of New York Life* (Hartford, CT: Worthington, 1891). Digitized at http://www.archive .org/details/darknessdaylight00campuoft.

52. Campbell, Knox, and Byrnes, *Darkness and Daylight*, frontispiece.

53. Hutchins Hapgood, *Types from City Streets* (New York: Funk & Wagnalls, 1910; repr. New York: Garrett Press, 1970), 13.

54. Charles Baudelaire, "To the Reader," translated by Eli Siegel (1861).

55. Jean Norton Cru, *Témoins: Essai d'analyse et de critique des souvenirs de combattants édités en français de 1915 à 1928* (Paris: Les Étincelles, 1929; repr. Nancy: Presses Universitaires de Nancy, 1993), 148.

56. Julia Kristeva, *Pouvoirs de l'horreur: Essai sur l'abjection* (Paris: Seuil, 1980); Julia Kristeva, *Powers of Horror: Essay on Abjection*, trans. Leon Roudiez (New York: Columbia University Press, 1982), chap. 1.

57. Paul Ricoeur, *Temps et récit*, vol. 3, *Temps raconté* (Paris: Seuil, 1985), 273; Paul Ricoeur, *Time and Narrative*, vol. 3, trans. Kathleen Blarney and David Pellauer (Chicago: University of Chicago Press, 1990), 188.

58. Marcel Proust, *Sodome et Gomorrhe* (Paris, 1921; repr. Paris: Gallimard, 1988), 12; Marcel Proust, *Cities of the Plain*, trans. Scott Moncrieff (New York: Albert & Charles Boni, 1927).

59. Koven, *Slumming*, 198–205, whose fine analysis inspired the following paragraphs.

60. Koven, 200–201.

61. Koven.

62. Barrès, *Les déracinés*, 370.

63. Lucienne Favre, *Tout l'inconnu de la Casbah d'Alger* (Algiers: Baconnier, 1933), 10.

64. Georges Brassaï, *Le Paris secret des années 1930* (Paris: Gallimard, 1976), 9.

65. Miriam Cendrars, *Blaise Cendrars* (Paris: Balland, 1985).

66. Francis Carco, *Revue de Paris*, October 1,1952.

67. Francis Carco, "Envoutement de Paris," *Revue de Paris*, October 1,1952, 9–10.

68. Kessel, *Bas-fonds de Paris*, 8.

69. Peter Stallybras and Allon White, *The Politics and Poetics of Transgression* (Ithaca, NY: Cornell University Press, 1986).

70. Colette, *L'ingénue libertine* (Paris: Ollendorff, 1909).

71. Charlie Chaplin, *My Wonderful Visit* (London: Hurst & Blackett, 1922),130.

72. Ashelbé, *Pépé le Moko*, 18.

73. Olivier Bosc, *La foule criminelle: Politique et criminalité dans l'Europe du tournant du XIXᵉ siècle* (Paris: Fayard, 2007), 231–39.

74. Luc Bihl-Willette, *Des tavernes aux bistrots: Une histoire des cafés* (Lausanne: L'âge d'homme, 1997), 179.

75. Evans Lansing Smith, *The Descent to the Underworld in Literature, Painting and Film, 1895–1950* (Lampeter, Wales: Edwin Mellon Press, 2001); David L. Pike, *Metropolis on the Styx: The Underworlds of Modern Urban Culture, 1800–2001* (Ithaca, NY: Cornell University Press, 2007).

76. Robert L. Stevenson, *The Strange Case of Dr. Jekyll and Mr. Hyde* (London: Longman, Green, 1886).

77. Jacob Riis, *The Children of the Poor* (London: Sampson Low, 1892), publisher's blurb.

CONCLUSION

1. Victor Hugo, *Les misérables*, vol. 5, trans. Isabell Hapgood (New York: T. Y. Crowell, 1887), book 2, chap. 2.

2. François-René de Chateaubriand, *Mémoires d'outre-tombe* (Paris, 1830–1841; repr. Paris: Classiques Garnier, 1998); François-René de Chateaubriand, *Memoirs from Beyond the Grave*, trans. A. S. Kline (New York: New York Review of Books, 2018), book 35, chap. 4.

3. Cyril-Berger, *Les têtes baissées* (Paris: Ollendorff, 1913), 1.

4. Sergio González Rodríguez, *Los bajos fondos* (México: Cal y arena, 1990), 24.

5. Guy Rosa, "Histoire sociale et roman de la misère, *Les Misérables* de V. Hugo," *Revue d'histoire du XIXᵉ siècle*, no. 11 (1995): 95–110.

6. Michel Biron and Pierre Popovic, eds., *Écrire la pauvreté* (Toronto: Editions du Gref, 1996); the quotation is from Charles Grivel, "Les déchets de la littérature," in Biron and Popovic, eds., *Écrire la pauvreté*, 35.

7. Alain Corbin, *Le temps, le désir et l'horreur* (Paris, Aubier, 1991).

Index

Christian duty and, 40; criminals associated with, 171–72; dangerous locations and, 128–30; decriminalization of, 162–71; degeneration signs in, 42; detention and, 43–44; distribution of aid for, 89–90; exploitation of, 188; false, 106; human misery of, 18–19; in lower depths, 169–70; in Paris, 110, 143–44; pauperism in, 62–63; protestants wanting to eradicate, 41–42; queer slumming and, 119; semi-criminal class and, 163–64; social agitation from, 64–65; society with bad, 63–64; stench of, 22–23; stigmatization of, 41; underworld and, 113. *See also* beggars; pauperism; poor people
Powers, Tim, 196
Prévert, Jacques, 156–57
Princess Alice (ferry), 20
Princess of the Gutter, A (Meade), 215–16
Priollet, Marcel, 140
prisoners, 29, 91, 95, 182–83
prisons, 23, 183–84; Belém, 206; Blackwell's Island, 30; in Europe, 45; La Force, 69; in lower depths, 27
prisons de Paris: Histoire, types, moeurs, mystères, Les (Alhoy), 95
prisonships, 19
Pritchard, George, 69
prohibition, 178–79
Prolongeau, Hubert, 247n40
Propos rustiques (du Fail), 50
prostitution, 24, 35, 116–17; Babylon as great, 38; bordellos and, 25; in lower depths, 27–29; in Paris, 151–52; slave trade and, 221. *See also* brothels; pornography; sexuality
protestants, 41–42
public misery, 148
pulp fiction writing, 191
punishment, 53
punks à chiens (gutter punks), 188

Quai de la Fesse (Quay of the Ass), 29
Quai des brumes, Le (film), 156
Quasimodo, 59
Quay of the Ass (Quai de la Fesse), 29
queer slumming, 119

Raban, Louis-François, 23
race of detainees, 185–86
racialization, of Europe, 42
Radcliffe, Ann, 18
Ragged Dick, or Street Life in New York with the Bootblacks (Alger), 131
ragged proletariat (lumpenproletariat), 68
ragpickers, 69, 106
Ramaseeana (Sleeman), 70
Ramos, Vital, 126
Raoul (Baume), 21
Raynal, Hippolyte, 69
recherche du temps perdu, La (Lorrain), 215
reductive binary mode, 170–71
relégués, in France, 185–86
Renoir, Jean, 180
residuum, 18, 65, 165
respectable peoples, 214–20
resurrectionists, 14
Revelation, book of, 38
Reynolds, George, 56, 75, 210
Richard, Elie, 30, 135, 138, 146–50, 187; Montmartre myth from, 126; subhuman neighborhood comment of, 128; sub-men mentioned by, 24
Richepin, Jean, 147
Ricoeur, Paul, 215
Rictus, Johan, 148
righter of wrongs, 103
Rights of Man, 182
Riis, Jacob, 93, 168, 212, 219–20
rioting, in underworld, 66
robbery terms, 94
Robert, Raymond, 78
Robert Taylor Homes, 115
Rob Roy, 56
Robustel, Jean, 43
Rocher, Pierre, 213
Rockwood (Ainsworth), 56
Rogosin, Lionel, 224
roguery (gueuserie), 35, 47–52, 161–62
Rohmer, Sax, 133–34
Rome, marginal types in, 39
Romero, George, 195
Rook, Clarence, 211
Roosevelt, Theodore, 212
Roosevelt Island (Blackwell's Island), 30

European Perspectives
A Series in Social Thought and Cultural Criticism
Lawrence D. Kritzman, Editor

Michel Pastoureau, *The Devil's Cloth: A History of Stripes and Striped Fabric*

Alain Cabantous, *Blasphemy: Impious Speech in the West from the Seventeenth to the Nineteenth Century*

Julia Kristeva, *The Sense and Non-Sense of Revolt: The Powers and Limits of Psychoanalysis*

Kelly Oliver, *The Portable Kristeva*

Gilles Deleuze, *Dialogues II*

Catherine Clément and Julia Kristeva, *The Feminine and the Sacred*

Sylviane Agacinski, *Time Passing: Modernity and Nostalgia*

Luce Irigaray, *Between East and West: From Singularity to Community*

Julia Kristeva, *Hannah Arendt*

Julia Kristeva, *Intimate Revolt: The Powers and Limits of Psychoanalysis*, vol. 2

Elisabeth Roudinesco, *Why Psychoanalysis?*

Régis Debray, *Transmitting Culture*

Steve Redhead, ed., *The Paul Virilio Reader*

Claudia Benthien, *Skin: On the Cultural Border Between Self and the World*

Julia Kristeva, *Melanie Klein*

Roland Barthes, *The Neutral: Lecture Course at the Collège de France (1977–1978)*

Hélène Cixous, *Portrait of Jacques Derrida as a Young Jewish Saint*

Theodor W. Adorno, *Critical Models: Interventions and Catchwords*

Julia Kristeva, *Colette*

Gianni Vattimo, *Dialogue with Nietzsche*

Emmanuel Todd, *After the Empire: The Breakdown of the American Order*

Gianni Vattimo, *Nihilism and Emancipation: Ethics, Politics, and Law*

Hélène Cixous, *Dream I Tell You*

Steve Redhead, *The Jean Baudrillard Reader*

Jean Starobinski, *Enchantment: The Seductress in Opera*

Jacques Derrida, *Geneses, Genealogies, Genres, and Genius: The Secrets of the Archive*

Hélène Cixous, *White Ink: Interviews on Sex, Text, and Politics*

Marta Segarra, ed., *The Portable Cixous*

François Dosse, *Gilles Deleuze and Félix Guattari: Intersecting Lives*

Julia Kristeva, *This Incredible Need to Believe*

François Noudelmann, *The Philosopher's Touch: Sartre, Nietzsche, and Barthes at the Piano*

Antoine de Baecque, *Camera Historica: The Century in Cinema*

Julia Kristeva, *Hatred and Forgiveness*

Roland Barthes, *How to Live Together: Novelistic Simulations of Some Everyday Spaces*

Jean-Louis Flandrin and Massimo Montanari, *Food: A Culinary History*

Georges Vigarello, *The Metamorphoses of Fat: A History of Obesity*

Julia Kristeva, *The Severed Head: Capital Visions*

Eelco Runia, *Moved by the Past: Discontinuity and Historical Mutation*

François Hartog, *Regimes of Historicity: Presentism and Experiences of Time*

Jacques Le Goff, *Must We Divide History Into Periods?*

Claude Lévi-Strauss, *We Are All Cannibals: And Other Essays*

Marc Augé, *Everyone Dies Young: Time Without Age*

Roland Barthes: *Album: Unpublished Correspondence and Texts*

Étienne Balibar, *Secularism and Cosmopolitanism: Critical Hypotheses on Religion and Politics*